*Beyond Moral Judgment*

# Beyond Moral Judgment

ALICE CRARY

HARVARD UNIVERSITY PRESS

*Cambridge, Massachusetts*
*London, England   2007*

ISBN-13: 978-0-674-02457-1
ISBN-10: 0-674-02457-5

The Cataloging-in-Publication Data is available from the Library of Congress

For Anne
and
in loving memory of Jen

# *Contents*

# Acknowledgments

I would like to thank the individuals and institutions who, in different ways, assisted me with this book. I completed a first draft in 2003–2004 while holding a Laurance S. Rockefeller Visiting Fellowship at the Princeton University Center for Human Values, and I am grateful to the Center, as well as to the New School for Social Research, for supporting my work. My largest debts are to Stanley Cavell, Cora Diamond and John McDowell, and the extent of what I owe to them will be evident to anyone familiar with their thought. I am also greatly indebted to Nancy Bauer and James Conant, who have shared insights about relevant topics in conversations reaching back two decades, as well as to a number of people who have given me useful comments since I began circulating material from the book. I especially want to thank Jay Bernstein, Richard Bernstein, Akeel Bilgrami, Lisabeth During, Nathaniel Hupert, Elijah Millgram, Richard Moran, Stephen Mulhall and Ross Poole, all of whom have been not only helpful with suggestions but gracious with support. I want to acknowledge in addition, for their constructive feedback on individual chapters, Anita Avramides, Annette Baier, David Cerbone, Simon Critchley, Ben Eggleston, Eli Friedlander, Pablo Gilabert, Robert Haraldsson, Elizabeth Harman, Agnieszka Jaworska, David Kishik, Francesca Recchia Luciani, Hilary Putnam, Mark Richard, Bruce Robbins, Carol Rovane, Lisa Shapiro, Sanford Shieh, Peter Singer, Martin Stone, Margaret

Walker, Stephen White, Edward Witherspoon and John Wright. I am thankful to Anne van Leeuwen and Rocio Zambrano for their tactful and intelligent aid with research, to Matt Congdon for his extemely capable help with proofreading and with the index, and to Phoebe Kosman and Lindsay Waters at Harvard University Press, whose guidance has been invaluable in bringing the project to completion. Finally, a special word of gratitude to Cora Diamond, with whom I have productively discussed nearly every part of this book and on whose friendship and advice I have relied throughout its writing.

*Beyond Moral Judgment*

# Introduction

We take almost all the decisive steps in our lives as a result of
slight inner adjustments of which we are barely conscious.
~ *Austerlitz in W. G. Sebald,* Austerlitz *(2001), p. 134.*

Ethics is concerned with moral thought, and a survey of recent conversations in ethics reveals the existence of extensive agreement about
where to find such thought. Despite differing over wide ranges of issues, moral philosophers generally agree in assuming that the moral
work of language is the prerogative of moral concepts, where these are
understood as concepts that are specifically in the business of articulating a moral outlook. Further, despite lacking a clear consensus about
which concepts are the moral ones, moral philosophers generally agree
in assuming that moral thought invariably comes in the form of moral
judgments, where these are understood as judgments that apply some
moral concept or other. One definite sign of agreement on these matters is the widespread, if also mostly tacit, acceptance of a view of ethics
on which it is taken to be distinguished by a preoccupation with moral
judgments or, alternately, with judgments that make up one particular
region of language and specify one particular (practical or theoretical)
subject matter.

This familiar view of ethics is the central critical target of this book.
In the pages that follow, I trace some of its main sources and attempt to
counter it, arguing both that it is wrong to restrict moral thinking to
moral judgment-making and that moral thinking comes in other forms.
A guiding suggestion of my argument is that what at bottom prevents
the recognition of these additional forms is a set of deeply engrained

assumptions about the workings of language—assumptions that, in addition to dominating ongoing discussions in philosophy of language, also inform most research in ethics. Taking my bearings from this suggestion, I approach the task of expanding our inventory of forms of moral thought by criticizing the pertinent assumptions and exchanging them for a very different account of what our lives with language are like.

The alternative account I defend can be characterized as having a philosophically irregular *pragmatic* emphasis. The relevant contrast here is with an emphasis on pragmatics that is relatively routine in contemporary philosophy of language. A common refrain of recent conversations is that a good grasp of a linguistic expression is unavailable apart from an understanding of its public use, and discussions about the need for attention to use frequently conclude with proposals for some kind of pragmatic addendum to traditional semantic theories. If we take pragmatics to be concerned with those aspects of linguistic expressions that are functions of their use, and if we take semantics to be concerned with those aspects of the relation between linguistic expressions and the world that determine truth and falsity, then we can say that the prevalent idea is that we should recognize the significance of pragmatics while at the same time treating it as at best an addendum, or accessory, to semantics. This observation makes it possible to capture, in preliminary fashion, what is distinctive about the account of language presented in this book: it is distinctive in that it directly opposes this idea. One of its fundamental tenets is that propensities and sensitivities an individual acquires in learning to use expressions—propensities and sensitivities that are more commonly treated as of 'merely pragmatic' interest—make necessary contributions to all her linguistic capacities, including those that semantic theory aspires to illuminate.

This is the basic account of language that, I contend, obliges us to broaden our conception of moral thought so that it encompasses more than moral judgments. My case for showing this pivots on a claim about how the account bequeaths to us a (striking and philosophically heterodox) image of language as an irredeemably moral acquisition. My defense of this claim in turn centers on the idea that we are justified both in accepting the account's representation of certain acquired sensitivities and propensities as internal to a person's linguistic capacities and in representing these same sensitivities and propensities as composing her moral outlook. What I argue is, in brief, that, if we see what is right about this idea, we can also see that there is good reason to allow that a stretch of thought that does not make use of moral concepts, and that is not concerned with 'moral topics', might nevertheless play the kind of role in expressing a person's moral outlook that establishes it as genuine moral thought. Now we are in a position to see that moral reflection need not invariably take the form of moral judgments.

I just offered a summary outline of this book's main argument against a view of ethics on which its preoccupation with moral thought is interpreted as an exclusive preoccupation with moral judgments. What primarily interests me about the argument is that, in challenging this familiar view, it provides support for a very different one. Insofar as it presupposes that an individual's moral outlook is a function of a sensibility internal to all her linguistic capacities, the argument speaks for a view on which ethics is distinguished by a preoccupation not with judgments in one region of discourse but with a dimension of all of discourse—and on which a responsible ethical posture involves forms of attention that, far from being restricted to moral judgments, extend to webs of sensitivities informing all of individuals' modes of thought and speech.

This unorthodox view, while largely foreign to recent work in ethics, is not without antecedents in Anglo-American moral philosophy. It is possible to identify a small number of moral philosophers who, in different ways, express hostility to the fixation on moral judgments characteristic of recent work in ethics, and below I touch on the writings of some of the most original and interesting of these thinkers.[1] Relevant elements of their work have not, however, been engaged—or even acknowledged— within currently mainstream conversations in moral philosophy. Although this is in part simply a reflection of the philosophically radical character of these thinkers' projects, it is also in part because they tend not to make cases for their distinctive ethical orientations by explicitly and systematically attacking the kinds of philosophical assumptions that are taken to speak for understanding moral judgment as the locus of moral thought. These reflections allow me succinctly to describe the unique ambition of this book. Its ambition is to make a case along these lines and thereby to mount a thoroughgoing defense of a view of ethics

---

1. I have in mind, above all, Iris Murdoch, Stanley Cavell, and Cora Diamond.

that, despite its noteworthy local history, remains almost wholly alien to contemporary moral philosophy.[2]

My goals in what follows are not restricted to mounting such a defense. A successful defense would suggest the need for a significant shift in our conception of possible forms of moral thought, and a second important goal is to provide illustrations of what moral thinking is like when this shift is appropriately registered. A third and final goal is to demonstrate that the envisioned reorientation in ethics has consequences for what counts as a morally responsible stance and that the question of what speaks for it is therefore of real moral moment. The book's chapters are divided into three parts, corresponding to these three goals.

The three chapters in Part I contain the book's main argument for taking the concerns of ethics to reach beyond moral judgments to the whole sensibilities characteristic of individuals as language-users. The centerpiece of this argument is an account of language with an unusual emphasis on the practical, and I am preoccupied with this account in different ways in each of these three chapters. In Chapter 1, I make an initial case for the account in connection with a central and quite well-known strand of thought in Wittgenstein's *Philosophical Investigations*, and I do so in the context of offering an overview of my larger argument for the view of ethics with which the book is concerned. Then, in Chapter 2, I make a more detailed case for the account in connection both with the argument of J. L. Austin's *How to Do Things with Words* and with pragmatic lines of thought in more recent philosophy of language that this argument has inspired. Finally, in Chapter 3, I return to Wittgenstein's preoccupation with the account, now paying special attention to how Wittgenstein himself takes it to speak for a view on

2. Let me stress that what distinguishes this view is a conception of moral thoughts as including more than moral judgments and that no view that fails to incorporate this conception of moral thought is properly understood as deeply akin to it. Thus, it would, e.g., be wrong to suggest that because the view invites us to understand a person's acquired sensibility as internal to her capacity for moral thought, and because it in this respect resembles many views that get placed under the heading of "virtue ethics," it is correctly conceived as nothing more than a—perhaps slightly irregular—member of this set of views. Virtue-oriented views tend to be exclusively concerned with showing that sensibility plays a role in moral judgment-making that differs from the role consequentialist and deontological theories assign to it, and, insofar as virtue-oriented views thus fixate on the importance of sensibility for moral judgment, they help themselves to the assumption that it is the first business of this book to repudiate: viz., that moral thought is limited to such judgment.

which the concerns of ethics extend to the full range of sensitivities individuals possess as linguistic beings.

Given that I devote significant time in each of these three chapters to interpreting texts of Wittgenstein's and Austin's, it is worth stressing that my aims here are not merely exegetical. To say this is not to deny that I have some real exegetical concerns. One of my objectives in the book is to illustrate that, despite its neglect within philosophy of language, the account of language in which my preferred view of ethics is grounded has important sources in the Anglo-American philosophical tradition. But I devote significant time to careful interpretation of certain texts of Wittgenstein's and Austin's, not simply to attain this first objective, but also to show that these texts are rightly seen as laying the groundwork for compelling arguments for the pragmatic account of language that I defend as well as for the view of ethics that I take it to underwrite. It is above all these arguments, and not their sources in the work of particular philosophers, that interest me.

In addition to containing the book's main argument for its distinctive ethical view, the three chapters in Part I also contain its most tightly argued passages. Since Chapter 1 presents the entire argument in a preliminary form, it follows that the reader who, for one reason or another, prefers to forego more detailed discussion of the argument's central and philosophically most controversial steps might reasonably proceed directly from this chapter to Part II, returning to the skipped chapters when questions arise about the philosophical credentials of the ethical view for which they provide support.

The two chapters in Part II offer illustrations of the forms of moral thought that get described in the argument of Part I. In Chapter 4, my interest lies with moral thought that does not take the form of moral judgment. I claim that literature is a rich source of such moral thought and that many literary works are designed to elicit it. (Here I discuss, in particular, works of Jane Austen, E. M. Forster and Leo Tolstoy.) Then, in Chapter 5, I consider moral thought that *does* take the form of moral judgment. Having in earlier chapters already argued that philosophical considerations that speak for extending moral thought beyond moral judgments also speak for adopting a philosophically irregular view of what moral judgments are like, I now turn to showing that the view in question finds confirmation in existing traditions of moral thought. (Here I focus, in particular, on the tradition of feminist thought.)

The concluding chapter in Part III—Chapter 6—addresses moral implications of the larger view of ethics defended in the book. My central claim is that a fixation on moral judgments is a sign of attachment to modes of thought and conduct that are rightly impugned as *moralistic*, and I expand on this claim by considering studies of moralism in novels of Theodor Fontane and Henry James. One of my objects in thus representing the view I favor as opposed to moralism is to emphasize that the quarrel this book picks with more traditional, moral judgment-centered views has a significant moral dimension and that, without regard to where our sympathies initially lie in it, it therefore merits serious philosophical attention.

~ *I*

*ARGUMENT*

# ~ 1

## *Wider Possibilities for Moral Thought*

> Beliefs are not the only ethical supports we have.
> ~ *Elizabeth Costello in J. M. Coetzee,*
> Elizabeth Costello *(2003), p. 203.*

ETHICS IS CONCERNED with moral thinking, but where do we find such thinking? It is possible to speak, in reference to contemporary ethics, of a consensus about the locus of moral thinking that is so general it is rarely even explicitly commented on. The backdrop for this consensus is a widespread (albeit largely implicit) assumption to the effect that the moral business of language is the monopoly of *moral concepts*, where moral concepts are conceived as concepts specifically suited to articulate a moral outlook.[1] This assumption coexists with various differences over how the class of these concepts is best characterized. While sometimes the accent is on very broad concepts such as "duty," "right," "wrong," "good," "bad," etc., at other times, and especially recently, it is on concepts for virtues and vices such as "courage," "brutality," "kindness," "selfishness," etc. But, abstracting from such differences, we can speak of a general consensus about how moral thinking is a matter of making *moral judgments*, where moral judgments are conceived as judgments that apply members of one or another of these classes of moral concepts to, say, actions, persons, or personal qualities. Further, we can say that this consensus provides the impetus to a prevalent view

1. Throughout this book, I speak of a person's *moral* outlook in reference to her view of how best to live, or of what matters most in life. I do not adopt the practice of some moral philosophers of making a technical distinction between "the moral" and "the ethical," and I also sometimes speak in this connection of a person's *ethical* outlook.

of ethics as charged with illuminating the nature of these judgments or, in other words, as charged with illuminating the nature of judgments that represent one particular region of discourse and spell out one particular (practical or theoretical) subject matter. And, finally, we can add that this view is manifest in an emphasis within contemporary ethics on questions about, for instance, whether such judgments are appropriately conceived as cognitive or non-cognitive, or whether they are appropriately conceived as internally or externally related to action and choice.

One of the larger projects of this book is to argue, against the consensus that surrounds this view of ethics, that moral thinking should not be restricted to moral judgment-making, and that there are other possibilities for it.[2] Because it is difficult unambiguously to describe the alternatives that I discuss apart from an examination of philosophical assumptions that tend to obscure them, I get started in this chapter by considering some of the most important of these assumptions. I trace philosophers' fixation on moral judgments to a traditional philosophical conception of objectivity that, in addition to being influential in a very general sense, shapes the problem-space within which most conversations about the nature of moral judgments take place. My main goals in doing so are threefold. To begin with, following up on recent conversations about ethics and objectivity, I aim to make an initial case for thinking that the pertinent conception misrepresents what objectivity is like (1.2).[3] Further, I aim to bring out how, if we refashion the conception along more appropriate lines, we make room for an account of moral judgments on which they are characterized by a distinctive mode of engagement with the world (1.3).[4] Finally, I aim to establish— and this third goal is the one that gives this chapter its distinctive interest—that the refashioned conception of objectivity I favor is inseparable from an account of language hospitable to the view that

2. I am here using "moral judgment" specifically to mean an episode of moral thought that involves the application of a moral concept. Philosophers sometimes understand "moral judgment" as a generic label for any episode of moral thought whatsoever, and, against the backdrop of this understanding, there is a straightforward sense in which it would be paradoxical to claim—as I am claiming here—that moral thinking includes more than moral judgment-making. But there is nothing paradoxical about the thesis that I am advancing: viz., that moral thinking does not always involve the application of moral concepts.

3. I present a second case for this in Chapter 2.

4. With an eye to attaining this second goal, I will, in section 1.3ii, return to the conversations about the nature of moral judgments from which I begin and discuss a respect in which their characteristic terminology bears the imprint of the very conception of objectivity that I am setting out to question.

moral thinking is not exclusively, or even primarily, a matter of making moral judgments (1.4).

By taking these different steps, I lay the groundwork for showing that there are wider possibilities for moral thought than most work in contemporary moral philosophy, with its emphasis on moral judgments, would lead us to believe and, further, that these additional possibilities, when appropriately registered, speak for a significant reorientation in our conception of the concerns of ethics. My overarching thesis in this book is that our habits of moral thought and action need to reflect this reorientation if we are to do justice to challenges that we confront in trying to overcome limitations of our own moral understanding and in trying to negotiate moral differences that separate us from others (1.5).

## 1.1  A Brief Overview of Recent Conversations about Moral Judgment

> Ethical thought has no chance of being everything it seems.
> ~ *Bernard Williams*, Ethics and the Limits of
> Philosophy *(1985), p. 135.*

A central, organizing theme of recent conversations in ethics is that no plausible theory can simultaneously incorporate, without some qualification or correction, both of two very basic features of our intuitive understanding of moral judgments. The first of these two features is one that often gets placed under the heading of *objectivity*. At issue is the fact that moral judgments typically seem to be essentially a matter of sensitivity to how things really—or objectively—are in the world. (Thus, e.g., it generally strikes us as natural to treat claims to the effect that some action or person is "bad" or "selfish" as claims that we assess by attending to what the relevant action or person is like.)[5] The second feature is one that often gets placed under the heading of *internalism*. What is in question here is the fact that moral judgments typically seem to us, at least when they pertain to our immediate practical situation, to have a direct bearing on—or to be internally related to—what we have

---

5. There is an important difference between "the objectivity of moral judgments" in the sense in which I just explained it and what Kantian moral philosophers have in mind when they talk about the objectivity of moral judgments. I discuss the latter species of moral objectivity later in this section.

reason to do. (Thus, for instance, it generally strikes us as perverse to respond to a claim to the effect that some immediately available course of conduct represents the "right" or "courageous" thing for us to do by saying "yes, but that doesn't give me any reason at all to do it.")

The existence of widespread agreement about obstacles to straight-forwardly incorporating both of these features of our intuitive under-standing of moral judgments is a function of a deeply engrained metaphysical assumption to the effect that there can be no such thing as properties that are both objective in a full-blooded sense and also im-mediately related to action. It is widely assumed that, if we tried to make room for such properties, we would be forced to appeal to some metaphysically singular (or, in J. L. Mackie's argot, "queer") quality.[6] And this assumption is generally taken to show that any ethical theory that tries straightforwardly to accommodate both of the above two fea-tures of our ordinary understanding of moral judgments—that is, any ethical theory that endeavors to be both *objectivist* in that it represents moral judgments as essentially in the business of answering to how things stand and also *internalist* in that it represents such judgments as internally related to action and choice—has to be rejected as untenable.

Although widely accepted, the view that there are metaphysical ob-stacles preventing us from representing moral judgments as both es-sentially concerned with the layout of the world and also intrinsically practical has encountered increasing resistance over the last several decades. One sign of this is the growth of interest in the prospects for some kind of *moral realism*. The new trend toward moral realism seems to bespeak a willingness to contest the suggestion of metaphysical ob-stacles of the relevant sort, for the idea of moral realism is naturally in-terpreted as suggesting properties that are both fully objective and also internally related to action.

There is an obvious worry we might have about moral realisms inso-far as we understand them as tied to the idea of such properties. Given this understanding, it may seem as though any genuine moral realism will need to invoke some metaphysically unique quality in order to account for the properties with which our moral judgments are supposedly con-cerned. And, as a result, it may seem as though any such moral realism is doomed to bring upon itself the charge of a "strange metaphysic."

6. J. L. Mackie, *Ethics: Inventing Right and Wrong* (London: Penguin, 1977), pp. 38–42.

There are moral realisms that successfully evade this charge. But many do so only because they insist on trying to reconcile their realist aspirations with the exclusion of objective and intrinsically practical properties. Consider a few influential strategies for affecting such a reconciliation. A number of theories that get discussed under the heading of "moral realism" undertake to accommodate the exclusion of objective and intrinsically practical properties by abandoning any effort to be internalist and aiming only to qualify as objectivist. The set of such *externalist* realisms openly give up the idea of an internal connection between moral judgment and motivation.[7] At the same time, other self-avowedly realist theories—and, in particular, a set referred to collectively as "response-dependent accounts of moral concepts"—try to combine the exclusion of objective and intrinsically practical properties with both internalism and objectivism by offering dispositional analyses of moral concepts.[8] And, if we bear in mind that Kantian ethical

---

7. Any adequate list of the most interesting externalist realisms would need to mention the theory laid out by Philippa Foot in *Virtues and Vices* (Berkeley, CA: University of California Press, 1978). (In more recent work Foot champions a realist theory that reclaims the idea of an internal connection between moral judgment and motivation. See *Natural Goodness* [Oxford: Clarendon Press, 2001].) There's also a loose family of externalist realisms put forth by a group of philosophers—including Richard Boyd, Nicholas Sturgeon and David Brink—who share affiliations to the Cornell Philosophy Department and are for this reason sometimes thought of as forming a "Cornell School."

8. The label "response-dependence" stems from Mark Johnston, "Dispositional Theories of Value," *Proceedings of the Aristotelian Society*, suppl. vol. 63 (1989): 139–174. What unites different response-dependent accounts is, very generally, the suggestion of some equivalence between statements to the effect that "X is good or right" and statements to the effect that "X tends to elicit certain responses from certain people in certain circumstances." Individual response-dependent accounts disagree over which kinds of responses, people and circumstances are in play on the right side of such an equivalence and also about the status of the equivalences. But it is possible to make sense of the interest the accounts have generated without entering into such disagreements. The accounts characterize moral judgments as strictly descriptive. By their lights, moral judgments describe specific responsive dispositions and are thus essentially concerned with the objective world. At the same time, the role they typically assign to affective responses seems to make it possible to depict moral judgments as intrinsically practical. The accounts thus appear to be able to deliver both objectivism and internalism and to do so, moreover, without appealing to any idea of objective and intrinsically practical properties. I am inclined to think that this appearance is misleading and that response-dependent accounts can't help but fall short of furnishing what by their own lights qualifies as a satisfactory moral realism. But I can't discuss these issues further here. For a helpful discussion, see Simon Blackburn, *Ruling Passions: A Theory of Practical Reasoning* (Oxford: Clarendon Press, 1998), pp. 104–119.

theories are sometimes described as realist theories, we can speak of yet another set of self-avowedly realist theories that try to accommodate an exclusion of this kind. We can say that there are realist theories that try to combine such an exclusion with both internalism and a species of objectivism by changing our view of what objectivism amounts to. For Kantian ethical theories maintain that if we're to appreciate the sense in which moral judgments aspire to objectivity we need, as it were, to recognize that such judgments are governed not by our ordinary theoretical ideal of objectivity but by a distinctively practical ideal. The kind of practical ideal that is supposed to be at issue is one modeled, more or less faithfully, on Kant's categorical imperative. The basic idea is that the objective correctness of a moral judgment is a matter of its affirming a practical principle or maxim to which everyone could in some sense consent. And since here the objectivity of a moral judgment is a matter not of getting a substantive claim about the world right but of specifying a maxim with a universalizable form, it appears to be possible to represent moral judgments as both objective and intrinsically practical without needing to appeal to any objective and intrinsically practical properties.[9]

The different realist strategies that I just surveyed are not uncontroversial, and there is a great deal of discussion in contemporary moral philosophy about whether they in fact furnish satisfactory accounts of morality. But this isn't the discussion that I want to join here. What interests me is stepping back from it and asking why the charge of meta-

9. For an especially clear and explicit description, along these lines, of Kantian ethical theories as realist doctrines, we can turn to writings of Christine Korsgaard. Korsgaard maintains that one of the central ethical lessons bequeathed to us by Kant is that ethics is not "a theoretical or epistemological subject" (*Sources of Normativity* [Cambridge: Cambridge University Press, 1996], p. 44). She claims that philosophers who represent moral judgments as having a theoretical logic—philosophers she describes as advocating forms of "objective realism" about moral values (*Creating the Kingdom of Ends* [Cambridge: Cambridge University Press: 1996], p. 278) or "substantive moral realisms" (*Sources of Normativity*, pp. 35*ff.*)—can't help but lapse into metaphysical obscurity when they try to account for the practical authority of moral claims and, by the same token, can't help but fail to make this authority transparent to individual agents (ibid., pp. 38*ff.*). And she depicts this claim as supporting the Kantian conclusion that an adequate account of moral objectivity needs to represent moral judgments as governed by a distinctively practical ideal of objectivity—an ideal whose logic she thinks is partly, but not entirely, captured by Kant's categorical imperative (ibid., pp. 98*ff.*). The upshot as Korsgaard sees it is an understanding of Kantian ethical theories as kinds of realist theories (see, e.g., ibid., pp. 35*ff.*) that are at home within a metaphysics that excludes any idea of objective and intrinsically practical properties.

physical strangeness that all three strategies are designed to respect appears to be one that we need to take seriously.[10] Why, after all, does a thinker's willingness to entertain the idea of objective and intrinsically motivational properties seem to merit such a charge?

The charge is helpfully understood as depending for its force on a traditional philosophical conception, or rendering, of objectivity. Let me stress that when I talk about such a conception, I have in mind something that is distinct from the concept of objectivity. Throughout this book, I speak of the *concept* of objectivity in reference to our concept of a feature of the world that is such that anyone who fails to recognize it is missing something and I speak of different *conceptions* of objectivity in reference to different specifications of what falls under this concept.[11] The philosophical conception of objectivity that governs ongoing debates about the nature of moral judgment, and that is my concern right now, consists in such a specification.

This conception invites us to understand a property as objective if it excludes everything that counts as subjective by the lights of a traditional philosophical conception of *subjectivity*. A traditional philosophical conception of subjectivity asks us to understand as subjective properties such that no fully satisfactory conception can be formed of what it is for an object to possess them except in terms of mental (i.e., perceptual or affective) responses the object elicits. Thus understood, the set of subjective properties includes what might be called *merely* subjective properties—properties an object can be said to possess just insofar as it in fact elicits a certain response from some subject (e.g., "appearing red to me" or "seeming funny to me"). It also includes what might be called *problematically* subjective properties—properties an object can be said to possess insofar as it is the kind of thing that would elicit certain subjective responses in appropriate circumstances. The set of problematically subjective properties comprises affective properties like "amusing." Further, given a fitting story about how, for example, a

10. It follows that for my purposes it doesn't matter whether the above list of realist theories that attempt to duck this charge is complete.

11. It is no part of my aim here to deny that it is possible to speak of objectivity in connection with other concepts—such as, e.g., the concept of a rigorously accurate (or consistent or unbiased) mode of thought. My choice of terminology here reflects the concerns of the particular debates about ethics and objectivity that interest me in the opening chapters of this book.

thing's being red can't properly be understood apart from its having a tendency to seem red in suitable circumstances, it also comprises perceptual properties like "red."[12] Now, according to a traditional philosophical conception of objectivity, the mark of the objective is the exclusion of all subjective properties—both the *merely* and the *problematically* subjective.[13]

It is not difficult to see how this conception of objectivity makes it seem natural to exclude the idea of objective and intrinsically motivational properties. According to its logic, if a given property stood in the sort of internal relation to sensibility or affective propensities that allowed it to be essentially practical, it would not count as properly objective. Conversely, if it had the sort of independence from human subjectivity that would distinguish it as fully objective, it would fail to be essentially practical. So here there can be no properties that are both objective and intrinsically motivational. Moreover, if, within the framework of this conception, someone insisted that there were such properties, it would sound as though she were captivated by the—genuinely strange—idea that features of the world that are absolutely independent of human subjectivity nevertheless possess some special quality that enables them to have an essential purchase on the will.

The result is that, within the framework of a traditional philosophical conception of objectivity, we seem to be obliged to incorporate our ordinary understanding of moral judgments without invoking any idea

12. The inclusion of perceptual properties like colors within the problematically subjective will seem wrongheaded to those who equate, e.g., a thing's being red with categorical grounds for its disposition to appear red. (For a well-known defense of this equation, see Michael Tye, *Ten Problems of Consciousness* [Cambridge, MA: MIT Press, 1995].) But the inclusion should seem appropriate to advocates of a familiar view on which such properties are taken to be subjective properties with a derivative sort of objectivity. The familiar view I have in mind is one that stipulates both that an object's being, e.g., red needs to be understood in terms of its having a tendency to present a certain perceptual appearance and that redness is therefore disqualified from objectivity. The view then adds that colors like red are correlated with microphysical properties that an object can be said to possess independently of its having any such tendency and that, as it were, therefore qualify as objective. The result is that colors are taken to be—in my sense—problematically subjective properties with a qualified claim to objectivity.

13. I am calling the set of subjective properties that I just described "problematically subjective" to flag the fact that their status as subjective is problematic—specifically in the sense that it's possible to raise a question, of a sort that wouldn't be appropriate in reference to the subjective status of *merely* subjective properties, about whether or not this status condemns them to exclusion from the realm of the objective. I address this question in section 1.2.

of objective and intrinsically practical properties. Moreover, it is a testament to the influence of this conception of objectivity that contemporary ethical theories are by and large designed to respect this constraint. In addition to the different realist theories I just touched on, this includes also *non-cognitivist theories* of all different stripes. Non-cognitivist theories try to avoid appealing to an idea of objective and intrinsically practical properties by relinquishing an understanding of moral judgments as essentially answerable to objective reality. Thus, some relatively *primitive* non-cognitivisms (e.g., the types of emotivist or "boo-hooray" theories associated with various logical positivists) represent moral thought as concerned with non-objective properties that are merely subjective.[14] And more *sophisticated* non-cognitivisms (e.g., various prescriptivisms, error theories and expressivisms) represent moral thought as concerned with non-objective properties that are problematically subjective.[15]

In the next section, I critically examine the line of reasoning that leads moral philosophers to exclude the idea of objective and intrinsically practical properties by raising a question about the traditional philosophical conception of objectivity that drives it. I ask whether we are right to accept the wholesale a priori exclusion from objectivity of problematically subjective properties, or whether we should instead endorse an alternative conception of objectivity that includes the problematically subjective.

The very idea of a conception of objectivity that takes certain subjective properties within its scope may seem to conflict with our ordinary understanding of objectivity and subjectivity as conceptual opposites. So it is worth emphasizing that the appearance of a conceptual barrier is in fact nothing more than a product of the traditional philosophical vocabulary that I just described. The vocabulary in question is one on which "subjective" is used both to denote properties that can only adequately be conceived in terms of our sensibility and to denote non-objective properties. This way of talking may seem simply to mirror our ordinary forms of thought and speech. For in ordinary linguistic contexts we often take claims to the effect that some judgment is subjective

14. The classic defense of such a primitive non-cognitivism is given in chapter 6 of A. J. Ayer's *Language, Truth and Logic* (New York: Dover Publications, 1952).

15. I discuss the internal logic of what I call sophisticated non-cognitivisms in greater detail in section 1.3.ii.

to mean that its appearance of truth or appropriateness is a reflection of someone's subjective makeup and that it therefore needs to be regarded as falling short of objectivity. But there is a philosophically decisive misfit between this ordinary way of talking and the traditional philosophical conception of objectivity at issue. When we use "subjective" in such ordinary contexts, we are typically using it to refer to properties that are merely a projection of someone's subjectivity—or *merely* subjective properties—and not to the kinds of subjective properties that I am describing as problematically subjective. Indeed, our everyday discursive practices encode an understanding of these properties as objective. This means that it is possible to contemplate a question about the merits of a conception of objectivity that takes problematically subjective properties within its scope without worrying about offending against our ordinary understanding of objectivity and subjectivity as conceptually opposed.[16]

For the sake of convenience, I use the following monikers for the competing conceptions of objectivity at play. I describe the traditional philosophical conception that I want to challenge—on which objectivity is construed as too restrictive to incorporate problematically subjective properties—as *the narrower conception*. And I describe the alternative,

---

16. There is another consideration that might seem to speak against even seriously entertaining such a question. A conception of objectivity that incorporates the problematically subjective might seem to be excluded on the ground that it comes into conflict with a familiar moral psychology that gets described as "Humean." What distinguishes this moral psychology is a sharp contrast between the beliefs and desires in which our cognitive and conative faculties deal. On its terms, desires are taken to be active expressions of our affective natures, and beliefs, to the extent that they are undistorted, are taken to owe their contents to wholly passive processes. The point here is that the philosophically less traditional conception of objectivity that I am considering makes room for beliefs that fail to conform to this view. The conception treats problematically subjective properties as objective, and it thereby makes room for a class of undistorted beliefs—viz., beliefs about such properties—that have contents that are available not in the (wholly passive) manner of Humean moral psychology but only via the (active) exercise of the subjective propensities in terms of which the properties need to be understood. It is, however, unclear why we should take the fact of conflict between this conception of objectivity and the view of belief internal to Humean moral psychology as a reason for refusing seriously to entertain the conception. Although the Humean view has a certain intuitive appeal, and although it currently enjoys significant philosophical respect, attempts to discredit it also have a venerable history, and nothing bars us from representing our efforts to grapple with a question about the merits of the pertinent conception of objectivity as an extension of this history. (For a further comment on Humean moral psychology, see note 35.)

philosophically heterodox conception of objectivity that I explore—on which objectivity is conceived as capacious enough to encompass problematically subjective properties—as *the wider conception.* The question that I address in the next section, to put it in these terms, is whether there are grounds for rejecting the narrower conception and helping ourselves instead to its wider counterpart.

Although my aim in defending the wider conception of objectivity is to explore its implications for ethics, and, although this conception promises to eliminate certain obstacles to assimilating our ordinary understanding of moral judgments as both essentially concerned with the world and intrinsically practical, my central goal is not to use the conception for this project of assimilation. A number of contemporary moral philosophers have undertaken projects along these lines,[17] and, while I here make use of what I see as some important insights from their work, my emphasis is on a point that receives relatively little attention. My primary concern is not to show that the wider conception of objectivity better prepares us to take our ordinary understanding of moral judgments at face value. Rather, I am concerned to show that, in doing so, it sheds light on the way in which moral judgments are concerned with the world. One of my main contentions below is that a proper grasp of what speaks for the wider conception equips us, not to defend a moral realism that preserves the stress on moral judgments characteristic of other realist theories, but rather to revise our understanding of how moral judgments are engaged with the world in a way that discourages us from prejudicially limiting the moral interest of language to moral judgment-making alone.

## 1.2 Rethinking Objectivity

> The more narrowly we examine actual language, the sharper
> becomes the conflict between it and our requirement . . . The
> conflict becomes intolerable; the requirement is now in danger of

---

17. The most original contemporary philosophers to do so are John McDowell, David Wiggins, and Sabina Lovibond. See esp. McDowell, *Mind, Value and Reality* (Cambridge, MA: Harvard University Press, 1998); Wiggins, *Needs, Values, Truth: Essays in the Philosophy of Value,* 3rd ed. (Oxford: Clarendon Press, 1998); Lovibond, *Realism, Imagination and Ethics* (Minneapolis: University of Minnesota Press, 1983), and *Ethical Formation* (Cambridge, MA: Harvard University Press, 2003).

> becoming empty.—We have got on to slippery ice where there is no
> friction and so in a certain sense the conditions are ideal, but also,
> just because of that, we are unable to walk. We want to walk: so we
> need *friction*. Back to the rough ground!
>
> ~ *Wittgenstein*, Philosophical Investigations, §570.

The common denominator of a classic set of strategies for defending
the narrower conception of objectivity is an idea that is simple and not
without a certain intuitive appeal: namely, that the subjective (i.e., perceptual and affective) endowments we draw on in thinking and talking
about how things are have an essential tendency to distort our view of
reality, and that it is therefore only by abstracting from such endowments that we can assure ourselves of having our minds around more
than mere appearance.[18] This idea is sometimes formulated in terms of
a requirement to survey the world from a maximally abstract (i.e., dispassionate and dehumanized) vantage point, and, thus formulated, it
seems to lend clear support to a conception of objectivity that counts as
"narrower" in that it excludes not only merely subjective properties but
also problematically subjective ones.[19] For, to the extent that we take
seriously the requirement for an abstract or non-subjective vantage
point, we seem obliged to conceive progress toward an objectively accurate view of the world as involving a winnowing process that leaves ever
fewer properties with an essential reference to subjectivity (i.e., ever
fewer properties that are either merely or problematically subjective).[20]

---

18. For a couple of influential (but to my mind overly sympathetic) contemporary discussions of this idea about how to distinguish between reality and appearance, see Bernard
Williams, *Descartes: The Project of Pure Enquiry* (London: Penguin, 1978), esp. chapter 2; and
Thomas Nagel, "Subjective and Objective," in *Mortal Questions* (Cambridge: Cambridge Uni-
versity Press, 1979), pp. 196–214, and *The View From Nowhere* (Oxford: Oxford University
Press, 1986), esp. chapter 1. For a more recent (and to my mind appropriately skeptical) dis-
cussion of the idea, see Barry Stroud, *The Quest for Reality: Subjectivism and The Metaphysics of
Colour* (Oxford: Oxford University Press, 2000).

19. There are strategies for defending the narrower conception of objectivity that, unlike the strategies that are my initial concern here, aim to avoid reliance on the idea of an
ideally abstract vantage point. I broach the topic of such strategies toward the end of this
section.

20. Both Williams and Nagel use the classic strategy described in this paragraph to motivate the narrower conception. They agree in endorsing not only a familiar philosophical account of how perceptual, or secondary, properties are excluded from objectivity (see, e.g.,

When the narrower conception of objectivity is conceived as encoding an abstract epistemological requirement—or, as I will hereafter put it, an *abstraction requirement*—it has significant implications for how we understand discursive activity or the use of concepts. In speaking here of the use of concepts, I am employing "concept" as a technical term. In my parlance, a *concept* is something that determines objectively the same content in different circumstances, and, by the same token, a *sound conceptual practice* is one that deals in genuine, objective regularities. Employing this terminology, we can say that it is an implication of the imposition of an abstraction requirement that the regularities constitutive of a sound conceptual practice must transcend the practice in the sense of being discernible independently of any subjective responses characteristic of us as participants in it.

The different arguments against the narrower conception that I explore in this book turn on a question about whether we are right to understand our conceptual practices as thus beholden to an abstraction requirement. The particular argument of this kind that I want to sketch right now draws its inspiration from central passages of Wittgenstein's *Philosophical Investigations*. Part of what interests me about the pertinent passages has to do with the fact that they already enjoy a certain familiarity in this context. A number of philosophers—most originally and influentially, Stanley Cavell and John McDowell—have appealed to these considerations in suggesting that Wittgenstein is hostile to what I call the narrower conception of objectivity.[21] The work of these philosophers is, however, generally greeted with a certain degree of confusion. Even when they explicitly argue that Wittgenstein is urging us to revise traditional philosophical assumptions about what objectivity is like

---

Williams, *Descartes*, pp. 236–237, and "Ethics and the Fabric of the World," in *Making Sense of Humanity and Other Philosophical Papers 1982–1993* [Cambridge: Cambridge University Press, 1995], pp. 172–181, esp. pp. 177–179, and also Nagel, *View From Nowhere*, p. 14) but also a familiar philosophical account of how affective properties like "humorousness" are incapable of figuring within an undistorted description of objective features of the world (see Williams, *Descartes*, p. 243, and "The End of Explanation?" *New York Review of Books* 45 [1998]: 40–44, and also Nagel, *The Last Word* [Oxford: Oxford University Press, 1997], p. 40).

21. See esp. Stanley Cavell, "The Availability of Wittgenstein's Later Philosophy," in *Must We Mean What We Say?* (Cambridge: Cambridge University Press, 1969), pp. 44–72, and Parts One and Two of *The Claim of Reason* (Oxford: Oxford University Press, 1979). For references to relevant parts of McDowell's work, see the next note.

along more adequate lines, as McDowell, for instance, does,[22] they are often portrayed as doing nothing more than confusedly proposing to reject our concept of objectivity wholesale.[23] Moreover, this tendency toward misinterpretation extends to the work of those who—and, once again, this includes McDowell—sound Wittgensteinian themes in criticizing narrowly objective philosophical assumptions that inform ongoing conversations in ethics.[24] For these reasons, I want to revisit the suggestion that a central strand of Wittgenstein's later thought positions us to question the authority of the narrower conception of objectivity. In doing so, I want to anticipate a predictable interpretative error by arguing that it would in fact amount to a misappropriation to represent this strand of thought as inviting us to do away with our concept of (full-blooded) objectivity altogether.

One place in the *Investigations* at which Wittgenstein's critical preoc-

22. See the papers reprinted as chapters 3, 10 and 11 of McDowell, *Mind, Value and Reality.* Here McDowell argues that Wittgenstein favors a view on which there is something intrinsically confused about the idea that our linguistic practices might satisfy an abstraction requirement and on which "there is nothing but shared forms of life to keep [those practices in line]" (p. 61). McDowell depicts Wittgenstein both as trying to combat our tendency to regard a view of this kind as incapable of accommodating talk of something's being "objectively the correct move" within a linguistic practice and as trying to get us to relocate "the desired objectivity *within* the conceptual framework" represented by the view (ibid.). McDowell thus explicitly invites us to understand Wittgenstein as moving from the rejection of an abstraction requirement to a call not for jettisoning our concept of objectivity but rather for revising our rendering or conception of it.

23. For a vivid illustration of this tendency toward misinterpretation, we might turn to a book of Onora O'Neill's in which she criticizes "Wittgensteinians" for, among other things, representing the ideal of objectivity as hopelessly beyond our reach (*Towards Justice and Virtue: A Constructive Account of Practical Reasoning* [Cambridge: Cambridge University Press, 1994], esp. pp. 77–88). The "Wittgensteinian" with whose work O'Neill is primarily concerned is McDowell. Drawing almost exclusively on the passage from McDowell's work touched on in the last note—in which McDowell claims that Wittgenstein wants us to exchange a traditional philosophical conception of objectivity for a more accurate understanding of what objectivity amounts to—O'Neill argues that, according to McDowell, Wittgenstein holds that "nothing objective lays down right interpretations of concepts, right projections of predicates, right implementations of rules" (ibid., p. 83). She thus represents McDowell as advancing a view from which he takes pains to distance himself.

24. In two of the three of his papers cited in note 22, McDowell brings the philosophically unorthodox conception of objectivity that he finds in Wittgenstein directly to bear on conversations in ethics. And when O'Neill wrongly represents McDowell as calling in Wittgenstein's name for the repudiation of the very concept of objectivity—see the last note—she is attacking what she sees as the implications of such a move for ethics.

cupation with an abstraction requirement is clearly in evidence is the well-known section in which he observes that we are inclined to think of the regularities constitutive of our conceptual practices on the model of the stages of an infinitely long and ideally rigid rail.[25] What recommends this particular image is its fitness for expressing the thought, internal to an abstraction requirement, that a concept's correct projection is in some special sense already laid out in front of us—so that it is in principle accessible apart from any subjective responses that we acquire in mastering the concept.

It is tempting to think that we have a clear idea of what it would be for a conceptual practice to satisfy the requirement expressed by this rail imagery, and that we can therefore easily explain what would entitle us to say that someone had mastered a practice that did so—say, to mention only the seemingly most unproblematic of cases, the practice of developing simple mathematical series. Suppose that, picking up on the narrative of the *Investigations*, we envision a scenario in which we teach a student the series of natural numbers[26] and then teach her to develop the series of even natural numbers; we instruct our student by suggesting exercises and administering tests until she produces the series correctly up to 1,000 and we're inclined to say that she has mastered the capacity expressed by our instruction "add two."[27] What is tempting, to put it in terms of this scenario, is the thought that we can easily explain what would entitle us to construe our student's mastery as a matter of the internalization of some sort of algorithm that generates correct behavior independently of features of her subjective makeup, and that accordingly invites the image of a car gliding along ideally rigid rails.

It is, however, fundamentally unclear how this thought might be defended. Given that we want to explain what would entitle us to construe our student's mastery as essentially independent of features of her subjective makeup, it follows that we can't mention any sensitivity to instruction she manifests (say, a sensitivity she manifests by greeting a correction we give her with "*Now* I see!" and then giving a suggestive description of an error she had been making). At the same time, it also follows that we need to restrict ourselves to mentioning the bare fact

25. Wittgenstein, *Philosophical Investigations*, 3rd ed., G. E. M. Anscombe, trans. (New York: NY: Macmillan Publishing, 1958.) §218.

26. Ibid., §§143*ff.*

27. Ibid., §185.

that she produces correct linguistic behavior. But this restriction represents a problem. The problem has to do with the fact that we are interested in a form of mastery that, qua conceptual or linguistic, manifests itself in an indefinitely extended display of correct behavior. This is a problem because any stretch of bare behavior that we accept as correct, no matter how prolonged, will be consistent with incorrect behavior, and will accordingly be incapable of supplying anything more than a merely partial and hence inconclusive demonstration of conceptual mastery. Thus, the bare fact of our student's writing the series of even natural numbers up to 1,000 won't testify to mastery because it is consistent with her subsequently going on to write 1,004, 1,008, 1,012, etc.[28] What emerges is that we invariably frustrate our own efforts to explain what would entitle us to construe our student's mastery in terms of an image of travel along ideally rigid rails. For we are inclined to insist *both* on a restriction to bare behavior *and* on an understanding of what it would be for our efforts to succeed that is incompatible with respect for this very restriction.

One point of these reflections is, then, to get us to recognize that we ourselves impose conflicting restrictions on what it would be for a person's conceptual mastery to invite the image of progress along ideally rigid rails and that, however tempting it may be for us to think otherwise, we ourselves have no clear idea of what this would be like.[29] Another point is to get us to recognize that, in consequence, we have no clear idea of what it would be for the regularities constitutive of a concept's projection to be open to view independently of sensitivities that we acquire in mastering the concept. The end result is a view of our

28. Ibid.

29. Notice that these reflections are intended to lead us to this recognition even in the case in which the person whose conceptual mastery interests us is our own self. If we want to explain what, as we see it, entitles us to construe our own acquisition of some concept as essentially independent of any subjective endowments, we need to restrict ourselves to mentioning our own bare linguistic behavior. The trouble is that any bare bit of our own behavior that we take to demonstrate mastery of a concept will be inconclusive—now in the sense that registering this behavior will be consistent with discovering that it strikes us as correct to go on projecting the concept in a manner that no longer harmonizes with the projections of those around us. The upshot is that we are bound to upset our attempts to represent ourselves as entitled to construe our own acquisition of a concept in terms of an image of travel along ideally rigid rails. For we are in a position of wanting to insist both on a restriction to bare behavior and on an understanding of what it would be for our attempts to succeed that is inconsistent with respect for this restriction.

concepts as essentially integrated into, to use some of Wittgenstein's signature terms, *customs* or *practices* that instill us with the relevant sensitivities.[30] We might say that here Wittgenstein is inviting us to see that our concepts, far from being instruments for picking out contents that are independently available (as the image of an ideally rigid rail suggests), are resources for thinking about aspects of the world to which our eyes are only open insofar as we develop certain practical sensitivities.

A view of our concepts as essentially integrated into practices may seem to leave them too compromised to deliver full-blooded objectivity, and it may accordingly seem reasonable to insist that, if our conceptual practices in fact accommodate talk of unqualified objectivity, the image of an infinitely long rail must capture an important truth about them. It would not be an exaggeration to say that a tendency to insist on thus employing the image as a standard for full-blooded objectivity is characteristic of the greater portion of commentary on Wittgenstein's later philosophy. Critics and champions of his work by and large agree in interpreting his efforts to get us to distance ourselves from the abstraction requirement that the image symbolizes as an assault on the concept of (unqualified) objectivity, and they thus effectively assume that there is a conceptual tie between such a requirement and our concept of objectivity.[31] This assumption in turn inspires the tendency, mentioned earlier in this section, toward misinterpreting the work of the few commentators who argue that Wittgenstein's attack on an abstraction requirement is intended not to discredit the concept of objectivity per se but rather to correct what he sees as an inaccurate conception of it. For, given the assumption, it appears that there can be no question of distancing ourselves from an abstraction requirement without qualifying our entitlement to the notion of objectivity, and, as a result, it seems only charitable to find some alternative account of the work of commentators who appear to be arguing that Wittgenstein thinks there is a real possibility here (say, an account on which these commentators are now taken to be calling in Wittgenstein's name not

30. See, e.g., Wittgenstein, *Philosophical Investigations*, §§198, 199 and 202.

31. The group of commentators who agree in endorsing this basic interpretative strategy includes but is not limited to those who, following in the footsteps of Michael Dummett, read Wittgenstein as some kind of anti-realist. See Dummett, *The Logical Basis of Metaphysics* (Cambridge, MA: Harvard University Press, 1991), chapters 14 and 15.

for revising a received rendering of our concept objectivity but for rejecting it in favor of a watered down alternative).

There is a straightforward sense in which these interconnected interpretative trends are open to question. To the extent that they are informed by the assumption of a conceptual tie between an abstraction
requirement and our concept of objectivity, they repeat the very pattern of thought that the above reflections from Wittgenstein are intended to expose. These reflections aim to elicit the recognition that
there is something internally confused about the idea of an abstraction
requirement, and that we therefore need to distance ourselves from any
renderings of our basic logical concepts that get spelled out in its terms.
If we take for granted for the moment that the reflections attain their
aim, we can say that there can be no question of preserving an assumption about how to construe our concept of objectivity that retains an essential reference to this idea.

One way to illustrate this point is to consider what abandoning the
idea of an abstraction requirement as inherently confused would involve. To begin with, it would mean giving up an image of ourselves as
capable of discoursing about the world in a manner that doesn't draw
on our acquired sensitivities or subjective responses. At the same time,
it would also mean giving up as intrinsically confused the idea of a linguistically formulable conception of the world that is accessible to us
independently of such sensitivities or subjective responses. Now there
can no longer be any question of our adducing, as if from a vantage
point furnished by such a conception, a priori metaphysical considerations in favor of regarding our current conception of the world as
merely relative to whatever features of our subjective makeups we draw
on in formulating it. For it is essential to the philosophical position in
play that there is no such thing as an alternative conception that is
somehow available apart from any subjective endowments, and hence
no such thing as a comparison between our current conception and
such an alternative. If we in fact jettison the idea of an abstraction requirement as intrinsically confused, we at the same time commit ourselves to jettisoning the idea of a standpoint from which to discern that
our efforts to do so cut us off from objectivity. The upshot is that an attack on an abstraction requirement, of the sort that I am suggesting is
at issue in central remarks of Wittgenstein's, supports the conclusion
not that we are at risk of losing our entitlement to the very concept of

objectivity but rather that we are obliged to relinquish a conception (or rendering) of this concept that depends for its cogency on such a requirement.[32]

This conclusion only seems to speak against the narrower conception when the narrower conception is understood as having an essential reference to an abstraction requirement. So I should mention that, although the conception is classically understood in this manner, there are philosophers who explicitly undertake to defend it while at the same time distancing themselves from the very idea of such a requirement. It is, however, by no means clear that this project has any real prospect of success. Philosophers who reject the idea of an abstraction requirement are committed to representing our subjective endowments as making a necessary contribution to our efforts to get our minds around genuine, objective features of the world. How, given this commitment, can they defend the narrower conception of objectivity? Typical strategies presuppose that it is in some sense possible to survey our discursive practices from an ideally abstract or transcendent standpoint. The basic idea is that from such a standpoint we can see, not only that our practices are at bottom guided by genuine, objective features of the world, but also that these features are there independently of human subjectivity and qualify as objective in a narrower sense. A foray into the transcendent thus supposedly brings within reach a defense of the narrower conception of objectivity that is free from any appeal to an abstraction requirement.[33] But this type of defense is manifestly unstable. It takes

32. It would be possible to summarize this paragraph by saying that the kind of criticism of an abstraction requirement that Wittgenstein develops does not entail a form of *idealism*—where idealism is understood as inseparable from the loss of entitlement to the concept of full-blooded objectivity.

33. For one influential project along these lines, see the writings of Wilfrid Sellars. In his treatments of perceptual experience, Sellars attacks the idea that we somehow encounter experiential content in an ideally abstract manner, independently of sensitivities we draw on in deploying concepts (this is a way of summarizing Sellars' famous attack on the "myth of the Given" in "Empiricism and the Philosophy of Mind," reprinted as a monograph in 1997 by Harvard University Press). At the same time, elsewhere he takes it for granted that in philosophy it is possible to survey our experiential exchanges with the world from a transcendent standpoint. Sellars takes such a survey to reveal that experience is guided by a "manifold of sensibility" that is there anyway and that qualifies as objective in a narrower sense. (See, e.g., "Philosophy and the Scientific Image of Man" in *Science, Perception and Reality*, Hascadero, CA, Ridgeview Publishing Company, 1991, pp. 1–40.) He thus in effect attempts to defend the narrower conception without taking for granted the cogency of an abstraction requirement.

for granted at a transcendent level the very abstraction requirement that it treats as unintelligible at an immanent one. That is, it both rejects as intrinsically confused the idea that we can, immanently, grasp regularities constitutive of a conceptual practice independently of sensitivities acquired in learning it and, at the same time, helps itself to this idea, in a transcendent manner, long enough to observe that such regularities must be expressive of features of the world that qualify as objective in a narrower sense. What ultimately emerges is a strategy for motivating the narrower conception that only appears to progress at the cost of a deep internal inconsistency.[34]

These reflections suggest that it would be inappropriate to conclude from a successful attack on an abstraction requirement *either* that we are in danger of losing our entitlement to the very concept of objectivity *or* that we remain in a position to retain the narrower conception of it. A more appropriate lesson to draw is that such an attack obliges us to refashion our conception of this concept so that an abstraction from everything subjective no longer appears to be its touchstone.

This lesson bears directly on the quarrel between the narrower and wider conceptions of objectivity. The conception of objectivity that emerges here, on which there is no longer any question of an abstraction requirement, is one on which there is also no longer any question of an ideally abstract standpoint from which to make the a priori, metaphysical determination that every (even problematically) subjective property is as such disqualified from objectivity. Moreover, insofar as such a conception of objectivity allows the task of determining the status of subjective properties to devolve upon our ordinary, non-metaphysical ways of finding out how things are, it leaves open the possibility that, while in some cases we may discover that the ascription of a given subjective property is grounded in a *mere* projection of particular subjective propensities, in others we may discover that such an ascription figures in the best, objectively most accurate account of how things are and, further, that the person who lacks the subjective endowments that would allow her to recognize them is simply missing something. The result is a conception of objectivity that is in principle capable of bringing certain—

---

34. For the suggestion of this kind of internal inconsistency in Sellars' philosophical project (see the last note), see John McDowell, "Having the World in View: Sellars, Kant and Intentionality," *Journal of Philosophy*, no. 95 (1998): 431–491.

problematically—subjective properties within its scope and that is therefore justly placed under the heading of the "wider conception."[35]

The Wittgensteinian argument for the wider conception of objectivity presented in this section is, as I have emphasized, philosophically extremely controversial, and it would therefore be strategically unwise to
rest a case for the conception exclusively on it. Taking my cue partly from
this observation, in Chapter 2 I describe and defend a further, comple-
mentary argument—specifically, one inspired by the work of J. L. Austin.
For the time being, however, I assume that the Wittgensteinian argument laid out here at least establishes that it is possible coherently to
raise a question about whether the narrower conception accurately captures what objectivity is like or whether the wider conception is perhaps
more satisfactory. My thought is that, even within the context of this
relatively weak assumption, it would be irresponsible not to take an interest in what is at stake for ethics in how this question gets answered.

## 1.3 Some Further Reflections about Moral Judgment

> We continue to think that children have to be taught the difference
> between right and wrong, but we know in our bones that this
> teaching is not a species of either factual or technical instruction.
> What sort of teaching, then, is the teaching of the difference
> between right and wrong? What sort of learning is the learning of
> this difference? What kind of knowing is the knowing of it?
> ~ *Gilbert Ryle*, Collected Essays, *vol. 2 (1990), p. 385.*

What implications does the introduction of the wider conception of
objectivity have for ethics? In section 1.1, I observed that the wider

---

35. Notice that this conception poses a *global* challenge to the view of belief internal to
Humean moral psychology. (For a description of what I have in mind in speaking of Humean
moral psychology, see note 16, above.) Insofar as it incorporates problematically subjective properties, the conception introduces a *local* set of beliefs—beliefs concerned with such properties—
that have contents available to us not in the passive style of Humean moral psychology but only
via the active exercise of the subjective propensities in terms of which those properties need to
be understood. At the same time, insofar as it relies for its legitimacy on the rejection of the very
idea of an abstraction requirement, the conception also invites the recognition of a sense in which
*all* of our beliefs (i.e., without regard to whether they are concerned with the problematically
subjective) are available to us only via the active exercise of certain subjective propensities—
and hence in a manner offensive to Humean moral psychology.

conception's narrower counterpart is generally taken to place obstacles in the way of efforts straightforwardly to incorporate two fundamental features of our ordinary understanding of moral judgments (viz., the features that I placed under the headings of "internalism" and "objectivism"). This section outlines an argument for thinking that the wider conception equips us to eliminate these obstacles. Its basic argument is one that a number of moral philosophers—starting with John McDowell and David Wiggins—have used in defending accounts of moral judgment that are both internalist and objectivist in the plainest sense.[36] I am generally sympathetic to the work of these moral philosophers, and I am going to follow up on it in arguing that the wider conception removes some barriers to such an account. Nevertheless, I am not going to offer a full-fledged defense of this account. My interest lies elsewhere. My main aim is to show that, to the extent that the wider conception permits us to eliminate certain obstacles to taking our ordinary understanding of moral judgments at face value, it transforms our picture of how moral judgments engage with the world—and, as I argue in the next section, does so in a manner that we can only fully accommodate if we accept the view that moral thinking is not originally a matter of moral judgment-making.

### 1.3.i Toward an Intuitively Satisfying Account of Moral Judgment

> The rationality of virtue . . . is not demonstrable from an external standpoint. But to suppose that it ought to be is only a version of [a more general] prejudice. It is only an illusion that our paradigm of reason, deductive argument, has its rationality discernible from a standpoint that is not necessarily located within the practice itself.
>
> ~ *John McDowell, "Virtue and Reason," in*
> Mind, Value and Reality, *p. 71.*

Let me start with an observation about how we naturally understand moral concepts—one that, as will emerge, I see no reason to treat as anything but accurate. The observation concerns how we naturally take our moral concepts to determine features of the world that can only be fully grasped in terms of particular attitudes and, more specifically, how it comes naturally to us to think that a person lacks a fully satisfactory

---

36. For relevant references to the work of McDowell and Wiggins, see note 17.

conception of what it is for something (say, an action, person or personal quality) to be, for instance, "generous," "cowardly," "right" or "wrong" in an entirely plain sense if she doesn't conceive whatever is in question as the kind of thing that, in appropriate circumstances, merits certain attitudes of approval and disapproval. This observation suggests an understanding of moral concepts as concerned with what above I called the "problematically subjective," and, although at the close of section 1.3.ii I discuss a sense in which it is misleading to speak of *properties* in this connection, for the moment I describe the understanding as one on which moral concepts determine problematically subjective properties.

It would not be implausible to suggest that this understanding of moral concepts equips us to treat moral judgments as standing in the sort of immediate relation to affect that allows them to be internally related to action and choice. (I return to this point at this section's close.) So, given that my goal is to demonstrate in reference to this understanding that the wider conception of objectivity enables us to eliminate narrowly objective obstacles to an account of moral judgments as both internalist and objectivist, it makes sense to proceed by critically examining the kinds of considerations that, within the context of the narrower conception, seem to speak against construing the account on strictly objectivist lines.

These considerations are often presented in connection with an analogy, suggested by the relevant understanding of moral concepts between the properties our moral concepts pick out—moral values—and perceptual properties like colors. What prompts talk of an analogy is the reflection that, on the terms of the understanding, our attitudes play a role in our conception of what it is to be sensitive to moral values that is similar to the role played by our perceptual apparatus in a reasonable conception of what it is to be sensitive to colors.[37] Descriptions of this analogy are typically closely followed by mention of a significant

37. For a set of influential discussions of this analogy, see McDowell, "Values and Secondary Qualities" and "Projection and Truth in Ethics," reprinted as chapters 7 and 8 of *Mind, Value and Reality*, pp. 131–150 and 150–166, and Wiggins, "Truth, Invention and the Meaning of Life," "Truth, and Truth as Predicated of Moral Judgments," and "A Sensible Subjectivism?" reprinted as essays 3, 4, and 5 of *Needs, Values, Truth: Essays in the Philosophy of Value*, pp. 87–138, 139–184 and 185–214. The idea of an analogy here will obviously be unacceptable to those who identify, say, colors with categorical grounds for objects' dispositions to appear colored. See note 12.

respect in which the analogy breaks down. As we ordinarily understand them, moral values are not the kinds of things that merely call for appropriate attitudes in the way that colors are the kinds of things that merely cause appropriate perceptual experiences. Moral values are, instead, the kinds of things that *merit* appropriate attitudes.[38] And, since the question of whether something merits the attitudes internal to a given moral concept is a moral question, it follows that in underlining this disanalogy we are pointing out that, according to the understanding in question, our moral judgments are governed by standards that essentially reflect our substantive moral beliefs. This brings me to the sense in which the understanding is often seen as hostile to objectivism. On its terms, efforts to assess moral judgments are guided by the very body of moral beliefs to which these judgments belong. The understanding is thus aptly taken to represent moral judgments as encoding a form of *circularity*, and philosophers who register this circularity sometimes conclude that it prevents the understanding from, in the words of the members of one influential group of moral philosophers, "serv[ing] to license cognitivism or objectivity about goodness or rightness."[39]

There are different ways of interpreting this circularity worry, and on one interpretation the worry is clearly overblown. Consider a situation in which, in a quite ordinary conversation, someone draws your attention to how standards to which you appeal in trying to justify a given moral judgment bear the imprint of some of your other moral beliefs. ("But you only think *this* is unkind because you think *that* is really important in life.") One thing your interlocutor may be doing is raising a question about the credentials of your judgment by impugning some of those other moral beliefs. In such a case, you may be able to respond satisfactorily, and establish your judgment on a more secure footing, simply by showing that the other beliefs are not mere moral prejudices. This kind of exchange suggests an interpretation on which a worry about circularity is philosophically innocuous. But the interpretation fails to capture the intended force of the particular circularity worry

---

38. See, e.g., McDowell, "Values and Secondary Qualities," pp. 143–146, and Wiggins, "A Sensible Subjectivism?" pp. 187–189.

39. Stephen Darwall, Allan Gibbard and Peter Railton, "Toward *Fin de siecle* Ethics: Some Trends," *Philosophical Review* 101, no. 1 (January 1992): 115–189, 163*f.* Bernard Williams arrives at the same conclusion in "Truth in Ethics," in *Truth in Ethics*, ed. Brad Hooker (Oxford: Blackwell, 1996) pp. 19–34.

that gets raised in conversations about objectivity and ethics. It is not possible to dispel *this* worry simply by noting that there is a respect in which ordinary moral judgment-making, while circular, is nevertheless self-critical. For what at bottom drives it is insistence on regarding as a sign of epistemic limitation the mere fact of circularity itself.[40]

If we want to question the appropriateness of the worry, we accordingly need to ask whether this tone of insistence is warranted. It seems clear that the tone depends for its appearance of soundness on the idea of a non-circular mode of thought. That is, it seems clear that we need some minimally coherent grasp of this idea in order to preserve our entitlement to the assumption that any relevantly circular mode of thought must as such cut us off from how things really are. It is not difficult to find sympathetic philosophical treatments of the requisite idea of non-circularity, for instance, in reference to natural scientific discourse. Natural scientific discourse is sometimes represented as progressing not only toward the development of concepts that are as far as possible intelligible independently of any particular cultural perspectives but also toward a state in which its characteristic concepts bear directly on the world, in an ideally non-circular manner, without the intervention of argumentative standards that reflect scientific opinion at a particular historical period.[41] What I want to point out here is that a mode of thought, natural scientific or otherwise, that is conceived as non-circular is thereby conceived as satisfying the kind of abstraction requirement that is traditionally taken to underwrite the narrower conception of objectivity.[42]

An ideally non-circular form of discourse would be suitably abstract insofar as, within it, applications of concepts would be beholden to standards that have content apart from the beliefs the pertinent mode of discourse embodies and that can accordingly be conceived as accessible independently of any practical sensitivities that we acquire in arriving at those beliefs. In the last section, I presented an argument from Wittgenstein against the idea that a mode of discourse might somehow satisfy an abstraction requirement or, to return to the trope of Wittgenstein's touched on earlier, attain to the image of an ideally rigid rail. At this juncture, I want to add that if—say, in accordance with the

40. These remarks bear directly on the two texts cited in the last note.
41. See, e.g., Williams, *Ethics and the Limits of Philosophy*, pp. 136ff.
42. See section 1.2.

Wittgensteinian argument—we reject this idea we at the same time reject the idea that a mode of discourse might somehow qualify as ideally non-circular. This is noteworthy because, in rejecting the latter idea, we are depriving ourselves of a position from which to insist that the circular character of a practice of judgment-making—for instance, our practice of moral judgment-making—by itself disqualifies it from having an essential concern with how things objectively are. One result of the transition to the wider conception of objectivity is, then, that we appear to be justified in dismissing what is generally regarded as the deepest objection to an objectivist interpretation of the account of moral judgment from which I began.

This conclusion depends for some of its interest on our ability to demonstrate that the account does in fact assign affect a role in moral judgment that entitles us to represent moral judgments as internally related to action and choice. The account, as we are now construing it, is one on which moral concepts are concerned with properties that, while objective, are only properly conceived in terms of their tendency to merit certain attitudes. And, in supporting this understanding of moral concepts, the account eliminates obstacles that, within the context of the narrower conception of objectivity, seem to prevent objectivist views from representing the aspects of the world with which our practices of moral judgment-making are concerned as normative and hence as capable of rationalizing actions. The account thus overcomes at least some of the barriers that seem to prevent more traditional, "narrower" objectivisms from laying claim to an unqualified internalism.

To be sure, quite a bit more would need to be said to establish that this account qualifies as a fully satisfactory internalism. It is a familiar reflection that we ordinarily conceive reasons for acting as possessing, in addition to the normative dimension just mentioned, an *explanatory* dimension in virtue of which they are capable of motivating actions.[43] (The idea is that it typically strikes us as perverse to ask why we should do what we (admit we) have reason to do, and that in this respect we intuitively treat the acceptance of a claim about our reasons as including the acceptance of a motive.)[44] And I haven't said anything

43. See Bernard Williams, "Internal and External Reasons," *Moral Luck: Philosophical Papers 1973–1980* (Cambridge: Cambridge University Press, 1981), pp. 101–113, esp. pp. 104–105.

44. See Nagel, *The Possibility of Altruism*, Princeton, NJ, Princeton University Press, 1970, esp. p. 9, and Korsgaard, "Skepticism About Practical Reason" in *Creating the Kingdom of Gods*, p. 317.

about how this new account of moral judgment enables us to do justice to the pertinent explanatory dimension in the case of moral reasons.

We might try to make progress here by observing that the account asks us to conceive moral development as involving forms of instruction that simultaneously instill attitudes and make direct contributions to our mastery of legitimate modes of thought and, further, that it thus presents us with an image of such development as, in McDowell's words, necessarily a matter of the acquisition both "of a way of seeing things and of a collection of motivational directions or practical concerns, focused and activated in particular cases by exercises of the way of seeing things."[45] I am inclined to think that, by following up on this observation, we could show that the basic account of moral judgment I have been discussing amounts to a satisfactory internalism, but I do not pursue this topic here. My larger concern in what follows is not showing that the account enables us to conceive moral judgment as an intrinsically practical endeavor but rather exploring how it calls on us to see our sensibility as implicated in fully legitimate, moral modes of thought about the world—and how it at the same time invites us to rethink our image of language so that it now accommodates an understanding of moral thought as extending beyond such judgments.

## 1.3.ii  Moral Concepts

> Here . . . a moral concept seems less like a movable and extensible ring laid down to cover a certain area of fact, and more like a total difference of *Gestalt*. We differ not only because we select different objects out of the same world but because we see different worlds.
>
> ~ *Iris Murdoch, "Vision and Choice in Morality," in*
> Existentialists and Mystics: Writings on
> Philosophy and Literature *(1997), p. 82.*

A helpful way to capture what is distinctive about this account of moral judgment is to contrast it with the superficially similar account de-

---

45. "Might There Be External Reasons?" in *World, Mind and Ethics: Essays on the Ethical Philosophy of Bernard Williams*, ed. J. E. J. Altham and Ross Harrison (Cambridge: Cambridge University Press, 1995), pp. 68–85, p. 73. David Wiggins makes a similar observation in "Deliberation and Practical Reason," in *Essays on Aristotle's Ethics*, ed. Amélie Rorty (Berkeley, CA: University of California Press, 1980), pp. 221–240.

veloped within certain non-cognitivist theories—in particular, non-cognitivist theories that conceive moral concepts as determining (not merely subjective but) problematically subjective properties and that accordingly qualify as "sophisticated" in my sense.[46] The hallmark of the particular theories that I have in mind is the thought that, even within the framework of the narrower conception of objectivity, it is possible to represent moral concepts, thus conceived, as genuine concepts that determine objectively the same contents in different contexts. What makes this seem possible is the assumption that the problematically subjective properties that, by the theories' lights, moral concepts determine have non-subjective correlates in reference to which the projection of a moral concept can be understood, in a manner congenial to the narrower conception of objectivity, as a matter of going on and doing objectively the same. Below I suggest that this assumption stands or falls with the narrower conception of objectivity. I approach this suggestion by first highlighting a fundamental difference between the account of moral judgment at play in the non-cognitivist theories that draw on the assumption and the account that interests me.

The two views agree in asking us to conceive of moral concepts as simultaneously guided by the objective world and concerned with features of the world that can only be understood in terms of their tendency to elicit certain attitudes. But this similarity is relatively superficial. To the extent that the particular non-cognitivisms that I have in mind take for granted the narrower conception of objectivity, they are committed to conceiving the objective contents that (as they see it) are correlated with our moral concepts as available apart from the possession, or even imaginative appreciation, of propensities toward any particular attitudes.[47] This means that, by the lights of these non-cognitivisms, the cognitive or objective dimension of our practice with a moral concept must be

---

46. For the introduction of talk of "sophisticated" non-cognitivisms, see section 1.1.

47. The "sophisticated" non-cognitivist theories at issue here come in two basic versions. On one version—e.g., R. M. Hare's "prescriptivism" and Simon Blackburn's "expressivism"—our moral judgments are genuinely about the problematically subjective properties that we take their characteristic concepts to determine, and they earn their intellectual legitimacy through the non-subjective contents that those concepts are envisioned to have as correlates (see R. M. Hare, *Freedom and Reason* [Oxford, Clarendon Press, 1963], esp. §10.1, and Blackburn, *Ruling Passions*, especially chapter 4). On the other version—e.g., J. L. Mackie's "error-theory"—our

separable from any attitudes characteristic of us as participants in the practice.[48] The result is an understanding of moral concepts as instruments for tracing out patterns in a neutrally available region of fact—an understanding that implies that a person could in theory learn to recognize correct and incorrect applications of a moral concept even if she lacked any appreciation of the attitudes in terms of which the concept is intelligible.[49]

Our practices with moral concepts look very different on the account of moral judgment that I am laying out here. Insofar as this account takes for granted the wider conception of objectivity, it sanctions a representation of moral concepts as determining features of the world that,

---

practices of moral judgment-making encode a projective error and are best understood as concerned not with the subjective properties that we erroneously take their characteristic concepts to determine but rather with the concepts' alleged non-subjective correlates (see Mackie, *Ethics*).

48. For an account of this demand for "separability," see Simon Blackburn, "Through Thick and Thin," a contribution to a symposium on "Morality and Thick Concepts," *Proceedings of the Aristotelian Society*, suppl. vol. 66 (1992): 285–299. Blackburn's discussion in this paper is of particular interest because he himself was, at an earlier stage in his career, inclined to assume, wrongly, that a consistent non-cognitivist could deny separability while nevertheless representing our practice of moral judgment-making as rationally respectable (in the latter connection, see Blackburn "Rule-Following and Moral Realism" in *Wittgenstein: To Follow a Rule*, ed. Steven Hotzman and Christopher Leich [London: Routledge and Kegan Paul, 1981], pp. 163–187). For a criticism of this assumption, see the next note.

49. There are some sophisticated non-cognitivist theories that, while similar to those cited in note 47 in taking themselves to be entitled to represent our practices of moral judgment-making as rationally respectable, nevertheless differ in rejecting what I am calling a requirement of "separability." Here we might mention, in addition to some of Simon Blackburn's earlier ethical writings (see the last note), the variant of prescriptivism Williams advocates in *Ethics and the Limits of Philosophy*, and the species of expressivism that Alan Gibbard advocates in *Wise Choices, Apt Feelings: A Theory of Normative Judgment* (Cambridge, MA: Harvard University Press, 1990). What justifies the neglect of these particular non-cognitivisms here is the fact that they are threatened by a serious internal tension. Like other non-cognitivisms, these theories depend for their fundamental appeal on the narrower conception of objectivity. But, to the extent that they reject "separability," they effectively refuse to represent our practices of projecting moral concepts as cognitively respectable by the narrower conception's lights. They thus bequeath to us an image of such practices on which the connection between two applications of (what they represent as) legitimate moral concepts can be discredited by (what they represent as) fully objective considerations. Williams underlines the presence of this tension in his own work when, in a refreshingly frank gesture, he declares, "Reflection destroys [ethical] knowledge" (*Ethics and the Limits of Philosophy*, p. 148). I return to relevant aspects of Williams' work in Chapter 6.

while they need to be understood in terms of our attitudes, are nevertheless fully objective. By the same token, it deprives us of the grounds that the narrower conception of objectivity seems to furnish for insisting that, if our moral concepts are to count as determining objective regularities, their cognitive component must be accessible independently of, or separately from, the attitudes in terms of which they make sense. Now it appears that the objective regularities traced out by our moral concepts are revealed by the non-neutral considerations that count in favor of applying them. Further, it also appears that any tendency we manifest to impugn those considerations, or to insist that they must depend for any authority they possess on their success in tracking independent (or "separable") features of the world, is nothing more than an expression of an unjustified attempt to resuscitate the narrower conception of objectivity.[50] What thus emerges is that here moral concepts trace out objectively consistent patterns, not (as certain sophisticated non-cognitivists would have it) in a neutrally available region of fact, but rather in the moral outlooks within which they function.[51] The result is an account that implies that, in contrast to what certain sophisticated non-cognitivists believe, there can be no question of regarding the person who lacks an (even imaginative) appreciation of the attitudes in terms of which a given moral concept makes sense as capable of authoritatively determining whether a given application of it is correct or incorrect. It is an account on which projecting a moral concept is a matter of discerning regularities in, as we might put it, a vision of the world that is itself already moral.[52]

50. It is sometimes suggested that the simple fact that moral categories supervene on non-moral ones obliges us to respect something like a requirement of "separability." (See Simon Blackburn, *Essays in Quasi-Realism* (Oxford: Oxford University Press, 1993), esp. chapters 6–8.) The suggestion is that supervenience obliges us to insist that the regularities determined by a moral concept be recognizable as justifying its application when they are described in non-moral terms and are thus treated as separable from any attitudes in terms of which the concept makes sense. But this is wrong. Supervenience requires that we be able to find differences in the non-moral level supervened on for discriminations that we want to make in the supervening moral one, but it doesn't by itself require that the patterns traced out by a moral concept be recognizable as licensing its application when they are described in—separate—non-moral terms.

51. For an elegant expression of this understanding of moral concepts, see the passage from Iris Murdoch's writings that serves as an epigraph to this section.

52. Contemporary moral philosophers often speak of "thickness" in connection with moral concepts that, like those just described, trace out patterns that are not indifferently

There is a respect in which some of the terminology of this chapter can now be seen as misleading. At the chapter's outset, I characterized a central set of debates about the nature of moral judgment as partly organized by the exclusion, internal to the narrower conception of objectivity, of the idea of objective and intrinsically practical *properties*. Further, I characterized the ethical interest of the wider conception in terms of its tendency to bring the idea of these properties within reach. At this point, it is possible to identify a sense in which these characterizations are flawed. Talk of properties has its original home in the natural sciences, and I have been discussing a view on which moral judgments, far from determining a set of properties in the same way that, for instance, biological judgments do, are distinguished by an irredeemably moral mode of engagement with the world. In the light of this discussion, it seems advisable to find a new jargon for talking about the ethical interest of the wider conception of objectivity. We might say that this conception positions us to understand moral judgments not as preoccupied with a special set of properties but rather as playing an intellectually respectable role in articulating an already moralized image of the world.

I return to this view of moral judgment in a moment, after discussing how the account of language in which it is at home accommodates an understanding of moral thought that encompasses more than such judgment.

## 1.4 Beyond Moral Judgment

> When we apprehend and assess other people we do not consider only their solutions to specifiable practical problems, we consider something more elusive which may be called their total vision of life, as shown in their mode of speech or silence, their choice of words, their assessments of others, their conception of their own lives, what they think attractive or praiseworthy, what they think funny: in short the configurations of their thought which show continually in their reactions and conversation. These things, which may be overtly and

---

available. I have avoided this terminology because it fails to discriminate between the views of sophisticated non-cognitivists who reject "separability" (see note 49, above) and the view that I myself prefer, and because it thus threatens to confuse. Talk of "thickness" in the relevant sense enters conversations in Anglo-American moral philosophy with Williams's *Ethics and the Limits of Philosophy* (see p. 129).

comprehensibly displayed or inwardly elaborated and guessed at,
constitute what, making different points in the two metaphors, one
may call the texture of man's being or the nature of his personal
vision.

~ *Iris Murdoch, "Vision and Choice," pp. 80–81.*

It would be absurd to deny that moral thinking sometimes consists in
the application of a moral concept, or moral rule, to some aspect of a
situation.[53] For it clearly often does. But we can acknowledge this while
also claiming, not only that moral thinking takes other forms but,
moreover, that these other forms qualify as moral in the same way that
moral judgments do. This is the claim defended in this section, and a
helpful way to see what speaks for it is to follow up on the basic account
of language that emerges from the Wittgensteinian argument against
the idea of an abstraction requirement that I presented in section 1.2.[54]

There is a straightforward sense in which this account can be described as a *pragmatic* one. It is an account that, in repudiating as confused constraints that an abstraction requirement seems to impose on
the use of concepts, brings into question the coherence of the idea that
we can pick out regularities constitutive of a sound conceptual practice
in an ideally abstract manner. Additionally, it is an account that depicts
our capacity to pick out such regularities as necessarily involving sensitivities acquired in the process of learning language and that thereby issues an invitation to understand linguistic competence as an essentially
practical accomplishment. It is insofar as the account issues this invita-

53. Although absurd, this gesture of denial, which is sometimes thought of as the mark of
"ethical particularism," is often wrongly associated with the work of moral philosophers who
champion what I call the wider conception of objectivity. One philosopher whose work has
been wrongly criticized in this manner is McDowell. For a useful criticism of this kind of misinterpretation of McDowell's work, see Jay Garfield, "Particularity and Principle: The Structure of Moral Knowledge," in *Moral Particularism*, ed. Brad Hooker and Margaret Little
(Oxford: Oxford University Press, 2000), pp. 178–204.

54. In assuming that the Wittgensteinian account of our conceptual lives presented in section 1.2 is correctly described as an account of *language*, I am not overlooking the possibility
that a person's conduct may have the kind of sophistication that warrants us in crediting her
with a particular concept in a case in which she herself lacks words for the concept in question. My thought is simply that, even in a case in which appropriate verbal resources are thus
lacking, the relevant kind of conceptual ability is rightly characterized as linguistic and, further, that an account of this kind of conceptual ability is therefore rightly conceived as an account of language.

tion that it merits the label "pragmatic," and what interests me right now is bringing out how, in virtue of its pragmatic nature, it bequeaths to us an image of a natural language as a non-neutral, intrinsically moral acquisition.

Consider what it amounts to to claim, in accordance with the account, that mastering a concept is essentially a matter of acquiring a certain practical ability. Following up on the argument of section 1.2, we can describe the pertinent practical ability as taking the form of a sensitivity to the importance of similarities and differences among members of some set of a concept's uses. Or, rather, we can describe the pertinent practical ability in these terms as long as we add that there is no question of rigidly specifying the content of the envisioned sensitivity. Since, by the lights of the pragmatic account of language under consideration here, there is no question of surveying the projection of a concept in an ideally abstract manner, it follows that there is also no question of determining ahead of time, independently of efforts to cultivate the sensitivity, what shape it needs to take to justify talk of conceptual mastery. Further, since the sensitivity that the account thus represents as internal to conceptual mastery can in principle always grow, opening our eyes to new uses, it follows that, even when our facility with a concept reaches a level that plainly warrants talk of mastery, there is no question of a fixed linguistic competence.

One corollary of this is that different individuals may qualify as masters of a concept when they have developed sensitivities to the importance of different (and equally genuine) similarities and differences among its uses. This is not merely a point about cognitive maturation. It is true that we sometimes describe children as mastering a concept when their capacities to project it are more limited than the capacities of most mature speakers. Thus it is quite natural to say—and here I am adapting an example of Cavell's—that a young child has mastered the concept "dog" when, while she is capable of registering the correctness of greeting her family's dog, the neighbor's dog, and the dog in her favorite board book as "doggie!", she nevertheless cannot distinguish dogs from wolves and foxes. (Perhaps she comes out with "doggie!" when she sees them, too.)[55] At the same time, it is quite natural to wait

---

55. The example of Cavell's that I am drawing on here concerns a young child's learning of the concept "kitty." See *The Claim of Reason*, pp. 171–173.

to credit adults with mastering the concept "dog" until they have learned to recognize the correctness of a larger set of uses. But the point here is not simply that the sensitivities children have to the importance of similarities and differences among a concept's uses may thus differ from those of mature speakers. The further point is that the sensitivities individual mature speakers have to these things may differ as well.

Nor is the prospect of such differences restricted to some special set of concepts. The pragmatic account of language under consideration leaves room for the possibility that, without regard to which concept is in question, the sense of importance it represents as internal to conceptual mastery can in principle always grow. If we speak in reference to this kind of growth—as some philosophers do—of the *deepening* of an individual's grasp of a concept, we can say that, while it may be easier to imagine such deepening in the case of some concepts (say, moral and aesthetic ones), the account treats it as in principle possible in every case. Thus, to mention but one simple example of a rich and variegated phenomenon, it may happen to the person who has clearly mastered the concept "dog" that her sensitivity to the importance of similarities and differences among its uses grows so that she is newly capable of understanding and assessing certain metaphoric uses (e.g., its use in the charge that "Tony Blair is Bush's lapdog"). What emerges is that the practical ability that, according to the pragmatic account of language, I am considering, conceptual mastery represents takes the form of a sensitivity that, in the case of any given concept, may vary not only within a single individual over time (i.e., because it may develop as she first arrives at mastery of the concept and as her mastery then deepens) but also among distinct individuals (i.e., because, in the case of each individual, it may develop in different ways and to different extents as her mastery of the concept deepens).[56]

Given that a natural language is composed of a rich network of concepts, it seems clear that something similar can be said about the practical ability that, according to the pragmatic account of language in

---

56. It would be wrong to protest that the kind of deepening of concepts described in this paragraph is characteristic only of concepts that fall short of being cognitively authoritative. What suggests this protest is the assumption that no application of a concept that comes into view only from the perspective afforded by certain refinements of sensitivity can qualify as genuinely correct. This assumption is, however, held in place by an abstraction requirement of the type rejected within the pragmatic account of language at issue here. For further discussion of the phenomenon that I am here calling deepening, see section 2.2.i. For discussion of it in reference to metaphoric uses of language in particular, see section 2.2.ii.

question, mastery of such a language represents. To be sure, we need to bear in mind that individual speakers of a language possess and employ different concepts and that it would therefore be wrong to equate a particular language with a fixed set of concepts. But, bearing these things in mind, we can say that, on the terms of the account, mastery of a language involves an array of the kinds of intra- and interpersonally variable sensitivities just discussed or, as I will also put it, a complex sensibility.

Since a sensibility of this kind is, in addition to being an individual affair, also a practical endowment, it follows that within the context of the pragmatic account of language at issue here, learning to speak is inseparable from the adoption of a practical orientation toward the world—specifically, one that bears the imprint of the speaker's individuality. And since such a practical orientation to the world cannot help but encode a view of what matters most in life or of how best to live, it follows that here there is a significant respect in which learning to speak is inseparable from the development of an—individual—moral outlook.

This conclusion does not depend for its force on assumptions about the presence of moral concepts.[57] At issue is a conclusion about how an individual's modes of thought and speech, when conceived as possessing a certain pragmatic character, also need to be conceived as embodying a moral outlook. And the point here is that there is no special problem about imagining a person whose modes of thought and speech, while qualifying as pragmatic in the sense that has moral overtones, is nevertheless quite poor in moral concepts. This point is significant because, if we represent language as having a moral character that is thus independent of the presence of moral concepts, we at the same time make room for the possibility—of central concern to me in this section and, indeed, in the book as a whole—that a stretch of discourse that does not make even implicit use of moral concepts may nonetheless contribute to the expression of an individual's moral outlook in a way that establishes it as genuine moral thought.

This possibility emerges as a real one when we make the following allowances: namely, (1) that a person's ability to correctly project any—moral or non-moral—concept necessarily depends on her possession of a sense of the importance of similarities and differences among some set of its applications and (2) that this sense of importance is (a) integral to a practical orientation toward the world that cannot help but encode a

---

57. For my understanding of moral concepts, see section 1.3.

moral outlook and therefore also (b) bound to play an either more or less significant role in expressing such an outlook. In making these allowances, we open the door for cases in which a person is correctly described as engaged in moral thought because, without regard to whether she is using moral or non-moral concepts, she is, in her use of concepts, drawing on a sense of importance that figures significantly in her moral outlook. These are the kinds of cases I have in mind in insisting on the possibility of moral thinking apart from moral judgment-making.

A slightly more expansive overview might be given as follows. We are allowing that a person's moral outlook may make a necessary and substantial contribution to her ability to recognize that even something we are inclined to think of as falling under a 'non-moral' subject heading invites the use of certain terms. More specifically, we are allowing that, independently of perspectives central to the person's moral outlook, it may be impossible to make the connection between the features of a thing that call for certain terms and other things that likewise call for them. The idea is that, if the person's thinking thus expresses her moral outlook, then, even where it deals with what we are inclined to think of as a 'non-moral' topic, it is rightly brought under the heading of moral thinking. The result is an understanding of moral thought as characterized by an indifference to subject matter that allows it to range over in principle *any* topic (e.g., the ways in which humans live and work with animals, the role of luck in human life, the role of imaginative games in the cognitive development of children, the manner in which sibling rivalries and relations of admiration and envy affect major life choices, etc.), and I submit that once we remove ourselves from the artificial atmosphere of academic moral philosophy, where a preoccupation with moral judgments is generally granted the status of a disciplinary requirement, this broad understanding of moral thought will strike us as entirely natural.

Far from being morally insignificant, the expansion of our inventory of possible forms of moral thought I just described is inseparable from a substantial revision of our conception of demands of moral reflection. This emerges clearly if we consider implications of the expansion for what *moral differences* are like. Within contemporary moral philosophy, it is generally assumed that moral differences take the form either of disagreements about whether to apply a given moral concept or of disagreements about whether some moral concept (or set of such concepts) is one we ought to operate with in the first place. In contrast, within the context of this more expansive catalogue of forms of moral thought, moral differences may exist between people who inherit and develop different ways of thinking and talking about the world even where there is no question of a disagreement of either of these types. The view of language that underlies this new account of moral thinking represents even those of an individual's modes of thought and speech that do not involve moral concepts as expressing a sensibility integral to her moral outlook, and it thus makes room for moral differences that are not in the first instance a matter of disagreements about how or whether to apply particular moral concepts. Now we can speak of such differences whenever we confront significant discrepancies between the sensibilities that inform individuals' ways of thinking and speaking or, in other words, significant discrepancies between the images, composed by these sensibilities, of what the world is like.

Once we acknowledge the possibility of these additional kinds of moral differences, we are obliged to admit that in order to cope responsibly with demands of moral discourse we need to consider not only individuals' moral judgments but also modes of thought and speech that do not employ moral concepts and the sensibilities that inform these additional modes of thought and speech. What becomes apparent is that *proper respect for challenges of moral conversation involves concern with nothing less than individuals' entire personalities, the whole complicated weaves of their lives.*

Since non-schematic illustrations of the alternative forms of moral thought I have been discussing are necessarily quite involved, I postpone a presentation of them until later chapters.[58] Right now, I address the following question: if, in accordance with the argument of this section, we assume that we are entitled to talk about forms of moral thought apart from moral judgments,[59] what should we say about the relationship of such forms to moral judgments?

---

58. In Chapter 4, I discuss examples of the alternative forms of moral thought in question, and, in Chapter 6, I discuss additional examples, now with examples on the alternative kinds of moral differences that these forms of moral thought underwrite.

59. It should be clear that this assumption depends for its soundness on the pragmatic account of language that I presented in section 1.2. We need an account with the pertinent practical emphasis in order to allow that a person's *moral* sensibility can directly contribute to her ability to apply even a non-moral concept in a rigorously consistent manner, and we need to make such an allowance if we are to treat this kind of conceptual activity as involving genuine, rational moral thought. Because a pragmatic account of language is thus central to the case I am making for expanding moral thought beyond moral judgment-making, I return to a defense of it in the next chapter.

One thing that I want to stress in response to this question is that both forms of moral thought earn their status as moral in the same way. According to the view of moral judgments developed in the last section (1.3), such judgments apply concepts that are essentially in the business not of picking out members of some set of properties but of tracing out patterns in an already moralized vision of the world. They do not owe their status as moral to concern with a subject matter (say, one constituted by a set of properties). They owe it instead to nothing more and nothing less than the role they play in expressing different moral outlooks, and in this respect moral judgments resemble the forms of moral thought apart from moral judgments that I have been discussing, which likewise belong to moral reflection simply in virtue of the role they play in expressing different moral outlooks.

Having just identified a sense in which certain alternative forms of moral thought are on a par with moral judgments (namely, in the way in which they earn their status as moral), I hasten to add that it is no part of my project to deny that moral judgments, and the concepts that they apply, play a special role in moral reflection. Admittedly, it *is* an implication of the line of reasoning that I have been presenting that there is a sense in which the pertinent alternative forms of moral thought are prior to moral judgments. To the extent that, according to this line of reasoning, an individual's moral judgments are in the business of articulating a moralized image of the world and to the extent that here it is via these alternative forms of moral thought that she first develops such an image, it follows that there is a sense in which her moral judgments need to be understood as taking the alternative forms for granted. Nevertheless, this section's central line of reasoning is consistent with the recognition that the explicit use of a set of moral concepts can advance our efforts to arrive at reflective awareness of our moral commitments and, further, that reflective awareness can in turn assist us in critically assessing our commitments (and perhaps thereby revising or extending them).[60]

These remarks bring to a close my initial presentation of this book's argument for a view of ethics grounded in an understanding of moral thought as including more than moral judgments. Since, on the terms of this view, all moral thought without regard to form is essentially con-

---

60. In Chapter 5, I return to the topic of moral judgment and present a couple of illustrations of the philosophically irregular account of it presented in section 1.3.

cerned with expressing individual moral outlooks, and since, on its terms, a person's moral outlook is taken to be shaped by a sensibility internal to all of her linguistic capacities, it follows that the view might be described as one on which ethics is conceived as distinguished by a preoccupation not with judgments in one region of language but with a dimension of *all* of language. Alternatively, it might be described as a view that expands the concerns of ethics so that, far from being limited to a person's moral judgments, they encompass her entire personality—her interests, fears and ambitions, her characteristic gestures and attitudes and her sense of what is humorous, what is offensive and what is profound.[61]

## 1.5  Conclusion: An Anti-Moralistic Ethic

> We have to learn to love, learn to be charitable, and this from our youth up; if education and chance offer us no opportunity to practice these sensations our soul will grow dry and even incapable of understanding them in others.
>
> $\sim$ *Nietzsche*, Human, All Too Human *(1996), p. 192.*

This view is the main concern of this book, so it is worth closing with a few remarks about terms that I use in discussing it. I began this chapter with a comment on recent trends toward moral realism, and, although the view I favor is very different from the realist theories that I surveyed, there is nevertheless a sense in which "moral realism" might seem to be an appropriate label for it. This view represents moral thinking as essentially a matter of openness to how things really (or objectively) are, and the demand for such openness is often taken to be the mark of a realist doctrine in ethics. There is, however, a sense in which talk of moral realism here is bound to be misleading. Such talk is typically associated both with a focus on moral judgments and with an account of such judgments as distinguished by a concern with a particular subject matter, or a set of properties, in the manner of natural scientific judgments. Given these associations, introducing the label "moral realism" cannot help but obscure the emphasis, within the view I prefer, on an image of language that asks us not only to understand moral judgments

---

61. Iris Murdoch is presenting a fundamentally similar view when she describes the concerns of ethics as extending to the whole "texture of [a person's] being." (See the epigraph to this section.)

as characterized by a distinctive mode of engagement with the world but also to see moral thought as reaching beyond such judgments. This strikes me as ample reason to avoid the use of the label here.

The label that I do use refers to a moral criticism that my preferred view implies of more traditional, moral judgment-centered approaches in ethics. It is possible to give an initial impression of the force of this criticism if we bear in mind that the view claims both that a certain sensibility informs all of an individual's linguistic capacities and that this same sensibility is inseparable from her moral outlook. These claims support the conclusion that stretches of thought that do not employ moral concepts, and that are not composed of moral judgments, may nevertheless directly express an individual's moral outlook and thereby qualify as moral. It is a consequence of this conclusion that, in order to avoid condemning ourselves to simply retaining certain defects of moral understanding, we need to be willing to explore sensibilities that inform divergent ways of thinking and speaking and, moreover, that we need to be willing to do so without regard to whether the ways of thinking and speaking in question involve the use of moral concepts. A further consequence is that there is a moral danger inherent in insisting—say, out of respect for the narrower conception of objectivity at play in more traditional moral judgment-centered ethical theories—that it must in principle be possible to bring our lives clearly into focus, and to act responsibly, in the absence of any refinements of our own sensibilities or modes of response to life. The danger arises because, in adopting this tone of insistence, we in effect commit ourselves to preserving any prejudices that are direct functions of limitations of our sensibilities and to allowing these prejudices to color our efforts to understand our own lives and our relations with others. So, however thoughtful, tolerant, and non-judgmental we are in other respects, we run the risk of exhibiting a kind of moral arrogance.

In Chapter 6, I argue that this moral arrogance is properly understood as a species of *moralism*, and that the view of ethics that I am defending is therefore helpfully described as an *anti-moralistic* one. Since the species of moralism at issue only comes properly into view from within the context of the wider conception of objectivity, and since this conception is anything but philosophically uncontroversial, I need first to examine and follow up on another argument in its favor.

# ~ 2

## Objectivity Revisited:
## A Lesson from the Work of
## J. L. Austin

> In real life, as opposed to the simple situations envisioned
> in logical theory, one cannot always answer in a simple
> manner whether [a statement] is true or false.
> ~ *J. L. Austin,* How to Do Things with Words *(1962), p. 142.*

THIS BOOK'S FIRST CHAPTER contains a comprehensive argument for the view of ethics that is its main concern—a view that represents the concerns of ethics as stretching past moral judgments to the entire webs of sensitivities individuals possess as linguistic beings. In arguing for this view, I questioned philosophical assumptions that seem to speak against understanding moral thought as including more than moral judgments. The main assumption I targeted is, very generally, one about how the concept of objectivity should be interpreted as excluding everything with an essential reference to subjectivity. I placed this assumption under the heading of "the narrower conception of objectivity," and I discussed how this conception of objectivity is traditionally defended in reference to the idea that our subjective endowments have an essential tendency to obstruct our view of the world and that it is therefore only by abstracting from such endowments that we can assure ourselves of having our minds around how things really are. One of my main projects was attacking this idea—in my terms, the idea of an "abstraction requirement"—specifically with an eye to discrediting the narrower conception. My attack, which drew its main inspiration from a central line of thought in Wittgenstein's later philosophy, represents the philosophically most controversial step in Chapter 1's argument, and my goal in the current chapter is to reinforce this argument by launching a second attack—this time one inspired by a central line of thought in the writings of J. L. Austin.

The moment in Austin's work that particularly interests me is one at which he distances himself from the view that sentences possess what philosophers sometimes call *literal meanings* (i.e., meanings they carry with them into different contexts of their use). What interests me about this Austinian gesture has to do with the fact that the idea of literal sentence-meaning is often taken to underwrite a conception of correspondence between language and the world that encodes an abstraction requirement. We can get a preliminary sense of what is at issue if we consider in slightly greater detail what literal sentence-meaning is supposed to be like.

To speak of literal sentence-meaning in the sense relevant here is not to deny that we need to refer to contextual cues in order to clear up ambiguities and to identify the contribution that, say, indexical features of a sentence make to its meaning. To speak of literal sentence-meaning is, rather, to assume both that there must be rules for making such determinations (e.g., rules for assigning values, in particular circumstances, to the parameters that indexicals pick out) and, further, that it must be possible to represent our mastery of these rules, when combined with our knowledge both of the meanings of the words that compose a sentence and of other rules of the language, as a kind of algorithm for generating the meaning of the sentence as uttered on particular occasions.[1] Now, if we assume that we can arrive at a grasp of the meaning of a sentence by thus applying a kind of algorithm, and if we also assume (as advocates of the idea of literal sentence-meaning generally do) that our ability to apply such an algorithm is independent of our possession of any particular subjective endowments, it will appear to be possible to grasp the meaning of a sentence and to determine whether it accurately represents the world in a manner that satisfies an abstraction requirement. This, roughly, is how the idea of literal sentence-meaning is taken to underwrite a conception of correspondence between language and the world that encodes an abstraction requirement, and what I want to stress right now is that it is because the idea is taken to underwrite such a conception that Austin's attack on it concerns me in this chapter.

---

1. For a variant on this standard account of literal sentence-meaning, see note 6.

I approach Austin's attack on the idea of literal sentence-meaning in two basic stages. An image of Austin as repudiating this idea is foreign to standard philosophical interpretations of his work, and, for this reason, I am initially largely preoccupied with exegetical questions. I start by arguing, in opposition to standard philosophical interpretations, that Austin's writings—and in particular, his 1955 lectures *How to Do Things with Words*—contain a thoroughgoing critique both of the idea of literal sentence-meaning and of the conception of correspondence between language and the world suggested by it (2.1). In the second stage of my discussion, I present an independent defense of Austin's critique and discuss how it brings into question the idea of an abstraction requirement and the narrower conception of objectivity that this idea seems to fund. In closing my discussion, I observe that this broadly Austinian case against the narrower conception of objectivity, despite turning on the rejection of a familiar philosophical idea of literal sentence-meaning, is not threatening to our ordinary conception of literal speech (2.2).

Having at this point provided a new argument against the conception of objectivity that seems to speak for limiting moral thought to moral judgments, I will have attained my main argumentative goal. I conclude by appending a set of reflections on how the standard interpretations of Austin's thought I criticize have governed discussions of its bearing on ethics, and on how, when these interpretations are exchanged for the alternative interpretation I advocate, his thought can be seen as speaking for the non-traditional view of ethics that is this book's main concern (2.3).

## 2.1  An In-Depth Attack on the Idea of Literal Sentence-Meaning: J. L. Austin's *How to Do Things with Words*

> The question of truth and falsehood does not turn only on what a sentence *is*, nor yet on what it *means*, but on, speaking very broadly, the circumstances in which it is uttered.
>
> ⁓ *Austin*, Sense and Sensibilia *(1962), p. 111.*

In *How to Do Things with Words*, Austin presents himself as contesting a picture of correspondence between language and the world on which corresponding to the facts is the prerogative of what might be called

*bipolar* 'statements' or propositions²—that is, 'statements' or propositions that always describe states of affairs either truly or falsely.³ He addresses himself to a philosophical audience whose members for the
most part regard this picture as containing an uncontroversial representation of what it is for language to correspond to the facts.⁴ However, here and elsewhere, Austin's particular target is not the logic of
bipolarity per se, but the view of meaning that he thinks feeds philosophical insistence on it—namely, the view that sentences have meanings that they import with them into different contexts of their use or
(to use the philosophical jargon that I employ here) "literal meanings."

It is accordingly noteworthy that most of Austin's philosophical commentators represent him as endorsing the idea of literal sentence-
meaning. Philosophical commentators typically assume that Austin
takes the bipolar 'statement' (or some other view of the 'statement' that
likewise presupposes the idea of literal sentence-meaning) to contain an
accurate representation of what it is for language to have a bearing on
the world. Thus, for instance, in his earliest writings on Austin, John
Searle claims both that Austin's study of speech acts constitutes a cri-

2. I am borrowing talk of "bipolar propositions" from the early Wittgenstein. Wittgenstein speaks of "the bipolarity of the proposition" in connection with the thought that it is essential to a proposition that it be either true or false. He writes: "Every proposition is
true-false. To understand it we must know both what must be the case if it is true and what
must be the case if it is false. Thus the proposition has two poles corresponding to the case of
its truth and the case of its falsehood" ("Notes on Logic" in *Notebooks 1914–1916*, 2nd ed., ed.
G. H. von Wright and G. E. M. Anscombe, trans. G. E. M. Anscombe [Oxford, Basil Black-
well], pp. 93–107, 98–99).

3. I am following Austin in placing single quotes around "statement." Austin uses this
notation to indicate his reservations about referring to a traditional linguistic ideal—often
characterized in philosophy as an "ideal of the statement"—as an ideal of the *statement*.
Throughout this chapter, I speak of 'statements' (with single quotes) when talking about the
philosophical ideal that Austin wants to challenge, and I speak of statements (without single
quotes) when talking about things that Austin himself says about statements. I discuss the
philosophical rationale behind this notation in section 2.1.i.

4. Austin does not address himself to philosophers (such as Lukasiewicz) whose attacks on
classical logic lead them to endorse many-valued theories of logic. But it is not obvious that such
theories can be excluded from the class that Austin is criticizing simply on account of their de-
piction of assertions as tripolar and not bipolar. Many-valued theories typically resemble the
views that Austin is attacking in representing the sense of a sentence as fixed by the conditions
under which it is true and all other conditions. That these other conditions include the conditions in which a sentence is false in addition to the ones in which it is neither true nor false
does not matter to Austin's critique. The heart of the critique, as will emerge, is that sentences
possess fixed senses prior to and independently of being used on particular occasions.

tique of traditional philosophical views of the 'statement' and also that his critique is compatible with respect for the bipolar 'statement.'[5] In slightly later writings, Searle distances himself from the view that Austin's doctrine of speech acts is best understood as consistent with bipolarity. However, although Searle now also introduces a philosophically heterodox account of the idea of literal sentence-meaning, and although his view of what it is to be committed to an ideal of the literal 'statement' thus in certain basic respects changes, he nevertheless continues to favor an image of Austin as wedded to this ideal.[6]

The assumption that Austin takes an ideal of the literal 'statement' to capture the notion of correspondence between language and the world also enters into discussions of his work within literary-theoretical circles, albeit in a very different manner. There has been a dramatic growth of interest in Austin's lectures within such circles since Jacques Derrida suggested that Austin's view of language has significant affinities with deconstructivist views.[7] Theorists who endorse this suggestion typically take Austin to be agreeing with representatives of deconstruction in claiming that there is something confused about the suggestion that language might have a fully objective bearing on the world. Further, they typically take him to be deriving this claim from an attack on the

5. At this stage in his career, Searle, although he acknowledges that some things Austin says about the truth and falsity of statements are at odds with a conception of the statement as bipolar, claims that Austin's hostility to this conception is a function of an error in his analysis of statements and that, when allowances are made for this error, the doctrine of speech acts becomes fully compatible with bipolarity. See John Searle, "Austin on Locutionary and Illocutionary Acts," *Philosophical Review* 77 (1968): 405–424, esp. 422–424, and *Speech Acts: An Essay in the Philosophy of Language* (Cambridge: Cambridge University Press, 1969), chapters 1–3.

6. The account that Searle now discusses in reference to Austin's work stipulates both that the notion of the literal meaning of a sentence for the most part only applies in connection with a set of "background assumptions" and that learning to make these assumptions is independent of learning the meanings of words and the rules of the language (John Searle, *Expression and Meaning: Studies in the Theory of Speech Acts* [Cambridge: Cambridge University Press, 1979], pp. 117 and 120). Searle's account is heterodox insofar as on its terms—the relevant contrast is with the terms of the more standard account of literal sentence-meaning touched on in this chapter's opening paragraphs—there can be no question of capturing mastery of a language in the form of an antecedently available algorithm for generating the meaning of sentences on particular occasions of their use. I touch on this account in connection with Searle's reading of Austin in section 2.1.iv.

7. Jacques Derrida, "Signature Event Context," reprinted in *Limited Inc.* (Evanston, IL: Northwestern University Press, 1988).

idea of literal sentence-meaning. The upshot is a picture of Austin as denying that sentences have literal meanings and as concluding from this gesture of denial that no sentence can describe how things are in a thoroughly objective manner.[8]

Although literary-theoretical commentators thus tend to disagree with philosophical commentators like Searle, who portray Austin as attached to the idea of literal sentence-meaning, their disagreement takes place against the background of philosophically significant agreement. These commentators by and large read Austin as claiming that there can be no such thing as literal sentence-meaning, and that *therefore* there can be no such thing as a mode of discourse that has a wholeheartedly objective bearing on the world. This means that they arrive at the conclusion that Austin rejects the possibility of objective correspondence because they take him to be maintaining that there is an important sense in which an ideal of the literal 'statement' accurately captures what such correspondence amounts to. Further, it means that they effectively agree with Searle and others in thinking that Austin is properly read as assuming that the literal 'statement' contains a faithful representation of what it would be for language to have an objective bearing on the world.

In the remainder of this section, I attempt to show that these different readings fail to do justice to the thrust of Austin's lectures and that Austin in fact sets out to repudiate not only the view that sentences have literal meanings but also the conception of correspondence between language and the world that this view seems to underwrite. Later in the chapter, I bring these features of Austin's thought into contact with the main argument of this book, arguing that Austin is right to reject the view that sentences have literal meanings and, further, that if we follow him in rejecting it we distance ourselves from the idea of an abstraction requirement and thereby discredit the narrower conception of objectivity that seems to speak for restricting the concerns of ethics to moral judgments.

8. Stanley Fish's writings contain one of the clearest and most influential readings of Austin along these lines. See especially "How to Do Things with Austin and Searle: Speech-Act Theory and Literary Criticism," in *Is There a Text in This Class? The Authority of Interpretive Communities* (Cambridge, MA: Harvard University Press, 1980), pp. 197–245. In more recent work, Fish explicitly claims that his interpretation of Austin resembles Derrida's in important respects. See, e.g., "With Compliments of the Author: Reflections on Austin and Derrida" in *Doing What Comes Naturally: Change, Rhetoric and the Practice of Theory in Literary and Legal Studies* (Durham, NC: Duke University Press, 1989), pp. 37–67.

## 2.1.i  Constatives and Performatives

> If . . . someone says that [a] sentence . . . makes sense to him, then
> he should ask himself in what special circumstances this sentence is
> actually used. There it does make sense.
>
> ~ *Wittgenstein*, Philosophical Investigations, §24.

Austin's argument against literal 'statements' (or independently meaningful sentences) begins with his involved and rightly famous treatment
of a distinction between constative and performative utterances. Austin
introduces the distinction by declaring that he wants to critically examine the assumption that "the business of a [grammatical] 'statement' can
only be to 'describe' some state of affairs, or to 'state some fact', which
it must do either truly or falsely" (1).[9] He then tells us that philosophers
are beginning to depart from this ideal of the 'statement' by insisting
that some sentences that have the grammatical form of 'statements' "do
not set out to be statements at all" (2) and hence should be regarded (not
as certain logical positivists aver, as nonsensical "pseudo-statements" but)
as linguistic formulae suited for other functions. In this connection he
mentions, for example, the efforts of emotivists to introduce a category
of "emotive utterances . . . intended . . . to evince emotion or to pre-
scribe conduct or to influence it in special ways" (2–3).

Notice that the approach to departing from a traditional ideal of the
'statement' that Austin thus describes presupposes that some sentences
are perfectly suited for describing the facts and, further, that in this respect the approach retains the category of the traditional 'statement'.
This is noteworthy because, when Austin turns to his distinction between constatives and performatives, he adopts the same approach. Like
the other philosophers he mentions, Austin suggests that while there are
some utterances that meet the specifications of a traditional ideal of the
'statement'—he calls them "constatives"—there are also utterances that,
although they have the same grammatical form as 'statements', are not
suited for describing states of affairs. What distinguishes Austin's particular suggestion is simply his account of the additional utterances that

9. The parenthical reference is to *How to Do Things with Words* (Cambridge, MA: Harvard
University Press, 1962). All unattributed page references in the text and notes of this chapter
are to this work of Austin's.

interest him—which he calls "performatives"—as those in which the production of a sentence ("I bet") is the doing of an action (e.g., betting) that "is not normally thought of as just saying something" (7). This means that his work on performatives resembles other strategies for achieving distance from a traditional ideal of the 'statement' in preserving the view, internal to the ideal, that some linguistic formulae are as such in the business of reporting on states of affairs.

This observation should *not* be taken as a sign that Austin thinks we can develop an adequate criticism of the traditional 'statement' without rejecting the view of meaning that informs it. Already at a couple of points in his first two lectures, Austin indicates that he thinks a deeper criticism is required. He tells us that he doubts that isolated linguistic formulae have meanings in virtue of which they can be classified into those suited for stating things and those suited for other purposes, and he says that he is inclined to think that what does the work of constating is "not a . . . sentence" but "an act of speech" (20; see also 1, n. 1). By thus hinting that he disputes the view of meaning that informs the traditional 'statement' (or constative utterance), Austin indicates his willingness to adopt a more radical critical stance. At the same time, he anticipates a conclusion he draws several lectures farther on—viz., that his original classification of utterances into constatives and performatives cannot, in the final analysis, be preserved.[10]

What precipitates the classificatory crisis is Austin's attempt to legitimate the category of the performative by describing dimensions within which performatives (which cannot be said to report on the facts truly or falsely) can be assessed. Austin characterizes the pertinent dimensions— which he refers to as forms of "happiness" and "unhappiness"—as follows. He claims that in order for a performative to be *happy*, the circumstances in which a speaker comes out with a set of words must meet the conditions of a conventional procedure having a certain conventional effect— a procedure that involves the uttering of these words by a person of a certain standing in a certain situation.[11] He mentions two kinds of unhappiness: (1) "misfires" that result in the relevant act—i.e., that for

---

10. It would not be unreasonable, in the light of these considerations, to describe Austin's discussion of constatives and performatives as having the structure of a *reductio*-proof. Austin's larger aim in introducing the distinction is to collapse it and thereby show that the view of meaning that seems to underwrite it (and that seems also to breathe life into the traditional 'statement') is bankrupt. For one of Austin's own suggestions to this effect, see 4, n. 1.

which the verbal form was produced—not coming off at all (e.g., I say "I christen this yacht *Mystic*," but I say it to myself in the bathtub, so the act in question, naming, doesn't come off) and (2) "abuses" that result in the act being performed in a less than ideal fashion (e.g., when I say "I guarantee that this food is good," knowing that the food is rotten, I do, despite my knowledge, offer a [false] guarantee) (18). These two forms of unhappiness initially appear to hold forth the promise of distinguishing the performative. But immediately after describing the two, Austin observes that utterances that are subject to them, and that in this respect qualify as performatives, may nevertheless bear on the facts in the same way that statements do.[12]

Austin mentions several utterances that, although they qualify as performatives, nonetheless resemble constatives in having a bearing on the facts. He considers, for example, a case in which a person comes out with the sentence "I warn you that that bull is about to charge" in a situation in which the relevant bull is *not* on the verge of charging. He points out that while this utterance is a performative (since the person who comes out with it is performing the act of warning) it fails to do justice to the facts in the same way that a statement might, and that what this person says is "false or (better) mistaken, as with a statement" (55).

Here Austin follows up on his observation that performatives may be true or false by observing that utterances that meet the specifications of constatives can be unhappy or, in his words, that "we can do wrong, speak outrageously, in uttering conjunctions of 'factual' statements" (47). What interests him is not only showing that there are statements of fact that qualify as "abuses" in that they are made in situations in which they are bizarre or inappropriate (e.g., I say "we're almost out of dog food" when a friend and I are in the middle of a serious conversation about our relationship). He also hopes to show that even factual utterances (e.g., "John's children are all bald") can *misfire* or, as he also puts it, turn out to be "null and void" (25; see also 11, 17, 20 and 23) if the circumstances are sufficiently inappropriate (e.g., John has no chil-

---

11. Thus—to mention one of Austin's favorite examples—for my uttering of "I pronounce you husband and wife" to be happy, there must be an established procedure for marrying, and I must be an appropriate person in appropriate circumstances.

12. Austin also claims that some utterances that seem to be clear cases of performatives nevertheless resemble constatives in that they are assessed in terms of how accurately they represent the facts (47*ff.*).

dren) (50–51).[13] Austin is claiming that when the conditions of a certain conventional procedure aren't met it can turn out not only that a supposed constative utterance is odd or awkward but that it's not clear what (if anything) it's in the business of saying. And he is thereby criticizing the assumption—internal to the traditional 'statement'—that we can isolate combinations of words as constative independently of a consideration of how they are used on particular occasions.[14]

Having at this point argued both that "considerations of the happiness and unhappiness type may infect statements (or some statements)" and also that "considerations of the type of truth and falsity may infect performatives (or some performatives)" (55), Austin now speculates that "perhaps indeed there is no great distinction between statements and performative utterances" (52). But instead of immediately giving up hope of "some precise way in which we can definitely distinguish the perfor-

---

13. See also 136*ff.* where Austin argues that factual utterances *misfire* not only when there is some breakdown of reference (as in the example that I just mentioned in parentheses in the text) but also when the circumstances are sufficiently inappropriate in other respects—e.g., when the speaker is "not in a position" to say what she utters (138).

14. A number of Austin's philosophical contemporaries hold that he overestimates the difficulty of preserving a sharp distinction between constatives and performatives. According to Max Black, Austin could have retained his original distinction if he had simply stipulated that no utterance in which a speaker makes a truth claim counts as a performative—not even if the speaker makes the claim in "a special way indicated by the utterance" (e.g., "I state that it is time to do it"). Black claims that if we impose this constraint on what counts as a performative "many if not all of the difficulties that Austin encountered [in attempting to distinguish constatives and performatives] will be overcome" ("Austin on Performatives," in *Symposium on J. L. Austin*, K. T. Fann, ed., London: Routledge & Kegan Paul, 1969, pp. 401–411, p. 406). Here Black is specifically concerned with passages in which Austin suggests that his initial distinction between constatives and performatives is threatened by the discovery that some performatives, while not true or false per se, have some bearing on the facts. Elsewhere Black also considers passages in which Austin suggests that statements, like performatives, are the performances of conventional procedures. Black says he agrees with Austin that there is a sense in which even statements are conventional. He adds that if we are to safeguard the constative/performative dichotomy we need to distinguish between the sense in which the action performed when a speaker utters a performative formula is conventional and the sense in which *any* act of speech is conventional, and he suggests that this task will be a quite straightforward one (ibid., pp. 406–408). The trouble is that Austin gives us reason to think that the task of making a general distinction between the conventional character of performatives and that of constatives will be more difficult than Black imagines. Indeed, Austin suggests that the task is a hopeless one. When he points out that constatives are in general subject to the same range of infelicities to which performatives are subject, he is effectively pointing out that (at least some) constative utterances are the performances of conventional procedures *in just the same way* in which performatives are.

mative from the constative utterance" (55), he explores several alternative strategies. He first searches for a *grammatical* criterion for isolating the performative and notes that "mood and tense . . . break down as absolute criteria" for the isolation of the performative (58).[15] He then considers the possibility that the performative is distinguished by a special *vocabulary* and finds that, for any candidate 'performative words', it is possible both to produce a certain performative without those words and to use the words without producing a performative (59). These failures lead him to ask whether a more complex criterion "involving both grammar and vocabulary" (59) is required, and to consider such a criterion for what he calls "explicit" performatives (61). The mark of an explicit performative is that it makes explicit the agent performing the pertinent action and also that its verb or verb phrase makes explicit what action is being performed on the occasion of utterance (e.g., "I promise to pay you tomorrow"). Austin's suggestion is that we can demarcate performative language by counting as performatives utterances that are "reducible, expandable, or analysable" into this explicit form (61). But, as he goes on to observe, some verbal formulae (e.g., "I approve") seem sometimes to be explicit performatives (e.g., "I approve" when it has the performative force of giving approval) and sometimes to be descriptives (e.g., "I approve" when it means "I favor this"). What these examples reveal is that, in different circumstances of its use, a given sentence may have entirely different discursive upshots—and may thus qualify as a different kind of utterance (or, in cases in which it "misfires," as no kind of utterance at all). It is after considering such examples that Austin gives up the project of sorting sentences as such into constatives and performatives (91).

It seems clear that Austin's narrative about his failure to find a grammatical criterion for distinguishing constative and performative utterances is intended to establish that there is something confused in principle about the idea of such a criterion. Austin presents himself as attacking the view that we can isolate constative combinations of words in

15. More specifically, he notes that the performatives he has thus far considered (e.g., "I name this ship . . . ," "I give and bequeath this watch . . . ," "I bet you sixpence that . . . ," etc.) all have verbs in the first person singular present indicative active. In this connection, he asks whether this mood and tense are distinctive of the performative. What he then recognizes is that there are performatives that do not observe this rule and, more specifically, that there are verbal formulae in the first person plural (e.g., "We promise . . ."), in the second person (e.g., "You are hereby authorized to pay . . .") and in the third person (e.g., "Passengers are warned . . .") that are sometimes issued with performative force (57).

advance of a consideration of ways in which the pertinent combinations are used on particular occasions. He challenges our tendency to regard the contexts in which we come out with strings of words as essentially irrelevant, or 'merely pragmatic.' This relatively dismissive treatment of context appears justified where the 'statement' is understood as perfectly suited (i.e., without regard to the circumstances in which it is made, the purpose for which it is made, or the audience to whom it is made) for describing a state of affairs either truly or falsely. Implicit in this understanding of the 'statement' is a picture of the sense of a sentence as fixed independently of its being used to say something to someone on a particular occasion. On this picture, the assignment of meaning to a combination of words is accomplished in a manner that is insulated from mishaps that would render it "void." The picture makes room for the idea of linguistic constructions that are 'purely descriptive (or constative)' in that they describe a bit of the world or make a factual claim about it in *any* context of use. Austin puts critical pressure on the picture, for instance, when he mentions cases in which putative constative utterances "misfire" so that we cannot isolate the 'proposition' that, according to the picture, is invariably expressed by a proper 'statement'.[16]

These remarks illuminate the significance of Austin's practice of placing the word "statement" in single quotes when he talks about a traditional philosophical ideal of the descriptive 'statement' (a practice I have adopted here). Since Austin rejects the idea that it is possible to determine the meaning of verbal formulae apart from a consideration of the circumstances of their use, he thinks it is important clearly to distinguish merely grammatical entities from the use of such entities to say things in particular contexts. He proposes to use the term *sentence* strictly for a class of merely grammatical entities and to use the term *statement* (without single quotes) for utterances of sentences in particular situations.[17] In putting single quotes around "statement" when he is discussing a familiar philosophical "ideal of the statement," Austin indicates that he thinks that a particular linguistic ideal, insofar as it depicts meanings as belonging to isolated combinations of words, is

16. Austin writes that "in order to explain what can go wrong with statements we cannot just concentrate on the proposition involved (whatever that is) as has been done traditionally" (52).

17. In "Truth" (*Philosophical Papers*, 3rd ed., edited by J. O. Urmson and G. J. Warnock, Oxford: Oxford University Press, 1979, pp. 117–133), Austin explicitly discusses this distinction between *sentences* and *statements* (see pp. 119–120). He sometimes restricts the application

properly understood as containing not (as it tends to be portrayed) an account of the workings of *statements* but rather an account of the workings of *sentences*.[18]

Although Austin repudiates the idea that we can somehow identify sentences as such as either constative or performative, he is not trying to prevent us from drawing distinctions among different ways in which language functions. He hopes to discourage us from studying the workings of language by looking at isolated sentences. But he thinks that we can productively study language if we take as our object what he regards as its minimal units: statements (without single quotes) or complete acts of speech. Austin represents his own investigations of language as exclusively concerned with language in this sense, with speech acts. He writes that "the total speech act in the total speech situation is the *only actual* phenomenon which, in the last resort, we are engaged in elucidating" (147). And he signals that he thinks we can classify bits of language with regard to the kind of speech act that they are—with regard, as he will put it, to their "illocutionary forces."[19]

### 2.1.ii  Isolating the Illocutionary

> The source of the mistake seems to be the notion of *thoughts which accompany the sentence*.
>
> ~ *Wittgenstein, MS. 110, in David Stern*, Wittgenstein on Mind and Language *(1995), p. 105.*

Austin begins his discussion of the illocutionary act by offering the following gloss. The illocutionary act is, he writes, the "performance of an

---

of the term "statement" to specific sorts of utterances (131). I touch on this restriction in note 24.

18. At the opening of his lectures, Austin claims that philosophers endorse a traditional ideal of the 'statement' in part because they fail to distinguish sentences from statements. He tells us that they tend to obscure the fact that "not all 'sentences' are (used in making) statements" and that they do so through "some loose use of 'sentence' for 'statement'" (1).

19. Indeed, Austin believes that we can classify bits of language as either constatives or performatives—as long as we are clear that what we are doing is classifying *acts of speech* according to whether or not, in performing them, the relevant speaker constates something and not classifying *sentences* according to whether or not they are suited for constating things. The fact that Austin is willing to use a vocabulary of "constatives" and "performatives" later in his lectures should, for this reason, not be taken as a sign that he equivocates about whether it is possible to sort sentences as such into constatives and performatives.

act *in* saying something as opposed to [the] performance of an act *of* saying something" (99). He announces that his "interest in [his] lectures is to fasten on [this] act and contrast it" both with the "locutionary act," the act of saying something "with a certain sense and a certain reference," and also with the "perlocutionary act," the act of producing certain consequential effects by saying something (103).

The distinction between locutionary and illocutionary acts is among the more controversial points of Austin's lectures.[20] Austin himself seems to invite debate on this topic by expressing reservations at several points about the adequacy of his own conception of the locutionary act. He says, for example, that he is inclined to think that "a great many further refinements would be possible and necessary if we were to discuss [the locutionary act] for its own sake" (95); and at one point he even says that a distinction between locutionary acts and illocutionary acts "is only adumbrated" in his lectures and that he himself is not sure *"if this distinction is sound"* (148, stress in the original). It would, however, be wrong to take the moments at which Austin voices a lack of confidence in his account of the locutionary act as a sign that he suspects that the things he says here, taken as a whole, are flawed. This becomes clear once we locate his worries about the account within the architectonic of the lectures.

The main point of Austin's treatment of the locutionary act is not to isolate this act itself but rather to avert what he regards as a natural misunderstanding of the *illocutionary* act. He wants to make it clear that when he talks about the illocutionary forces of utterances he is not talking about ways in which grammatically correct and meaningful sentences— or "locutions"—are used. He says that he believes that the "descriptive fallacy" (i.e., the fallacy of thinking that the proper business of all 'statements' is to describe a state of affairs truly or falsely) typically arises when questions about all different sorts of features of language, including the illocutionary forces of utterances, are conceived as questions of what he calls "locutionary usage" (99–100).

When Austin speaks of locutions (or locutionary usage) in thus anticipating a misunderstanding of his notion of the illocutionary act, he is not employing the term in a sense that he himself ultimately wants to endorse. His thought is that if we conceive questions about illocutionary force as questions about the manner in which particular locutions are used—where locutions are understood as independently meaning-

20. In this connection, see Searle, "Austin on Locutionary and Illocutionary Acts."

ful sentences—then, in speaking about the illocutionary force of a particular utterance, we will be at least tacitly assuming that we can make out what locution is at issue without first grasping how, in the situation at hand, the speaker is using a set of words to say something to someone. He worries that if we conceive of the meaning of a combination of words in this way as somehow fixed independently of its being used to say something to someone on a particular occasion—so that it appears possible to tell what locution is at issue even if we cannot, as it were, specify the illocutionary force with which it is intended—then it will seem to make sense to think that some sentences are (on account of the locutionary acts we imagine are invariably performed when they are uttered) ideally suited for making a factual claim. We will be inclined to embrace a version of the view of meaning, underlying a traditional philosophical ideal of the statement, that he attacks in his discussion of constative and performative utterances.

To the extent that Austin endorses a conception of the locutionary act at all, he favors one according to which "to perform a locutionary act is in general . . . also and *eo ipso* to perform an *illocutionary* act" (98, stress in the original). Austin stresses that he thinks that whenever I say anything (except things like "ouch" and "damn") I perform both a locutionary act (i.e., an act of saying something with a certain meaning) and an illocutionary act (i.e., an act of saying something with a certain force). (See, e.g., 113 and 132.) He is drawn toward this view by the thought that there is no such thing as identifying the meaning of a combination of words (or: no such thing as identifying the "locutionary act" performed when a combination of words is uttered) independently of an appreciation of how those words are being used to say something to someone on a particular occasion (or: independently of an appreciation of their "illocutionary force"). Our ability to say what a bit of language means, as he sees it, is parasitic on our understanding of it as a complete act of speech or illocutionary act. His refusal to regard locutionary and illocutionary acts as separate kinds of acts thus stems from the view that it is only insofar as the circumstances in which a combination of words is uttered satisfy the conditions of a certain conventional procedure—the conditions for performing a certain illocutionary act—that it is constituted as the (meaningful) utterance that it is.[21]

---

21. Given that, for reasons just touched on, Austin's treatment of the illocutionary might be represented as committing him to the view that language is *conventional*, we should note

In section 2.2, I have more to say about the kinds of considerations that lead Austin—and that may also lead us—to be suspicious of the idea that sentences have literal or conventional meanings that they carry with them into every context of their use.[22] For the moment, however, I want to close my discussion of Austin's attack on this idea with a remark about his method for distinguishing illocutionary and locutionary acts and also a further remark about how he distinguishes illocutionary and perlocutionary acts.

Austin takes his larger account of locutionary and illocutionary acts to bring into question the idea that we might develop a theory that could be used to identify the locutionary acts performed whenever particular sentences are used. But his strategy for combating this idea involves allowing himself at first to entertain it. After initially elaborating

---

that the claim about language's conventionality that he is rightly construed as making differs significantly from certain more familiar claims about the conventional character of language. When Austin insists that understanding the locutionary act performed in a given set of circumstances requires first seeing how those circumstances satisfy the conditions for performing some conventional, illocutionary procedure, he is suggesting that in order to understand what someone is saying in uttering certain words we need first to have a sense of the intelligible or illocutionary point of producing those words in those circumstances. His suggestion is that there is no question of authoritatively determining what someone is saying in a manner that does not presuppose such a sense, and what merits emphasis here is that this suggestion is foreign to various well-known attempts to show that language is conventional. Thus, e.g., when David Lewis develops his famous argument to the effect that the adoption of a particular language is a matter of convention (see *Convention: A Philosophical Study* (Cambridge, MA: Harvard University Press, 1969), he is not distancing himself from the idea that it is possible to grasp what someone is saying in uttering a sentence independently of an appreciation of the practical point of using the sentence on the pertinent occasion. It follows that Lewis needs to be understood as pursuing a project that, whatever interest it possesses on its own terms, is fundamentally different from Austin's.

22. It would be wrong to represent the kind of attack on the idea of literal sentence-meaning that Austin here launches, as Peter Geach once famously did, as undermined by the Fregean observation that a thought that occurs unasserted in discourse (say, because it is the antecedent in a condition or a disjunct in a disjunction) may nonetheless have a determinate content. See Geach, *Logic Matters* (Oxford: Blackwell, 1972) pp. 254–258. This observation only appears to amount to a telling objection if we assume that the attack has to do with whether thoughts are asserted in the sense that Geach has in mind. But this assumption is clearly false. Austin is claiming that sentences depend for their content not on being asserted in Geach's sense but rather on being used to say something to someone in a particular context. And this claim applies to complex sentences involving clauses that express unasserted thoughts just as it applies to simpler sentences. (For a helpful discussion of limitations of Geach's objection, see François Recanati, *Literal Meaning* [Cambridge, Cambridge University Press, 2004], pp. 154–155.)

his (suspect) notion of the locutionary act, he criticizes it by rejecting as flawed an idea that it presupposes—viz., that it is possible to isolate the locutionary act that is performed when a particular sentence is employed in the absence of a grasp of the illocutionary force with which it is being used. Austin's misgivings about the viability of his own notion of the locutionary act are best understood as directed toward his initial description of it and should not be interpreted as a sign that he lacks confidence in his overall treatment.

After contrasting the illocutionary act with the locutionary act, Austin goes on to contrast it with the perlocutionary act. He distinguishes the sorts of *conventional* effects that belong to the illocutionary act (e.g., my saying something that has the illocutionary force of a promise has the effect of my being committed by my promise [102]) from the sorts of *consequential* effects that uttering a string of words may have (e.g., your saying "Look what you're doing!" may have the effect of my stopping my work and looking to see whether I have perhaps spilled my coffee or put my elbow in the jam). He calls the production of the latter kind of effects a perlocutionary act (101), and says he wants to keep us from confusing illocutionary acts with perlocutionary ones (103). In urging us not to understand his remarks about illocutionary force as remarks about perlocutions, Austin is, once again, guarding against the picture of meaning at play in a traditional philosophical ideal of the 'statement'. What interests him is the fact that it is possible to identify the perlocutionary (or consequential) effects of an utterance without understanding what someone is saying in uttering the relevant string of words. His thought is that, insofar as it's possible to sort utterances according to their perlocutionary forces without understanding them, a system of classifying utterances according to such forces won't threaten the idea that we can grasp the meaning of a sentence without attending to a context of its significant use (114–115). It is because he realizes that we could accordingly study perlocutions without abandoning the idea of literal sentence-meaning that he insists on distinguishing his interest in illocutions—which is specifically driven by his efforts to rid himself of the idea of such meaning—from an interest in perlocutions.[23]

---

23. Although Austin's distinction between illocutions and perlocutions hasn't proved as controversial as his distinction between illocutions and locutions, this area of his work has in-

The aspects of Austin's account of illocutionary force that I have been discussing go unrecorded in most philosophical conversations about his work.[24] Austin's talk of illocutionary acts is typically understood, in a manner that simply obscures his efforts to discredit the idea of literal sentence-meaning, as talk of ways in which (what are thought of as) independently meaningful sentences are used. Philosophical commentators tend to characterize Austin's concern with questions of illocutionary force as concern with what he himself disparages as questions of "locutionary usage." And they then often proceed to represent themselves as following in his footsteps when they describe schemes for classifying illocutionary forces that are conceived in terms of such questions. One fundamental problem with this approach to Austin's work is that, in failing to register his critique of the idea of literal sentence-meaning, it also fails to register his interest in using such a critique to take a fresh look at what it is for language to correspond to the world.[25]

---

spired some interesting discussion about the philosophical interest of the category of the perlocutionary. I turn to relevant issues in section 2.3.

24. One further comment about this account is in order here. After contrasting illocutionary acts with locutionary and perlocutionary acts, Austin goes on to classify utterances according to their illocutionary forces. At this juncture, he starts to refer to those utterances that have the illocutionary forces of promises, bets, warnings, etc., as "promises," "bets," "warnings," and he starts to use the term "statement" (without single quotes) not, as he did previously, to refer to all historical utterances of sentences but rather to refer exclusively to those utterances that have the illocutionary force of statements. See note 17.

25. Another problem with this approach is that it obscures connections between theoretical concerns that guide Austin's analysis of the workings of language and the *linguistic method* he employs throughout his work. It is characteristic of Austin to proceed philosophically by investigating how particular expressions are ordinarily used and arguing that philosophers misuse those expressions, thereby lapsing into "nonsense" or "meaninglessness" (e.g., *Sense and Sensibilia* (Oxford: Oxford University Press, 1962), pp. 10, 15, and 19). Moreover, when Austin explicitly discusses his characteristic method (see esp. "A Plea for Excuses," *Philosophical Papers*, pp. 175–204), he makes it clear that he takes this charge of nonsense to represent not a *merely pragmatic* objection (i.e., one that is consistent with our having a grasp on what it is philosophers are saying) but rather a *logical* objection (i.e., one whose upshot is that, even though philosophers are employing sentences that we know perfectly well how to use in other contexts, it's not clear what, if anything, they are saying). This logical criticism depends for its cogency on Austin's rejection of the idea of literal sentence-meaning. It takes for granted his thought that it is impossible to grasp the locutionary act someone is performing in uttering a

## 2.1.iii The Happy Truth

> And forget, for once and for a while, that . . . curious question "Is it true?" May we?
>
> ~ Austin, *"A Plea for Excuses," in*
> Philosophical Papers *(1979), p. 185, n. 2.*

When, toward the end of *How to Do Things With Words,* Austin turns to the question of how we conceive correspondence between language and the world, his accent is on challenging a fixation on truth and falsity—or, in his parlance, a "true/false fetish" (142)—that he thinks is nourished by the idea of literal sentence-meaning. He realizes that, to the extent that it seems possible to identify sentences as such as constative, it will seem reasonable to think that we can characterize the relation of correspondence between language and the facts without investigating how what we say bears on the facts in particular circumstances. *Now* it will seem as though we are justified in conceiving "true" and "false" as terms of assessment which (because, by our lights, they pertain to a relationship between sentences and world that is not caught up with our conventional procedures for performing speech acts) are essentially different from the terms of assessment employed in assessing speech acts (e.g., "bizarre," "appropriate," "rough," "misleading," etc.). Austin accordingly believes that if we abandon the idea that we can grasp the meaning of sentences independently of a grasp of the (illocutionary) force with which they are used in particular contexts we will want to say that the terms we use for appraising statements "overlap with those we use in the appraisal of performatives" (141–142). One of his strategies for getting us to abandon this idea

---

set of words apart from a grasp of the illocutionary force with which she utters them and hence that *all* illocutionary performances—even, say, those philosophical ones that strike us as having the form of descriptive statements or constatives—are subject to circumstantial infelicities that render them "null and void." Stanley Cavell discusses Austin's interest in this logical form of criticism in "Must We Mean What We Say?" and "Austin at Criticism" (reprinted in *Must We Mean What We Say?: A Book of Essays* [Cambridge, MA: Harvard University Press, 1969], pp. 1–43 and 97–114). But Cavell's contribution to Austin scholarship is in this respect exceptional. The general tendency of philosophical commentators is either to overlook indications that Austin is interested in this sort of logical criticism (see, e.g., Paul Grice, "Prolegomena," *Studies in the Ways of Words,* (Cambridge, MA: Harvard University Press, 1989), pp. 1–22) or to treat such indications as signs that he is confused about methodological ramifications of his own view of language (see, e.g., Searle, "Assertions and Aberrations" in K. T. Fann, ed., *Symposium on J. L. Austin,* pp. 205–218.)

involves presenting sentences with a simple descriptive content (e.g., "France is hexagonal") and observing that they can be used to express thoughts that not only differ but, moreover, differ in their truth-values. (Thus, "France is hexagonal" may say something true when uttered by a top-ranking general and something false when uttered by a geographer [142].)[26] Austin's aim in confronting us with these kinds of observations is to remind us that we grasp what a sentence says, and thereby position ourselves to assess it in terms of truth or falsity, only if we imagine it being used in a particular situation to make a statement. By issuing this reminder, he hopes to move us to take "true" and "false" to stand, not for a "simple" relation (i.e., one 'uncontaminated' by conventions of illocutionary force), but rather for "a general dimension of being a right or proper thing to say as opposed to a wrong thing, in these circumstances, to this audience, for these purposes and with these intentions" (144). He writes:

> Is the constative, then, always true or false? When a constative is confronted with the facts, we in fact appraise it in ways involving the employment of a vast array of terms which overlap with those that we use in the appraisal of performatives. In real life, as opposed to the simple situations envisaged in logical theory, one cannot always answer in a simple manner whether it is true or false (141–142).[27]

By arguing along these lines, Austin wishes to get us to jettison the view that "true" and "false" are essentially different from evaluative terms we use in the assessment of speech acts and to leave room for the possibility that some bits of language that report on the facts are most accurately characterized not as either true or false but rather as, say, rough or deceptive.[28] But it would be misleading to portray him as simply claiming that sometimes statements are neither true nor false—that sometimes they are "approximately true" or "not strictly false." This claim is consistent with

26. In this connection, see also Austin's treatment of the sentences "Lord Raglan won the Battle of Alma" and "All snow geese migrate to Labrador" (142–143).

27. For the significance of Austin's willingness to continue to talk about constative and performative utterances even late in his lectures, see note 19.

28. Austin draws a similar conclusion elsewhere in his work. In "Unfair to Facts" (*Philosophical Papers*, pp. 154–174), he presents a list of adjectives, apart from "true" and "false," that we use in assessing statements ("precise," "exact," "rough" and "accurate") and then declares that he is happy to claim "that these are the important terms to elucidate when we address ourselves to the problem of 'truth'" (161).

the view of literal sentence-meaning that Austin rejects. Someone who endorsed the rejected view might maintain that there are cases in which we know the literal meaning of a sentence that is being used to make a 'statement'—and in which, moreover, we also know how the indexical elements of the sentence pin it to the particular context of use—but in which we nevertheless cannot determine whether the relevant 'statement' is true or false. The idea might be that our inability to make judgments of truth or falsity in these cases is a function of what might be thought of as the indeterminacy of literal meaning. However, although a conception of the indeterminacy of literal meaning might thus plausibly be taken to motivate various things Austin *says* in criticizing an ideal of the 'statement' as bipolar, the resultant critique of bipolarity would not be Austin's.[29]

This concludes my account of the line of reasoning in *How to Do Things with Words* for the view that correspondence with the world (whether truly, falsely or in some other manner) is the job not of independently meaningful sentences but of illocutions or speech acts. What primarily interests me about this line of reasoning is that, as I discuss in section 2.2.i, it raises a question about the coherence of the idea of the kind of abstraction requirement that appears to underwrite the narrower conception of objectivity. Before turning to this issue, I want to say a word about what leads many of Austin's readers to overlook the line of reasoning entirely.

## 2.1.iv  Contesting Austin's Legacy

> The truth or falsity of a statement depends not merely on the meanings of words but on what act you were performing in what circumstances.
> ～ *Austin,* How to Do Things with Words *(1962), p. 146.*

Consider the following structural feature of John Searle's interpretation of Austin. In his earliest writings on Austin, Searle acknowledges

---

29. Austin's critique of the bipolar 'statement' is grounded in his critique of the idea of literal sentence-meaning. It follows not only that there is no such thing as assimilating his critique of bipolarity while retaining this idea but also that he should be read as leaving undisturbed forms of bipolarity that do not presuppose it. Austin leaves us free to think of statements (as opposed to 'statements') as bits of language that state facts either truly or falsely as long as we acknowledge: (1) that statements are a class of utterances, (2) that there may be utterances that are like statements in every respect except that they are not either strictly true or strictly false and (3) that statements, in addition to being aptly described as either true or false, may aptly be described as, e.g., appropriate, bizarre, misleading, etc.

that Austin regards corresponding to the world truly (or falsely) as the business of speech acts. But at the same time Searle also suggests that this claim is confused and that charity speaks for reading Austin as holding that such corresponding is the work of independently meaningful sentences.[30] Searle is aware that Austin's description of statements as speech acts is intended to draw attention to the role that the circumstances in which a statement is made play in making up its content, and he duly observes that showing this is one of Austin's larger ambitions. Searle proposes to accommodate this moment in Austin's thought by claiming that features of the way in which a sentence is used (such as its "stress and intonation contour") affect what Searle calls its "intended meaning."[31] Searle's thought seems to be that, if he makes this initial claim about the significance of the circumstances in which linguistic expressions are used, he can then go on—without betraying the fundamental spirit of Austin's thought—to advance a further claim about how sentences have (in addition to their "intended meanings") "literal meanings" and about how correspondence to the world is a function of elements of such meanings.

A further feature of Searle's work deserves mention here. In a paper that he wrote approximately ten years after his first discussions of Austin—and that he subsequently followed up with a series of additional publications—Searle distances himself from more standard philosophical accounts of literal sentence-meaning.[32] While these accounts stipulate that it is necessary to appeal to contextual cues to eliminate ambiguities and pick out the contributions that indexical features of a sentence make to its meaning, they also claim, not only that there must be rules for mak-

---

30. In "Austin on Locutionary and Illocutionary Acts," Searle argues that Austin's claim that some speech acts have truth-values is the product of an error in his analysis of statements. His thought is that "statement" is ambiguous in that it can sometimes mean the act of stating (e.g., "The statement of our position took all of the morning session") and also sometimes mean what is stated (e.g., "The statement that all men are mortal is true" [ibid., p. 422]). Searle refers to the former as "statement acts" and to the latter as "statement objects," and he tries to show that Austin winds up defending the view that some speech acts are capable of being true or false because he unwittingly slides between these two meanings of "statement." According to Searle, when Austin says that statements are speech acts, he is talking about "statement acts," and when he says that statements are capable of being true or false, he is talking about "statement objects." So, as Searle sees it, it does not follow from Austin's discovery that statements are speech acts that some speech acts are capable of being true or false (ibid., pp. 421–423).

31. Ibid., pp. 415–416, and *Speech Acts*, pp. 44–49.

32. John Searle, "Literal Meaning," reprinted as chapter 5 of *Expression and Meaning*.

ing such determinations (e.g., rules for assigning values, in particular circumstances, to the parameters that indexicals pick out), but also that it must in principle be possible to capture our grasp of these rules, when combined with our knowledge of the meanings of the words that compose a particular sentence, in the form of an antecedently available algorithm for generating the meaning of the sentence as employed on particular occasions.[33] Searle rejects these familiar accounts in favor of an alternative on which "in general the notion of the literal meaning of a sentence only has application relative to a set of contextual or background assumptions" and in which the relevant assumptions are such that they cannot be captured in the form of a strict rule or algorithm.[34] Searle adds that, far from being easily enumerable, the envisioned "assumptions" may take the form of "our whole mode of sensibility" and may accordingly be resistant to full and explicit formulation.[35] What emerges is an account of literal sentence-meaning, fundamentally different from more standard philosophical accounts, on which grasping such meaning requires a sensitivity to occasions on which sentences are used.

Searle appears to be happy to integrate this philosophically irregular account of literal sentence-meaning into his interpretation of Austin. He does not renounce his resistance to Austin's suggestion that the meaning of a sentence is an abstraction from the speech act in which the sentence figures and that there is therefore a decisive sense in which corresponding to the world is the prerogative of speech acts. Instead, Searle seems to believe that, if he starts from a philosophically heterodox account of literal meaning, he can go on—without departing fundamentally from an Austinian orientation in the philosophy of language—both to represent the literal meaning of a sentence as something we arrive at independently of an appreciation of the practical point with which it is used on a particular occasion and to represent correspondence to the world as the business not of statements (or other speech acts) but of literally meaningful sentences.

Although Searle never defends the attribution to Austin of the particular idea of literal sentence-meaning in question here on internal, textual grounds, it is possible to find in Searle's writings the outlines of

33. See ibid., pp. 117–119.

34. Ibid., p. 117. In Searle's parlance, the point is that the relevant assumptions cannot be "realized in the semantic structure of the sentence" (ibid., p. 120).

35. Ibid., p. 130.

a defense that appeals to evidence of an external kind. Searle expresses sympathy for the thought that we need to retain some idea of literal sentence-meaning to preserve the notion of objective truth, and he signals that he takes this thought to speak in favor of searching for an interpretation of Austin's doctrine of speech acts that is consistent with the idea of such meaning.[36]

Despite the well-known (and notoriously divisive and unproductive) dispute between Searle and Derrida about how to read Austin, there is a basic sense in which Derrida's interpretative strategy resembles the Searlean strategy just sketched.[37] An assumption about a conceptual tie between literal sentence-meaning and objective truth also informs the exegetical efforts of Derrida and the group of literary-theoretical commentators influenced by him—albeit, as we saw (2.1), in a very different manner. Within Derrida's interpretation, the assumption seems to speak for representing Austin, not (as Searle suggests) as hostile to the idea of literal sentence-meaning, but rather as hostile to the notion of objective truth. What accounts for this difference is that Derrida straightforwardly registers Austin's concern with criticizing the idea that sentences have literal meanings.[38] Derrida acknowledges that Austin represents himself as receptive to a notion of unqualified truth. But Derrida suggests that such receptivity is in tension with (what he regards

36. See e.g., John Searle, "Rationality and Reason, What is at Stake?" *Deadelus* 122 (1992): 55–84. To be sure, Searle's introduction of an account of literal sentence-meaning as inaccessible except in terms of certain background assumptions does complicate matters. It is not obvious that this account is compatible with the conception of objective truth with which the idea of literal sentence-meaning is typically associated (i.e., a conception that represents our access to objective truth as essentially involving an abstraction from all sensitivities). Since Searle appears to be attracted to the thought that the idea of literal sentence-meaning, even as he conceives it, positions us to preserve this conception by allowing us to represent the business of corresponding to the world as 'untainted' by illocutionary conventions, it is worth recalling that the assumption that we can distinguish the conventional character of statements from the conventional character of other speech acts is one of the central targets of Austin's lectures. See note 14.

37. The dispute includes Derrida's "Signature Event Context," in *Limited Inc.*, first published in *Glyph* 1, no. 1 (1977); Searle's response in "Reiterating the Differences: A Reply to Derrida," in H. Sussman and S. Webster, eds., *Glyph* 1, no. 2, (1977); and Derrida's counter in "Limited Inc a b c . . . ," *Limited Inc*, pp. 29–110.

38. Derrida describes Austin's rejection of the idea of literal sentence-meaning in these terms. He says that Austin moves from a classical view of meaning to a view on which the distinguishing mark of linguistic signs is their "iterability" or "citability"—i.e., their capacity for projection into multiple contexts. (See, e.g., "Signature Event Context," p. 7.) Here Derrida refers specifically to the moment at which Austin declares that he cannot find a grammatical criterion to sort linguistic formulae as such into constatives and performatives. Derrida writes

as) Austin's appropriate hostility to literal sentence-meaning and that charity speaks for reading Austin as rejecting the notion of objective truth outright.[39] It is insofar as Derrida thus suggests that the only way in which Austin can consistently distance himself from the idea of literal sentence-meaning is by jettisoning the notion of objective truth that Derrida appeals to an assumption—of the same sort that tacitly informs Searle's interpretation—about how the notion of objective truth stands or falls with the idea of literal sentence-meaning.[40]

This brings me to my main quarrel with prevailing interpretations of Austin's lectures. An assumption about a direct conceptual dependence

---

that "[iterability] is what creates this embarrassment and makes it impossible . . . 'to lay down even a list of all possible criteria'" (ibid., p. 23, n. 10). Now, to the extent that Derrida thus represents Austin as rejecting the idea of literal sentence-meaning, his interpretation resembles the interpretation defended in the pages above. But this initial similarity coresides with a philosophically fundamental difference. (See notes 39, 40, and 52.)

39. Derrida offers the following diagnosis of Austin's alleged misstep. He argues that there is a moment at which Austin betrays his repudiation of the idea of literal sentence-meaning. Derrida's specific suggestion is that Austin holds that the *intentions* with which a speaker produces a set of words secure those words against mishaps that would deprive them of meaning ("Signature Event Context," pp. 14–15). But this suggestion—which has unfortunately been echoed by many theorists influenced by Derrida—is simply unfounded. Although Austin does mention intentions in connection with the "infelicities" to which he thinks all speech acts are subject, he plainly indicates, by classing those infelicities constituted by inappropriate intentions as "abuses" and not "misfires," that he does not believe that the presence of appropriate intentions represents any sort of semantic guarantee. Nevertheless, however misguided, the suggestion is the centerpiece of Derrida's explanation of how Austin is led—wrongly, as Derrida sees it—to "reintroduce the criterion of truth in his description of performatives" (ibid., p. 22, n. 7). Moreover, since Derrida thinks that Austin's interest in objective truth reflects philosophical confusion, it appears to him that Austin is best read as rejecting such truth and, more specifically, that he is best read as wanting "to free the analysis of the performative from the authority of the truth *value* . . . and to substitute for it at times the value of [illocutionary or perlocutionary] force" (ibid., p. 13, stress in the original).

40. In his paper on Austin, Derrida offers a brief argument for this assumption. He claims that there is an important sense in which a view of language that rejects the idea of literal sentence-meaning or, in his terms, an "iterable" view (see note 38, above) is paradoxical. Derrida writes that, within the context of iterability, "the condition of the possibility of [linguistic] effects is, simultaneously, once again, the condition of their impossibility" ("Signature Event Context," p. 10). His thought is that here the very thing that—allegedly—enables signs to convey meaning (viz., their iterability) at the same time prevents them from serving as metaphysical guarantees of the delivery of meaning (i.e., since their iterability is what exposes them to mishaps that render them "null and void"). This strikes him as paradoxical because he thinks that if signs lack meaning in isolation the validity of whatever meanings they have in particular contexts must be relative to the illocutionary conventions governing their use in those contexts. So the putative paradox is that the very iterability that enables signs to convey meaning at the same time prevents them from doing so except in a qualified (non-objective or relativistic) manner.

of objective truth on literal sentence-meaning is entirely foreign to Austin's thought. Moreover, it is just as foreign when made by philosophers like Searle as it is when it is made by literary-theoretical commentators like Derrida. What gives these interpretative shortcomings their deeper interest is the fact that they reveal a significant philosophical blind spot. There is, I submit, good reason to think not only that Austin is right to reject the idea of literal sentence-meaning but, moreover, that he is right to treat this gesture of rejection as unthreatening to his entitlement to talk about genuine, objective truth.

## 2.2 Objectivity Revisited

> I said that the application of a word is not everywhere bounded by rules. But what does a game look like that is everywhere bounded by rules? Whose rules never let a doubt creep in, but stop up all the cracks where it might?—Can't we imagine a rule determining the application of a rule, and a doubt which *it* removes—and so on?
>
> ~ *Wittgenstein*, Philosophical Investigations, *§84.*

I turn now to discussing considerations that, especially when combined with the argument of *How to Do Things with Words*, might lead us to share Austin's hostility to the idea of literal sentence-meaning. My goal in doing so is to suggest both that we should follow in his footsteps in rejecting this idea and that, if we do so, we lay the groundwork for a critique of the narrower conception of objectivity that, far from ushering in a form of skepticism about objectivity makes room for the philosophically heterodox conception of objectivity that I am describing as "wider" (1.1).

I proceed here by following up on an observation that Austin makes relatively late in his lectures. This observation needs to be understood against the background of Austin's claim that it is impossible to sort sentences as such into constatives and performatives and that we can only carry out the relevant task of sorting once we appreciate how sentences are being used in particular circumstances (2.1.i). Austin anticipates that this claim will be interpreted—wrongly—as presupposing that it is possible to determine ahead of time what thought a sentence expresses. He accordingly stresses that his point is not that we need to await a consideration of circumstances of use to determine the (constative or performative) force with which some allegedly pre-given thought is being produced. His point is rather that thoughts (or locutions) are abstractions from speech acts (or illocutions) and that it is only once we have grasped the intelligible force of a person's utterance that we are in a position to say which thought, if any, is in question (2.1.ii). One of Austin's methods for making this point involves showing us how, even when its indexical elements are held constant, a given sentence may be used to express thoughts that not only differ but, more specifically, differ in truth-values (2.1.iii). This is the moment in Austin's work from which I now start. It is a moment that is highlighted prominently and productively in the work of Charles Travis, and my initial point of reference is an example of what is at issue that, in addition to being Austinian in spirit, shares a structure with examples Travis adduces throughout his writings.

### 2.2.i Continuing the Case for the Wider Conception of Objectivity

> A philosopher says that he understands the sentence "I am here," that he means something by it, thinks something—even when he doesn't think at all how, on what occasions, this sentence is used.
>
> ～ *Wittgenstein*, Philosophical Investigations, §514.

Take the sentence "This vase is red." While this sentence appears to have a constant and unvarying descriptive meaning, it does not seem implausible to suggest that, even once its indexical elements are pinned down to a particular setting, it can be used to express different thoughts. Consider the following two scenarios:

(1) A and B are walking through a pottery studio, and A stops in front of a shelf that holds a set of finished items that have been painted with a green glaze. A is explaining to B that, while the other potters in the studio use a more standard gray clay, she herself works with a red clay found in parts of the American Southwest. Pointing to a vase she made that, like the other items, is glazed green, A says: "This vase is red."

(2) A is in the pottery studio when B, a painter, calls to ask whether she has any red pieces that could be used for color in a still life

painting. Standing in front of the shelf that holds her vase, A says "yes" and then adds, "This vase is red."

It seems natural to describe the example comprised of these two scenarios as illustrating that the sentence "The vase is red" can be used to say two distinct things—one of them (viz., [1]) true, the other (viz., [2]) false. Admittedly, a critic might want to reject the idea that the example illustrates this and to argue instead that the sentence as uttered in both scenarios has the same truth-value. But it is not clear what could underwrite this person's argument, justifying her in drawing either the conclusion that what A says in both cases is true or the conclusion that what she says in both cases is false. It would need to be shown that the meaning of "red" somehow fixes it that a painted object that is red underneath either does or does not qualify as red, and it is not clear what feature of the meaning of "red" could be in question. Nor does the difficulty here seem to be a function of anything special about color terms like "red." We need look no further than some of Austin's own examples to find the same point made in connection with different kinds of predicates.[41]

The critic who wants to deny that a sentence can be used to express different thoughts might seem to be on stronger ground in claiming that the reason the sentence in question ("The vase is red") can so be used is at bottom no more than a function of some particular *ambiguity* or *vagueness* in the meaning of "red." Consider the issue of ambiguity. Suppose for the moment that we do in fact use the expression "red" in two clearly different senses—in one in which it is true of red objects painted a different color and in the other in which it is false of such objects. Even if this were the case, it would not prevent us from finding that this expression when, say, taken in the second of these putative senses is sometimes true when used of a given object (say, a red vase covered with a translucent yellow glaze or a red vase decorated with delicate white stripes) and also sometimes false. Moreover, if we now take ourselves to have discovered that we use "red" in even more senses than we at first hypothesized, there is nothing to keep the same phenomenon from repeating itself in connection with these further puta-

41. See the Austinian examples touched on in the text and notes of section 2.1.iii (above), examples involving predicates such as "hexagonal" and "won the battle." For a wide assortment of further examples, see Travis's work, esp., *The Uses of Sense: Wittgenstein's Philosophy of Language* (Oxford: Clarendon Press, 1989) and *Unshadowed Thought* (Cambridge, MA: Harvard University Press, 2000.)

tive senses. Indeed, given that the phenomenon can in principle repeat itself indefinitely, and given that it is not limited to color terms like "red," there is no good reason to think—and this is a point Travis repeatedly makes—that our willingness to represent the expressions as possessing even a quite large number of senses equips us to challenge the suggestion that sentences like "The vase is red" can be used to express different thoughts.[42]

What about vagueness? It might seem reasonable to think that the sentence "The vase is red" fails to express a unique thought only because "red" picks out an especially vague concept. But why should talk of vagueness seem to help here? It is not unusual to speak of vagueness in reference to thoughts that are not clearly recognizable as either true or false. However, while there is a respect in which it might accordingly seem appropriate to represent the sentence "The vase is red" as vague (i.e., insofar as it can be used to express thoughts with different truth-values), it is also clear that—and this is another point Travis makes— the thoughts that the sentence is used to express may be far from vague. One moral we may reasonably draw from this observation is that, in order to arrive at a satisfactory non-vague account of what is said on a given occasion on which the sentence is used, we need to reach beyond both the meanings of its constitutive words and the rules of the language and appeal to the circumstances of its employment. And this moral, far from being helpful to the critic who hopes to challenge the view that sentences are vehicles for expressing various different thoughts, runs directly counter to her efforts.[43]

At this point, it is helpful to observe that, far from being alien to mainstream philosophy of language, the view that sentences are vehicles for expressing various different thoughts in fact enjoys widespread acceptance. At the same time, given the concerns of this section, we should observe that the view is generally taken to be consistent with the idea of literal sentence-meaning. Philosophers of language who endorse the view are generally at least implicitly committed to combining it with this idea.

---

42. See, e.g., Travis, *The Uses of Sense*, pp. 38*ff.*, 259*ff.* and 288*ff.* and *Unshadowed Thought*, pp. 18–19, 34*ff.* and 46–47. For a condensed discussion of the question of ambiguity, see also Travis's "Pragmatics" in Bob Hale and Crispin Wright, eds., *A Companion to the Philosophy of Language* (Oxford: Blackwell, 1999), pp. 87–107, p. 90.

43. See, e.g., Travis, "Pragmatics," p. 91.

The most prevalent—and initially most promising—methods of combination might reasonably be described as *indexicalist* or *parameters-based* methods.[44] These methods turn on the thought that, whenever what a sentence says is affected by the circumstances of its use, we are justified in concluding that the meanings of its constitutive words are properly understood (either individually or in virtue of aspects of their compositional structure) as encoding *indices* or *parameters* for which values need to be assigned by features of those circumstances.[45] The pertinent indices or parameters are supposed to be antecedently formulable as rules for arriving at the meaning of a sentence (i.e., rules that specify the kinds of functions from contextual factors to semantic values of which the sentence is composed), and this supposition is what appears to allow us to reconcile the view that context plays a role in determining what a sentence says on different occasions of its use with the idea of literal sentence-meaning. For if we can in fact formulate rules of the relevant kinds in advance, it appears that—for all of our concessiveness about the semantic importance of context—we are warranted in retaining the literalist idea that the meanings of the words that com-

44. The first of these labels is François Recanati's (see *Literal Meaning*, pp. 85–86), and the second is Travis's (see "Pragmatics," pp. 91*ff.*).

45. There is another method for combining the view that sentences are vehicles for saying various different things with the idea of literal sentence-meaning—a method grounded in the thought that a given sentence may say different things on different occasions of its use because it is in each case *elliptical* for a different longer sentence. The method of ellipsis depends for its success on the assumption that, once we formulate 'non-elliptical sentences', we will be entitled to represent the meanings of their words as determining what they say so that, once any indexical elements are tied down to a particular context, there can be no question of their being used to say different things. The idea is that as we move from generic and allegedly elliptical sentences like "The vase is red" to more specialized and allegedly less elliptical sentences like "The entire vase is covered in an even, one thirty-second of an inch deep layer of red glaze number eighteen" we eliminate the possibility that a particular sentence can be used to say different things. But this idea doesn't withstand scrutiny. Bearing in mind the moral of this section's remarks about ambiguity, we can say that there is in principle no more reason to exclude the possibility that a specialized sentence can be used to say different things than there is to exclude the possibility that a quite generic sentence can be used to do so. (I leave it to the reader to confirm in reference to, e.g., the specialized sentence just mentioned that the former possibility is indeed a real one.) Let me add that I believe that the reason that Austin and Travis and other philosophers who likewise hope to bring out how sentences can be used to say different things focus on quite generic sentences is, not that more specialized sentences wouldn't work for their purposes, but that consideration of more specialized sentences would detract from their efforts to underline a feature of language that is generic in the sense of being entirely universal.

pose a sentence determine what the sentence says on different occasions of its use.[46]

But can we formulate such rules in advance? If we focus exclusively on familiar indexical elements of language—for instance, "I," "here," "now," "he," "she" and "that"—then it will seem as though we are entitled to answer this question in the affirmative. This is so because it is internal to the meanings of such indexicals that they are in the business of picking out antecedently specifiable contextual features. (Thus, e.g., it is internal to the meaning of "here" that it is in the business of picking out the place in which a speaker or writer finds herself.) It follows that we can say ahead of time how different contextual features assign semantic values to parameters that these indexicals encode, and, by the same token, it also follows that there are respects in which the indexicals are rightly understood as permitting the antecedent formulation of the kinds of rules at issue.

But things look very different if we abandon an exclusive focus on familiar indexical elements of language and turn our attention to a broader selection of linguistic phenomena.[47] Here it is helpful to return to the guiding example of this section. One thing that reflection on various uses of the sentence "The vase is red" reveals is that, as I have suggested, "red" may make any of indefinitely many different contributions to what the sentence says. This observation (which resonates with the claim advanced in section 1.4 about how our concepts are subject to an open-ended process of "deepening") creates obvious problems for efforts to antecedently capture the meaning of "red" in the form of a set of rules that specify functions from contextual features to semantic values.

It might seem reasonable to proceed toward such a set of rules in the following manner. We might survey a large and variegated set of cases in which "The vase is red" is used and formulate a set of rules for the semantic contribution of "red" by appeal to these cases; we might then hypothesize that our rules capture the semantic contribution that "red"

46. Two of the currently most outspoken proponents of the kinds of indexicalist or parameters-based methods described in this paragraph are Jeffrey King and Jason Stanley.

47. The point here is not that the familiar indexicals just mentioned are the only elements of language that permit the antecedent formulation of rules specifying functions from contextual features to semantic values. Other elements of language also permit this. The point is simply that, if we avoid the temptation to fixate solely on these elements of language, we quickly encounter linguistic phenomena that speak strongly against the success of an indexicalist—or parameters-based—program in the philosophy of language.

makes to the sentence "The vase is red" on every occasion of its use; and, finally, we might repeat the procedure for sentences in which "red" is predicated, not of vases, but of different kinds of objects. Would we at this point be justified in crediting ourselves with a complete set of rules for the semantic contribution of "red" to speech acts in which it figures? The answer is clearly no. For, however complete our set of rules strikes us as being, we cannot foreclose the possibility that on some further employment "red" will play a role that our rules do not cover. Moreover, should this happen, it would be illegitimate to protest that it simply shows that we have not yet generated rules constitutive of all of the parameters that we operate with in using "red." Given that we cannot at any point say with authority that we have generated all of these rules, we seem obliged to conclude that, in our efforts to generate them, we are relying on a form of appreciation of what is said by uses of sentences involving "red" that is not even implicitly informed by such rules. Further, given that we are thus forced to recognize that, in our efforts to grasp what this and other sentences say on different occasions, we invariably rely on forms of linguistic appreciation that resist formulation in the kinds of rules in question, we seem obliged to conclude that our talk of literal sentence-meanings that are fully constituted by rules is no better than empty and that we should therefore reject as bankrupt the thought of grasping the meaning of a sentence in a manner independent of sensitivities characteristic of use as language-users.[48]

This argument against the idea of literal sentence-meaning exploits and expands on the main line of reasoning in Austin's *How to Do Things with Words* and is appropriately thought of as Austinian in spirit. It is accordingly noteworthy that the argument receives reinforcement from the passages of Wittgenstein's *Investigations* that I discussed in section 1.2. Where the Austinian argument takes as its central critical target the assumption, essential to a traditional philosophical idea of literal sentence-meaning, that we can somehow antecedently capture as a set of rules

---

48. For Travis's formulation of a similar conclusion, see, e.g., "Pragmatics," pp. 92–94. Notice that the conclusion applies even to sentences containing the familiar indexicals discussed earlier. In observing that there are features of the meanings of familiar indexical expressions that permit the antecedent formulation of rules specifying functions from contextual contributions to semantic values, we do not thereby exclude the possibility of other features of their meanings that resist the antecedent formulation of such rules.

the contribution contextual features make to the meaning of a sentence on different uses, these parts of the *Investigations* likewise target the assumption that applications of words are, in Wittgenstein's words, "everywhere bounded by rules."[49]

In the pertinent passages of the *Investigations*, Wittgenstein is—to use the terms that I used in Chapter 1—rightly seen as discrediting an "abstraction requirement," a requirement to the effect that regularities constitutive of a sound discursive practice must transcend the practice in the sense of being discernible from a vantage point that abstracts from any sensitivities that we acquired in mastering it. To say that Wittgenstein attacks such a requirement is to say that he attempts to subvert an understanding of the applications of words as fixed in a manner that is abstract in that it bypasses the need for reliance on acquired sensitivities. The point here is that he is flagging his efforts to subvert this understanding—and, more specifically, flagging these efforts by underlining his repudiation of the thought that (implicit or explicit) rules can do the relevant work of abstract fixing—when he presents himself as rejecting the assumption that language is everywhere "bounded by rules." So, in the passages of the *Investigations* considered in section 1.2, Wittgenstein is rightly understood as trying to discredit the view that rules can somehow relieve us, in our efforts to determine the meaning of a combination of words or a sentence, of the need to rely on sensitivities to the circumstances in which the relevant combination of words or sentence is used. And, by the same token, he is rightly understood as reinforcing Austinian attempts to show, in opposition to advocates of indexicalist or parameters-based programs in the philosophy of language, that no set of rules will equip us to save the idea of literal sentence-meaning.

These remarks demonstrate the legitimacy of speakng of a composite "Austinian-Wittgensteinian" argument against a familiar philosophical idea of literal sentence-meaning. While the idea of such an argument is not a novelty within philosophy of language, and while in the nineteen sixties and seventies various arguments taken to fall under this heading aroused significant philosophical excitement, today philosophers of language generally take it for granted that any Austinian-Wittgensteinian arguments of interest were conclusively answered

---

49. Wittgenstein, *Philosophical Investigations*, §84. See also the epigraph to this section.

decades ago and that they no longer merit sustained philosophical attention. Since Paul Grice is often credited with providing the first comprehensive rejoinder to Austin, Wittgenstein and their sympathizers, it is worth observing that, as far as the particular Austinian-Wittgensteinian argument just presented is concerned, the allegedly germane portions of Grice's work are quite beside the point.[50] They in no way speak against taking this argument seriously or seriously exploring its philosophical implications.[51]

This brings me to my main concern in this chapter. I am interested in implications of the above argument against the idea of literal sentence-meaning for how we conceive of objectivity. A helpful way to approach this topic is to observe that philosophical resistance to relinquishing the idea of literal sentence-meaning is at bottom driven by concern with protecting our claim to the concept of objectivity. Philosophers who insist

50. Grice agrees with advocates of this argument that, when a given sentence is used in different circumstances, it may, even when variations attributable to ambiguity and indexicality are held fixed, call for different interpretations. At the same time, he thinks he has a superior strategy for accommodating this fact. The centerpiece of this strategy is what he calls *conversational implicature* (see his *Studies in the Ways of Words*, pp. 26–27 and *passim*), and we can grasp what he has in mind by turning to the contrast we intuitively draw between what someone says in coming out with a set of words and what she thereby merely implies or hints at. If, with Grice, we take an interest in what is implied by what is said, some of what we find will be implied simply by the meanings that words have as used on a particular occasion. (Grice speaks here of *conventional implicature* [ibid., pp. 25–26].) Another part of what we find will be implied not merely by the meanings that words have on a particular occasion of their use but by those meanings taken together with circumstantial factors. This is what Grice means by conversational implicature. Grice thinks that the idea of such implicature equips us to account for the linguistic phenomena of primary interest to Austinian-Wittgensteinian philosophers because this idea makes it possible to explain how a sentence used in different contexts may call for different interpretations. The problem is that, in addressing these matters, Grice is concerned with different uses of a particular sentence that, while they have different implications—nevertheless say the same thing. This is a problem because advocates of the Austinian-Wittgensteinian argument that I just presented are concerned with how a given sentence can be used in different circumstances to say different things (e.g., things with different truth-conditions) and because this concern is what originally leads them to critically examine a traditional philosophical idea of literal sentence-meaning. It is to the extent that these philosophers are first and foremost committed to critically examining this idea, and to the extent that Grice's rejoinder to them simply takes the idea for granted (see, e.g., ibid., p. 25) that his rejoinder needs to be regarded as simply beside the point.

51. Another philosopher who is sometimes credited with answering the kind of argument against the idea of literal sentence-meaning that I just presented is Peter Geach. For a remark on how the allegedly pertinent parts of Geach's work leave the argument unscathed, see note 22.

on the idea of literal sentence-meaning are in effect insisting on an understanding of language as governed by an abstraction requirement, and, as we saw in Chapter 1, this requirement is internal to the deeply engrained philosophical conception of objectivity that I am describing as "narrower." This means that philosophers who worry that we will lose our entitlement to the very concept of objectivity if we give up the idea of literal sentence-meaning are doing nothing more surprising than giving expression to the logic of the narrower conception of objectivity.

However unsurprising, this posture is unwarranted. Where in the last chapter I argued that a rigorously consistent and sound attack on the idea of an abstraction requirement is rightly taken to threaten not the concept of objectivity per se but only this narrower conception of it (1.2), I now want to add that, insofar as it entails an attack on the idea of an abstraction requirement, a rigorously consistent and sound attack on the idea of literal sentence-meaning is also rightly taken to speak not for jettisoning the concept of objectivity altogether but only for refashioning the narrower conception of it.

At the heart of the last chapter's argument was the following reflection: insofar as we treat efforts to impugn the coherence of the idea of an abstraction requirement as undermining our entitlement to the concept of objectivity, we effectively present ourselves, in an internally inconsistent manner, both as abandoning the thought of an ideally abstract perspective on the world and as endorsing a view of language that (since it represents us as cut off from objectivity as a result of our failure to adopt such a perspective) continues to take for granted the intelligibility of this thought. In discussing these matters, I noted that this reflection will fail to interest those who believe that it is possible to defend the narrower conception of objectivity without appealing to an abstraction requirement, and I commented on the hopelessness of trying to realize this possibility. My conclusion was that the appropriate moral to draw from the reflection is that, where successful, efforts to impugn the coherence of the idea of an abstraction requirement oblige us not to relinquish our license to the concept of objectivity but to revise our conception of what objectivity is like so that an abstraction from all our subjective endowments is no longer a necessary prerequisite of access to it. My point right now is simply that we should draw the same moral in connection with attacks on the coherence of the idea of literal sentence-meaning. We should conclude that, where successful, such attempts oblige us to revise our conception of objectivity along the very same lines.[52]

The pertinent revisions are constitutive of what I am calling the wider conception of objectivity. In making them, we equip ourselves with a conception of objectivity that, to the extent that it is free from an abstraction requirement, is also free from the idea of a radically abstract vantage point from which to make the a priori determination that any (even problematically) subjective aspects of our lives are excluded from objectivity. And since, according to this conception, there can therefore be no question of antecedently determining whether an aspect of our lives that needs to be understood in terms of subjective responses qualifies as objective, it follows that here we are obliged to rely on quite ordinary, non-metaphysical intellectual resources in making determinations of the relevant kind and, by the same token, obliged to leave open the possibility that, while in some cases we may find that a subjective aspect of a situation is a *mere* projection of our subjectivity, in others we may find that such an aspect figures in the best, objectively most accurate account of our lives. The upshot is that, in attacking the coherence of an abstraction requirement, we equip ourselves to describe a conception of objectivity that is "wide" enough to incorporate aspects of our lives only properly conceivable in reference to human subjectivity.[53]

Now we have before us the additional argument for the wider conception of objectivity that is the main object of this chapter. Before closing my presentation of the argument, I want to say something about one way in which it may be misunderstood.

52. The line of thought traced out in this paragraph implies a criticism of the claim Derrida makes, in reference to Austin's work, about how there is something paradoxical about a view of language free from the idea of literal sentence-meaning. (See note 40, above.) The point of this paragraph is, as I can now put it, that the appearance of a paradoxical threat to objective truth is only sustained by the tacit retention of a bankrupt metaphysical perspective. Cavell concisely formulates this point in a discussion of Derrida on Austin. Cavell writes, "Derrida's sense of . . . 'paradoxicality' . . . seems to insist on the pathos of the philosophical view of language he combats" (in "Counter-Philosophy and the Pawn of Voice," *A Pitch of Philosophy: Autobiographical Exercises* [Cambridge, MA: Harvard University Press, 1994], pp. 53–128, 72).

53. I just made a case, via a reading of Austin's *How to Do Things with Words,* for concluding that rejecting the idea of literal sentence-meaning obliges us to refashion more traditional renderings of basic logical concepts such as "truth" and "objectivity." A list of the most influential thinkers to defend similar conclusions about the philosophical interest of Austin's work would need to include, in addition to Travis, Cavell (see the references to Cavell's work in notes 25 and 52, above) and George Lakoff (see, e.g., *Women, Fire and Dangerous Things: What Categories Reveal About the Mind* [Chicago: University of Chicago Press], 1987).

## 2.2.ii  Leaving Room for Our Ordinary
## Conception of Literal Language

> The Hatter [said], "Why is a raven like a writing-desk?"
>
> "Come, we shall have some fun now!" thought Alice. "I'm glad they've begun asking riddles—I believe I can guess that," she added aloud.
>
> "Do you mean that you think you can find out the answer to it?" said the March Hare.
>
> "Exactly so," said Alice.
>
> "Then you should say what you mean," the March Hare went on.
>
> "I do," Alice hastily replied: "at least—at least I mean what I say— that's the same thing, you know."
>
> "Not the same thing a bit!" said the Hatter. "Why, you might just as well say that 'I see what I eat' is the same thing as 'I eat what I see'!"
>
> ∼ *Lewis Carroll*, Alice's Adventures in Wonderland *(1946), pp.* 77–78.

It might seem reasonable to criticize this chapter's argument for the wider conception of objectivity on the ground that, in calling for the rejection of a familiar philosophical idea of literal sentence-meaning, it threatens our ordinary, philosophically innocuous conception of literal speech.[54] But this criticism, while suggestive, misses its mark. It turns for its apparent interest on the assumption that our ordinary conception of the literal needs to be understood in reference to the particular philosophical idea of literal sentence-meaning that the argument attacks, and there is good reason to think that this assumption is flawed and that the criticism of the argument it appears to underwrite is empty. Since we ordinarily talk about literal speech in connection with various different contrasts between the literal and the non-literal, a reasonable way to show this is to survey the notions of the literal—notions alike in belonging to our ordinary conception of literal speech—that inform some of the most prominent of these contrasts. For my purposes here, it will suffice to briefly examine the two such notions likeliest to be seen as causing trouble for this chapter's argument.

Consider, first, the notion of the literal that is internal to the contrast between literal and non-literal language that we are concerned with when we describe as non-literal modes of speech such as irony, indirection, hyperbole, understatement and sarcasm. When we describe these

54. I am indebted to Elijah Millgram for suggesting the need to respond to this criticism.

modes of speech as non-literal, we are typically concerned with the contrast between what someone says in coming out with a set of words (which we here think of as a literal matter) and what, in virtue of features of the circumstances of her utterance, she thereby implies or imparts (which we here think of as a non-literal matter). Thus, for instance, when we characterize as non-literal Elizabeth Bennett's ironic remark "Mr. Darcy is all politeness," we are likely to be taking an interest in the contrast between what Lizzie—literally—says in producing her remark and what, in the complex setting of Jane Austen's novel, she thereby—non-literally—implies (say, that Mr. Darcy lacks any true human feeling and that his merely formally fine manners are thus in some sense all there is to him).

Why should we think that our willingness to repudiate a familiar philosophical idea of literal sentence-meaning prevents us from making sense of the side of this contrast that is concerned with what is literally said? Our willingness to repudiate the relevant idea of literal sentence-meaning will only seem to represent an obstacle if we assume that the literal side of the contrast needs to be fleshed out in its terms, and it is not clear why we should accept this assumption. In repudiating this idea of literal sentence-making, we make room for the Austinian view of meaning that I have been defending in this chapter (viz., a view on which contextual features contribute to what is said when someone produces a sentence in a manner that is not antecedently codifiable), and our endorsement of this view does not impair our ability to draw distinctions between what is (literally) said and what is (non-literally) "conversationally implicated."[55] So there is no reason to take the fact that this chapter's overarching argument calls for rejecting the idea of literal sentence-meaning that is in question to show that the chapter fails to accommodate the notion of the literal that belongs to such distinctions.[56]

---

55. For an account of the Gricean notion of conversational implicature, see note 50.

56. Notice that we are warranted in drawing this same conclusion in connection with the notion of the literal that informs many distinctions we draw between literal and non-literal *interpretation*, as well as between literal and non-literal *translation*. For what is generally at issue in these further cases is the same basic notion of the literal. Here we for the most part again treat the question of what someone says when she utters or writes a sentence in a given context as the primary question of literalness. We tend to develop this question differently only in that we now take an interest not, as before, in the distinction between what she (literally) says in producing a sentence and what she thereby in a given context (non-literally) implies but rather in the distinction between offering a strictly accurate (and, as we here think of it, literal) account of what she says and somehow departing from such an account (in what we

The criticism of this chapter's argument that I am contemplating might seem to gain more traction if we turn from this first notion of literal speech to the notion at play in the contrast between the literal and the non-literal that concerns us when we represent metaphorical discourse as non-literal. Admittedly, it is difficult to find any terms for characterizing this further contrast that will not seem question begging to at least some philosophers. It is, however, fair to say that, when we are not philosophizing, we tend to take ourselves to be concerned here with a contrast between ordinary meaning (which for these purposes we think of as the mark of literal discourse) and a special sort of figurative or metaphorical meaning (which for these purposes we think of as the mark of non-literal discourse). Further, it is fair to say that the idea of such a contrast is originally suggested by two very basic aspects of the way in which metaphors naturally strike us. First, they naturally seem to us to have *forces* in virtue of which they are capable of producing insights that resist antecedent formulation in rules and are open-ended in scope.[57] Second, they naturally seem to us to have *meanings* in virtue of which they say things that can be the objects of genuine (i.e.,

---

here think of as a non-literal manner). Thus, e.g., when we describe as non-literal an interpretation of, say, a legal statute or a biblical passage, we are typically taking an interest in the distinction between rendering what the text says in a strictly accurate fashion and in some way (non-literally) expanding on or condensing this. Similarly, when we describe as non-literal a translation of, say, a foreign text, we are typically taking an interest in the distinction between rendering what the text says into another language in a strictly accurate fashion and in some way (non-literally) further developing or paraphrasing this.

57. Consider this aspect of a natural understanding of metaphor in reference to, for instance, the metaphor "X [some contemporary politician] is a tail-wagging lapdog of privilege." To say that this metaphor naturally seems to us to have a distinctive *force* is to say that we naturally take it, on different occasions of its use, to demand what Austin would call a certain *consequential* response—one whose special character might be captured by saying that it involves at least imaginatively adopting a certain perspective and surveying from there the elements of the metaphor (viz., X and a tail-wagging lapdog). This perspective is one that should enable us to see a range of things that, while open-ended, might include, e.g., that X is eagerly submissive to the powers that be; that she expresses devotion to them with slavish enthusiasm even when they fail to respect her interests; and that her highest pleasure is their indulgence. (I am here drawing on Richard Moran's treatment of this metaphor in "Seeing and Believing: Metaphor, Image and Force," *Critical Inquiry* 16 (1989): pp. 87–112, esp. 90.) Insofar as it strikes us as natural to represent metaphors as thus having forces in virtue of which they elicit certain consequential effects, it will seem appropriate to assimilate them to the realm of what Austin calls perlocutionary force. There is, however, a sense in which our natural understanding of metaphor speaks for qualifying this gesture of assimilation. In connection with this last point, see the next note.

cognitively legitimate) agreements or disagreements.[58] It is these two aspects of a very natural understanding of metaphors that, taken together, suggest a conception of metaphorical discourse on which it differs from plain or literal discourse in possessing a special type of meaning—in particular, a type of meaning that as such involves the conveyance of a distinctive force.

What account should we give of the notion of the literal that stands opposed to this conception of the metaphorical? There is a sense in which the idea of literal sentence-meaning that I have been attacking may seem particularly well suited to capture it—specifically, insofar as on its terms meaning is "everywhere bounded by rules," and insofar as here, a person's ability to grasp a meaning therefore cannot require any subjective response of the sort that might underwrite an indeterminate and open-ended insight and thus lead us to speak, as we are inclined to speak in reference to metaphors, of a distinctive force. There are, however, significant considerations against regarding an appeal to this idea of literal sentence-meaning as compulsory. To begin with, to the extent that this idea excludes the possibility of a conceptual tie between meaning and force, it seems to place insurmountable philosophical obstacles in the way of attempts to take at face value the natural understanding of metaphor under consideration. Moreover, while many philosophers and literary theorists are happy to accept the conclusion that this natural understanding should not be taken at face value and that it should instead be reconstructed, it is not clear why we should see ourselves as

---

58. Consider this second aspect of a natural understanding of metaphor in connection with the example touched on in the last note (viz., "X [a contemporary politician] is a tail-wagging lapdog of privilege"). To say that this metaphor naturally seems to us to have a *meaning* is to say that we naturally take the person who produces it on a given occasion to be thereby saying something with which it is possible to agree or disagree. Thus, for instance, if after someone utters it on a particular occasion we learn that X is willing to risk political capital in defending various long-cherished ideals, we will likely take ourselves to be justified in rejecting the utterance as false and misleading. Insofar as it strikes us as natural to represent metaphors as thus having meanings, it seems reasonable to move from our natural understanding of metaphors as having forces in virtue of which they elicit consequential effects (see the last note) to an assimilation of them to a philosophically distinct subcategory of what Austin calls the perlocutionary. For now the effects in question no longer appear consequential in a simple sense. They differ from other consequential effects that Austin classifies as perlocutionary in that a capacity to (at least imaginatively) register them is internal to a person's ability to grasp what the bit of language that produces them means. I return to this refinement to Austin's category of the perlocutionary in section 2.3.

compelled to embrace, as our guide to making sense of discourse that is literal in the sense of being plain or non-metaphorical, the very idea of literal sentence-meaning that seems to saddle us with this project of philosophical reconstruction.[59]

This brings me to a second and more significant consideration against thinking that our notion of literal qua non-metaphorical discourse needs to be spelled out in terms of a familiar philosophical idea of literal sentence-meaning. Throughout this chapter, I have been arguing that there are good reasons to replace this idea with an Austinian view on which meaning, or the application of words, is no longer entirely rule-governed. What merits emphasis now is that there are good reasons to think that such a view can do justice to our notion of literal, non-metaphorical discourse. To be sure, the view may at first glance seem better suited to our notion of metaphorical discourse. This is because it represents our ability to grasp a meaning as necessarily requiring the possession of certain capacities of subjective response and because, in consequence, it leaves open the possibility that grasping a meaning may in some cases require a response suggestive of the sort of force that we associate with metaphors. For the purposes of this discussion, it is accordingly important to stress that it is not an implication of the Austinian view that our grasp of a meaning inevitably requires this kind of special response. There is no good reason to think that this view is somehow disqualified from doing justice to discourse that is literal in the sense of being non-metaphorical.

We are, then, on good ground in concluding that the rejection of a familiar philosophical idea of literal sentence-meaning leaves intact our ability to account for the notion of the literal that informs our contrast between literal and metaphorical discourse. Indeed, partly for reasons adduced earlier in this section, we are also on good ground in drawing the more general conclusion that the rejection of this idea leaves intact our ability to account for the larger conception of literal speech to which this particular notion of the literal belongs. Despite the suggestiveness of allegations to the contrary, there is no compelling reason to think that, in calling for the repudiation of a familiar philosophical idea

59. For an overview of contemporary conversations about metaphor that helpfully describes philosophical pressures toward the kind of reconstructive project in question, see Richard Moran, "Metaphor," in Bob Hale and Crispin Wright, eds., *A Companion to the Philosophy of Language*, pp. 248–268.

of literal sentence-meaning, this chapter's argument for the wider conception of objectivity represents a threat to this ordinary conception.

This chapter's argument is the book's second in favor of the wider conception of objectivity. I set out to present a second argument both because the idea of such a conception is extremely controversial philosophically and because, as I discussed in Chapter 1, the conception plays a pivotal role within my larger case for a view on which ethics is no longer distinguished by an exclusive concern with moral judgments. Since what primarily interests me about the argument is its bearing on ethics, and since the argument draws its main inspiration from Austin's thought, this chapter closes with a brief addendum that describes some attempts to bring Austin's thought to bear on ethics.

## 2.3  Addendum: Conversations about the Bearing of Austin's Thought on Ethics

> In moral or practical affairs, we can know the facts and yet look at them mistakenly or perversely, or not fully realize or appreciate something, or even be under a total misconception . . . Even thoughtlessness, inconsiderateness, lack of imagination, are perhaps less matters for failure in intelligence or planning than might be supposed, and more matters of failure to appreciate the situation. A course of E. M. Forster and we see things differently: Yet perhaps we know no more and are no cleverer.
>
> ~ *Austin, "A Plea for Excuses," Philosophical Papers (1979), p. 194.*

Many of the most influential efforts to bring Austin's view of language to bear on ethics take for granted interpretations, of the sort criticized in section 2.1.iv, on which he is depicted as presupposing a traditional ideal of the literal 'statement.' Consider, to mention perhaps the best known effort of this kind, Jürgen Habermas's attempt to show that Austin's work on speech acts is capable of grounding a more or less Kantian account of morality.[60] Following in Searle's footsteps, Haber-

---

60. Habermas's most comprehensive accounts of what he sees as his inheritance from Austin are in "Universal Pragmatics: Reflections on a Theory of Communicative Competence," in *On the Pragmatics of Social Interaction: Preliminary Studies in the Theory of Communicative Action,* trans. Barbara Fultner (Cambridge, MA: MIT Press, 2001), pp. 67–84, "What is Universal Pragmatics?" *Communication and the Evolution of Society,* trans. Thomas McCarthy (Boston: Beacon Press, 1979), pp. 1–68, and *The Theory of Communicative Action,* vol. 1: *Reason and the Rationalization of Society,* trans. Thomas McCarthy (Boston, MA: Beacon Press,

mas defends an interpretation of Austin's work on speech acts that enshrines the idea of literal sentence-meaning.[61] Habermas reads Austin as taking an interest in "communicative failures" that are specifically pragmatic insofar as they result from the misuse of sentences that possess such meaning (and that are therefore presumably kosher from the point of view of syntax and semantics).[62] He claims that one of Austin's signature goals is showing that even describing is prone to the pertinent kinds of failures and that, far from monopolizing the serious business of language (as philosophers have often assumed), it accordingly represents one of a variety of ways in which we use what Habermas conceives as independently meaningful sentences. The strategy that Habermas thinks Austin adopts for attaining this putative goal centers on the development of a theory of speech acts that, as Habermas understands it, functions as a system for classifying different uses of such sentences.[63]

Habermas's account of the ethical interest of this allegedly Austinian theory proceeds roughly as follows. Habermas assumes, together with other Kantian moral philosophers, that a satisfactory account of morality must take at face value our intuitive understanding of moral judgments as both "objective" in the sense of aspiring to universal validity and intrinsically practical.[64] In addition, he assumes, in accordance with

---

1984). For a helpful overview of the roughly Kantian account of moral discourse Habermas thinks Austin's thought helps to fund, see "Discourse Ethics: Notes on a Program of Philosophical Justification," in *Moral Consciousness and Communicative Action*, trans. Christian Lenhardt and Shierry Weber Nicholsen (Cambridge, MA: MIT Press, 1999), pp. 43–115.

61. See, e.g., "What is Universal Pragmatics," pp. 27*ff.*, and *The Theory of Communicative Action*, vol. 1, pp. 297 and 335–337. For Habermas's more general and largely sympathetic remarks about Searle's interpretation of Austin, see, e.g., "Universal Pragmatics," pp. 82–83 and "What is Universal Pragmatics?" pp. 25–26. For basic similarities between Habermas's and Searle's approaches to Austin's work on speech acts, see the next two notes. For Habermas's account of certain differences, see note 67.

62. See, e.g., Habermas, "What is Universal Pragmatics?" pp. 27–34. For Searle's discussion of the same sorts of "communicative failures" or (in Searle's jargon) "linguistic improprieties," see "Assertions and Aberrations," and also chapter 6 of *Speech Acts*, pp. 131–156. Searle argues that Austin's remarks about misuses of language are confusing and that it is only by amending Austin's text that we arrive at a satisfactory picture of these linguistic improprieties. In this connection, see note 25.

63. This basic understanding of the nature of Austin's work on speech acts is faithful in fundamentals to the understanding that Searle describes in *Speech Acts*.

64. See, e.g., "Discourse Ethics," pp. 52–57. For a description of relevant features of Kantian approaches in ethics, see section 1.1.

the logic of the narrower conception of objectivity, that no universally valid descriptive (or theoretical) judgment can as such be intrinsically practical.[65] Because Habermas is committed to these two assumptions, he wants to resist the tendency of philosophers to focus on descriptive judgments and to think that the only way in which any judgment (and a fortiori any moral judgment) can be universally valid is by being descriptively true.[66] This is the background against which we need to understand Habermas's claims that the type of theory of speech acts that he ascribes to Austin is of ethical moment. What interests Habermas about such a theory is that it appears to equip us to depict moral judgments, in what he regards as a satisfactory (and strikingly Kantian) manner, as having non-descriptive claims to universal validity.[67]

There is another set of conversations about Austin and ethics that, while they resemble Habermas's work and conversations surrounding it in taking Austin to conceive correspondence between language and the world in terms of the idea of literal sentence-meaning, also differ from it in starting from the basic tenets of Derrida's reading of Austin.[68] Insofar as the theorists who participate in this further set of conversations agree with Derrida in reading Austin as denying even descriptive judgments a claim to objectivity or universal validity, it appears to them that it would be a sign of confusion to insist (say, with Habermas) that Austin makes room for additional, alternative claims to universal validity in connection with non-descriptive judgments. As these theorists see it, the appropriate way to start a conversation about Austin and ethics is to reflect on consequences, not of the discovery of what we may be inclined to think of as further universal validity-claims, but rather of the loss of

65. For a discussion of how the narrower conception seems to underwrite this assumption, see section 1.1.

66. See Habermas, "What is Universal Pragmatics?" pp. 41–44 and 55–57.

67. Habermas takes himself to be departing from both Austin and Searle in arguing that his allegedly Austinian theory of speech acts equips us to talk about non-descriptive modes of discourse with (non-truth-oriented) claims to universal validity. Although he thinks that Austin and Searle supply resources for combating philosophers' traditional fixation on the value of truth, he believes both philosophers nevertheless remain fixated themselves (see, e.g., "What Is Universal Pragmatics," pp. 55*ff.*). Further, he believes that this alleged fixation is reflected in limitations in the schemes for classifying speech acts both Austin and Searle propose (see, e.g., *Theory of Communicative Action*, vol. 1, pp. 309*ff.* and 319*ff.*). Although this criticism may have some merit where Searle's work on speech acts is concerned, where Austin's is concerned, it fails even to locate its target.

68. Central to these conversations are the writings of Stanley Fish's cited in note 8.

even the kind of universal validity-claim encoded in the notion of objective correspondence between language and world. Thus, for instance, the most outspoken theorists to adopt this allegedly Austinian approach to ethical matters—a group of "gender theorists" who are primarily concerned with its bearing on identity categories such as "woman"—argue that the categories that we employ in moral and political reflection, far from applying to our lives in an objective manner, are non-objective constructs that we undertake to "perform."[69]

The two suggestions about the ethical significance of Austin's thought just considered are unsatisfying in that both fail to record Austin's critical preoccupation with a conception of correspondence between language and the world that gets spelled out in terms of an ideal of the literal 'statement'. A more faithful account of the ethical interest of his thought would need to register his hostility to this ideal and the conception of correspondence between language and the world that it suggests, or, to put it in terms licensed by the argument of section 2.2, it would need to register his hostility to an abstraction requirement and the narrower conception of objectivity that this requirement seems to support.

Let me emphasize that my point here is *not* that Austin himself presents such an account of the ethical interest of his thought. On the contrary, there is a respect in which his own classificatory system frustrates efforts to bring some of his central insights into the workings of language to bear on investigations of moral thought.

We can see this if we return briefly to the argument of Chapter 1. One of the argument's central theses is that if we reject the idea of an abstraction requirement, we usher in a pragmatic account of language that obliges us to revise traditional moral judgment-centered theories of ethics. The pertinent pragmatic account of language represents certain sensitivities as internal to all of individuals' linguistic capacities (1.2; see also 2.1 and 2.2), and in presenting the account, I claimed that it invites both the recognition that these sensitivities make up individuals' moral outlooks and the further recognition that what distinguishes episodes of thought as moral is not the use of moral concepts

---

69. For an influential defense of this view of the ethical significance of Austin's work on speech acts, see Judith Butler, *Excitable Speech: A Politics of the Performative* (New York: Routledge, 1997).

but rather the way in which they express the outlook that these sensitivities compose (1.3 and 1.4). It follows from this claim that, within the framework of the pragmatic account of language in question, forms of instruction that address and cultivate our sensitivities may as such make direct contributions to moral understanding. This last point—to which I will return in later chapters—is what interests me right now. It is apposite because Austin, despite attacking an abstraction requirement and making room for a pragmatic account of language, does not include in his inventory of linguistic effects emotional responses with the relevant intellectual powers. Such responses would qualify as what Austin calls *perlocutionary* effects. They would belong to the class of *consequential* effects that saying something may produce on "the feelings, thoughts or actions of the audience" (*How to Do Things with Words*, 101). But they would not be consequential in a simple or undifferentiated sense. They would differ from other consequential effects in that a capacity to (at least imaginatively) register them would be internal to a person's ability to grasp what the bit of language that produces them can teach. And they would thus represent a philosophically distinct subdivision within Austin's category of the perlocutionary.

This observation underlines a respect in which Austin's linguistic apparatus obstructs efforts to investigate moral thinking in a manner respectful of the logic of his own pragmatic account of language. It suggests the need to criticize Austin for failing adequately "to articulate the perlocutionary" and, more specifically, for failing to isolate a set of perlocutionary effects that are capable of contributing directly to moral understanding.[70]

---

70. The inset quote is from Cavell, "Counter-Philosophy and the Pawn of Voice," p. 82. See also Cavell's more involved critique of Austin's treatment of the perlocutionary in "Performative and Passionate Utterance," *Philosophy the Day After Tomorrow* (Cambridge, MA: Harvard University Press, 2005, pp. 155–191. It would be difficult to exaggerate the extent of the difference between Cavell's treatment of Austin's category of the perlocutionary and other more standard treatments. Where commentators *do* take an interest in perlocutionary effects, their tendency is to understand them as without exception merely consequential in a sense that renders them incapable of making anything but an accidental contribution to the growth of understanding. Thus, e.g., Habermas, although he has on several occasions revised details of his view of perlocutionary effects, endorses this understanding throughout. His revisions target not fundamental tenets of the understanding but rather, more locally, his own early— and surely mistaken—suggestion that all intended or foreseeable perlocutionary effects are deceptive or, in his parlance, "strategic" (*Theory of Communicative Action*, vol. 1, pp. 288–289).

This basic criticism of Austin's treatment of the perlocutionary is developed in Stanley Cavell's writings. The backdrop for the criticism is an understanding of Austin—one that Cavell defends and that is congenial to the reading of *How to Do Things with Words* presented in this chapter—as championing a pragmatic account of language.[71] Cavell criticizes Austin's treatment of the perlocutionary because he holds that such an account suggests an understanding of moral thought that only a revised account of "perlocutionary effects" allows us to illuminate—specifically, an understanding on which such thought need not take the form of moral judgments and on which, without regard to whether or not it does take this form, it is a matter of the expression of a sensibility internal to all of a person's modes of thought and speech.

My overarching goal in this book is to develop the view of ethics that provides a home for this understanding of moral thought—a view on which the concerns of ethics reach all the way to the sensibilities individuals possess as linguistic beings. With an eye to advancing this project, I turn now again to the philosophy of Wittgenstein.

71. For comments on convergences between Cavell's approach to Austin and the approach defended in this chapter, see notes 25, 52, 53 and 70.

# ~ 3

## Ethics, Inheriting from Wittgenstein

> Ethics must be a condition of the world, like logic.
> ~ *Wittgenstein*, Notebooks 1914–1916 *(1979), p. 77.*

IN THIS BOOK'S FIRST CHAPTER I presented a comprehensive argument for a non-traditional view of ethics—a view that represents the concerns of ethics as stretching past moral judgments to the whole tissues of sensitivities individuals possess as linguistic beings—and in the second chapter I reinforced this argument by returning to the pragmatic account of language that the argument represents as underwriting this non-traditional view. In the current chapter, I am again concerned to reinforce my main argument, only now at a somewhat different point. Here I strengthen the case I made for moving from a pragmatic account of language to the basic view of ethics I favor by turning to the work of one philosopher who makes an analogous move—namely, Wittgenstein. I bring out how, in addition to describing the sort of pragmatic account of language that interests me, Wittgenstein depicts his preferred account as speaking for a non-traditional ethical view that, while in some respects different from the view defended in this book, resembles it in representing the concerns of ethics as extending to sensibilities that inform all of individuals' modes of thought and speech.

Wittgenstein is rarely read as advocating such a view of ethics, and, to make a good case for reading him on these lines, I need to distance myself from a prevalent interpretation of his later writings that takes conversations about "Wittgenstein and ethics" in a very different direction. The interpretation I have in mind represents Wittgenstein's pragmatic gestures as consistent with the philosophical idea of literal sentence-meaning that I attacked in the last chapter, and, when I turn to this interpretation below, I argue that, far from being receptive to this idea (or to the kind of abstraction requirement that seems to support the idea), Wittgenstein in fact aims to repudiate it. One of my guiding suggestions in this chapter is that we need to see that he cherishes this aim if we are to recognize his interest in a non-traditional view of ethics that resembles the view central to this book.

Since *On Certainty* is often taken to provide a good model both for the prevalent interpretation of Wittgenstein's pragmatic commitments that I oppose and for the claims about "Wittgenstein and ethics" that this interpretation is taken to fund, I focus my attention on this text. After first offering a general sketch of the interpretation and its ethical upshot (3.1), I turn to showing not only that *On Certainty* resists assimilation to the prevalent interpretation but also that this text of Wittgenstein's is properly read, in a manner that directly opposes the interpretation, as developing a pragmatic account of language that repudiates the idea of literal sentence-meaning (3.2). I close by pointing out that Wittgenstein takes the pragmatic account of language he thus presents to speak for a view on which the concerns of ethics extend to all of individuals' modes of thought and speech and, further, that in significant respects his work anticipates and reinforces the case for such a view that I am making in this book (3.3).[1]

## 3.1 The Standard View of the Bearing of Wittgenstein's Philosophy on Ethics

"So you are saying that human agreement decides what is true and what is false?"—It is what human beings *say* that is true and false; and

---

1. My primary topic in this chapter is the bearing of Wittgenstein's later philosophy on ethics. I say very little that pertains directly to ethical implications of the *Tractatus* or of Wittgenstein's pre-*Tractatus* writings. I am, however, sympathetic to the drift of the work of philosophers such as Cora Diamond and James Conant who have recently argued that there is significantly greater continuity between Wittgenstein's early and later thought than is traditionally assumed, and I am inclined to think that a significant portion—but not all—of what I say about Wittgenstein's later work in relation to ethics could also be said about the *Tractatus*. In this connection, see section 3.2.ii, especially note 31 and the associated text.

> they agree in the *language* they use. That is not agreement in
> opinions but in form of life.
>
>      ∼ *Wittgenstein*, Philosophical Investigations, *§241.*

It is a characteristic gesture of Wittgenstein's to insist on the importance, within philosophical investigations of the meanings of linguistic
expressions, of attention to how such expressions are used. This gesture
is often taken to show that Wittgenstein repudiates a classical theory of
meaning on which our use of particular expressions is in some sense a
consequence of the meanings the expressions already possess in favor of
what is sometimes called a "use-theory of meaning"—i.e., a theory on
which our manner of using expressions in some sense constitutes their
meanings.[2] Further, Wittgenstein is often taken to be moving from the
thought, internal to a use-theory, that the public practices to which an
expression is tied fix its meaning to the conclusion that those practices
determine what kinds of things can, and what kinds of things cannot,
coherently be said with the expression. What emerges is a familiar image of Wittgenstein as maintaining that investigations of how we use
expressions establish the bounds of sense by revealing regularities or
rules in accordance with which linguistic acts must be performed to be
fully intelligible.[3]

    When I turn to this image of Wittgenstein, one of my main preoc-
cupations is to underline the fact that it represents him as assuming that
some utterances are unintelligible on account of the kinds of things
they allegedly try to say (i.e., things not permitted by the structure of
our linguistic practices). More specifically, I am concerned to emphasize that when Wittgenstein is seen as making this assumption he is, by
the same token, seen as committed to the view that, even when the utterance of a combination of words or a sentence fails to perform an in-

---

2. For an early use of this label in connection with both Wittgenstein's and J. L. Austin's
writings, see, e.g., John Searle, *Speech Acts: An Essay in the Philosophy of Language* (Cambridge:
Cambridge University Press, 1969), p. 148.

3. One of the most influential readings to develop this image is presented in Gordon Baker
and P. M. S. Hacker, *Wittgenstein: Rules, Grammar and Necessity*, vol. 1 (Oxford: Basil Blackwell, 1985). Baker and Hacker tell us, e.g., that for Wittgenstein "[grammar's] rules determine
the limits of sense" so that "by carefully scrutinizing [these rules] the philosopher may determine at what point he has drawn an overdraft on Reason, violated the rules for the use of an
expression and so . . . traversed the bounds of sense" (p. 55).

telligible act of speech, and even when there is therefore no question of appreciating the practical point of producing it on the occasion at hand, it may nevertheless be possible to grasp its meaning—at least well enough to recognize what it is trying (unsuccessfully) to say. This point merits emphasis because, to the extent that Wittgenstein is represented as committed to this view, he is taken to be endorsing the familiar philosophical idea of literal sentence-meaning that I discussed in the last chapter, and, as I mentioned already, one of my central goals in what follows is demonstrating both that Wittgenstein is critical of this idea and that we need to understand how and why he is critical of it if we are to bring clearly into focus the pragmatic account of language that informs his reflections on ethics.

Some of the philosophical interest excited by an image of Wittgenstein as favoring a use-theory has to do with the fact that a use-theory appears to undercut the possibility of critical scrutiny of our linguistic practices. This theory can be developed so that it represents the meanings of terms for even our most basic epistemic or critical concepts as fixed by linguistic conventions. Thus extended, the theory represents our linguistic practices as immune to what might be thought of as "external" forms of criticism—forms that endeavor to round on our linguistic practices and supply them with rational foundations. Very roughly, the problem is that, insofar as these criticisms are intended to question even received critical practices, a demand to employ critical locutions in irregular and hence (by the lights of a use-theory of meaning) unsuitable circumstances appears to be internal to their aspirations. The result is that the very nature of such critical efforts seems to force us into a peculiar type of unintelligibility. We seem to be knocking up against a limit imposed by the structure of language— one that we would have to transgress if, *per impossibile*, we were to show that our linguistic practices are (or are not) rationally defensible. Admittedly this doesn't prevent us from offering rational criticisms of language when we can do so without flouting established critical practices. Nevertheless, even though "internal" forms of criticism (as we might think of them) remain within reach, external forms are prohibited. Our linguistic practices are immune to rational criticism, or inviolable.

Interpretations that proceed along these lines—hereafter *inviolability interpretations*—are often extended so that they seem to support some form of cultural relativism.[4] What suggests the extension is the thought that, in developing what is alleged to be a use-theory of meaning, Wittgenstein leaves room for the possibility of communities of speakers who have both very different linguistic practices and, by the same token, also very different critical standards. The idea is that when we encounter members of such communities we're not justified in regarding the distances that separate us as disagreements subject to rational resolution. In addition to being unable to critically survey our own linguistic practices, we are unable to demonstrate that our practices are rationally superior (or inferior) to those of others. Our hopes for convergence must accordingly be vested not in techniques of reason but in efforts to effect "conversions" using non-rational methods.[5]

Without regard to whether they are taken to underwrite this form of relativism, inviolability interpretations are the common denominator of most discussions about Wittgenstein and ethics. These discussions, which date back to the first reception of Wittgenstein's later thought, typically take the form of debates about the consequences of the allegedly Wittgensteinian view that our ways of thinking and speaking are inviolable. Some of the most outspoken commentators who ascribe this view to Wittgenstein and who also take an interest in its ethical implications insist that the view is inseparable from a form of ethical *conservatism*. The members of this group of commentators (which includes not only critics such as Bertrand Russell, Ernst Gellner and, more recently, Onora O'Neill but also fans such as David Bloor and J. C. Nyíri) trace the view's supposedly conservative character to what they see as its tendency to deprive us of resources required for making sense

4. An interpretation qualifies as an "inviolability interpretation" in my sense if it (1) attributes to Wittgenstein some version of the sort of use-theory of meaning described in this section's first paragraph and (2) suggests that it follows from this theory that there is no such thing as rational criticism of language games. One of the earliest readings that counts as an inviolability interpretation in this sense is developed by Norman Malcolm. According to Malcolm, Wittgenstein holds both that "*within* a language-game there is justification and lack of justification, evidence and proof, mistakes and groundless opinions, good and bad reasoning, correct measurements and incorrect ones" and, further, that "one cannot properly apply these terms to a language-game itself" (see "The Groundlessness of Belief," in *Thought and Knowledge* [Ithaca, NY: Cornell University Press, 1977], pp. 199–216, p. 208; stress in the original).

5. Among the most comprehensive discussions of Wittgenstein's alleged relativism are David Bloor, *Wittgenstein: A Social Theory of Knowledge* (New York: Columbia University Press, 1983), and Stephen Hilmy, *The Later Wittgenstein: The Emergence of a New Philosophical Method* (Oxford: Basil Blackwell, 1987).

of calls for rational improvements in our current modes of thought and speech. Many of them also represent the pertinent form of conservatism as tied to the species of relativism just described—on which our alleged inability to critically scrutinize our own practices leaves us incapable of comparing what we might have thought of as their rational credentials with those of the practices of others. The larger suggestion of these commentators is that Wittgenstein should be understood as maintaining that the only way for us to live consistently is to find a way to live within our current practices—while perhaps also withholding criticism of the practices of others.[6]

Not everyone who reads Wittgenstein along inviolability lines believes that the result is an image of him as a conservative thinker. A small number of such readers—including, famously, Richard Rorty—have wanted to rebuff the suggestion of "Wittgenstein's conservatism." These readers argue that Wittgenstein leaves room for the possibility of agitating for even radical changes in our linguistic practices. Their guiding thought is that, insofar as Wittgenstein represents efforts to transform our practices as unhampered by our current critical resources, he effectively maintains that we can bring about changes inconceivable from within those practices simply by getting our fellow speakers to pick up new linguistic habits.[7]

It is no part of my project in what follows to enter into the details of or try to arbitrate this dispute about implications of the allegedly Wittgensteinian view that our linguistic practices are inviolable. My initial goal is to show that, although passages in which Wittgenstein refers questions about meaning to a study of our public linguistic techniques may at first seem to provide support for the sort of use-theory of meaning distinctive of inviolability interpretations, a more careful

6. Gellner lays out one of the earliest criticisms of Wittgenstein on the grounds of his alleged conservatism in *Words and Things: An Examination of, and Attack on, Linguistic Philosophy* (London: Routledge and Kegan Paul, 1959). For a more recent criticism along similar lines, see O'Neill, "The Power of Example," reprinted in *Constructions of Reason: Explorations of Kant's Practical Philosophy* (Cambridge: Cambridge University Press, 1989), pp. 165–186. A list of significant defenses of Wittgenstein on the grounds of his alleged conservatism would include Bloor, *Wittgenstein: A Social Theory of Knowledge* and J. C. Nyíri, "Wittgenstein's Later Work in Relation to Conservatism," in *Wittgenstein and His Times*, ed. Brien McGuinness (Oxford: Basil Blackwell, 1982), pp. 44–68.

7. I discuss relevant aspects of Richard Rorty's work in "Wittgenstein's Philosophy in Relation to Political Thought," in *The New Wittgenstein*, ed. Alice Crary and Rupert Read (London: Routledge, 2000), pp. 118–146.

study reveals that he has no interest in such a theory. Nor is his lack of interest merely a matter of what a number of writers have disparaged as a "quietistic" reluctance to advance theoretical claims that he nevertheless requires to support his explicit philosophical commitments.[8] Wittgenstein is actively hostile to the tenets of a use-theory of meaning, and his hostility extends to the idea of literal sentence-meaning that, as we saw, informs the theory.

## 3.2  Ethics and Language in *On Certainty*

> We do not learn the practice of making empirical judgments by learning rules: we are taught *judgments* and their connection with judgments. *A totality* of judgments is made plausible to us.
>
> ∼ *Wittgenstein*, On Certainty, *§140*

Setting aside these larger issues for the moment, we can justly say that a prevailing tendency among commentators on Wittgenstein's later philosophy—without regard to whether they are specifically interested in questions of ethics—is to think that Wittgenstein is committed to some version of an inviolability view. Further, we can justly say that this tendency is especially marked in connection with *On Certainty*. Some of the most widely received accounts of *On Certainty*'s preoccupations both ascribe to its author a use-theory of meaning and suggest that the larger project for which he employs it is arguing that our own (and perhaps also others') linguistic practices are immune to rational scrutiny.[9] Given that *On Certainty* is often taken to speak especially strongly for some sort of inviolability interpretation, it follows that it

8. Simon Blackburn introduces this—widely used—but, by my lights, unhelpful and misleading—jargon ("Wittgenstein's quietism") in connection with what he understands as "the belief of the later Wittgenstein that [metaphysical] problems require therapy rather than solution." See Blackburn, *Spreading the Word: Groundings in the Philosophy of Language* (Oxford: Clarendon Press, 1984), p. 146.

9. In this section I take Marie McGinn's *Sense and Certainty* (Oxford: Basil Blackwell, 1989) as a paradigmatic instance of what I am calling an inviolability interpretation of *On Certainty*. For references to further readings that likewise qualify as such interpretations, see notes 20 and 22.

represents a particularly good test case for a challenge to such an interpretation.

### 3.2.i  On the 'Inviolability of Framework Judgments'

> Wittgenstein's own view . . . is that we should . . . recognize how very specialized the use of "I know" is . . . that is to say, that its use is restricted to propositions that are advanced *within* the framework of judgments which together constitute our view of the world.
>
> ~ *Marie McGinn,* Sense and Certainty *(1989), p. 119*

What lies in the background of Wittgenstein's remarks here is, famously, a couple of G. E. Moore's attempts to formulate a refutation of skepticism about the existence of the external world. Moore's most notorious procedure—the centerpiece of his "Proof of the External World"—involved placing himself in an epistemically optimal position for observing some standard object, such as his own hand or a tree, and then coming out with "I know this is a hand" or "I know that is a tree."[10] A second procedure—the crux of "A Defense of Common Sense"—involved listing sentences Moore took to express unquestionably true, or commonsensical, empirical propositions (e.g., "[My body has always been] either in contact with or not far from the surface of the earth"; "The earth had existed for many years before my body was born"; etc.) and then insisting that we can arrive at instances of knowledge by prefixing "I know" to each sentence.[11] Wittgenstein's remarks in *On Certainty* start from objections to both procedures—objections he frequently summarizes by charging that the types of utterances that preoccupy Moore (as well as the skeptic) are *meaningless* or *nonsense*.

This charge is most often construed as a direct expression of a use-theory of meaning. Moreover, it seems undeniable that there are remarks in *On Certainty* that, at least taken in isolation, can plausibly be represented as supporting such a construal. In *On Certainty*, as else-

---

10. G. E. Moore, "Proof of the External World," reprinted in *Philosophical Papers* (London: George Allen and Unwin, 1959), pp. 127–150.

11. G. E. Moore, "A Defense of Common Sense," reprinted in *Philosophical Papers*, pp. 32–59.

where, Wittgenstein is clearly concerned to emphasize the importance, within philosophical investigations of the meanings of particular expressions, of attending to how the pertinent expressions are used.[12] He also clearly traces what he sees as Moore's and the skeptic's lapses into nonsense to a failure to attend properly to uses of "I know" (e.g., §6). And he tries to address this failure by describing circumstances in which we ordinarily advance claims to know. What are in question are, Wittgenstein tells us, circumstances in which there is room for doubt (e.g., §§2 and 4); in which error is intelligible (e.g., §§66 and 74); in which there is a question of saying something informative (e.g., §468), etc. At first glance these different textual observations may seem to support the conclusion—drawn by many readers—that Wittgenstein's criticism of Moore is appropriately spelled out in terms of a use-theory of meaning. The familiar suggestion is that Wittgenstein thinks Moore cannot intelligibly assert the kind of thing he wants to say he knows because it is impossible to advance a claim to know *that* kind of thing within the circumstances in which we ordinarily advance claims to know (i.e., circumstances in which there is room for doubt, in which error is intelligible, etc.).

To the extent that it is thus spelled out in terms of a use-theory, Wittgenstein's charge of nonsense appears to depend for its force on the identification of some sort of misfit between—to use Wittgenstein's German—the *Sätze* to which Moore wants to prefix "I know" and the circumstances in which we ordinarily advance knowledge-claims. Since "*Sätze*" can be used to mean either sentences (i.e., merely grammatical entities) or propositions (i.e., entities that are as such in the business of expressing thoughts), it is important to note that, in order to capture the nature of the alleged misfit, we need to understand Wittgenstein's remarks about Moore's *Sätze* as remarks about propositions and not sentences. For it is only in virtue of our grasp of the nature of the propositions or judgments allegedly in question—they are, we are told, propositions about which there can be no doubt, no question of error, etc.—that we are supposed to be able to recognize that we are no longer dealing with circumstances in which we ordinarily claim to

---

12. See, e.g., *On Certainty* (G. E. M. Anscombe and G. H. von Wright, eds. and Denis Paul and G. E. M. Anscombe, trans. (New York: Harper & Row Publishers, 1972), §61. All unattributed section references in the text of this chapter are to this work of Wittgenstein's.

know things. So, as it gets analyzed here, Wittgenstein's charge of nonsense appears to amount to the charge that Moore slides into unintelligibility when he tries to assert his knowledge of certain independently proposition-expressing—or independently meaningful—combinations of words.

This allegedly Wittgensteinian mode of criticism is a central critical concern of one of James Conant's discussions of the philosophy of Wittgenstein.[13] In the context of arguing that it is wrong to represent the author of *On Certainty* as advocating it, Conant notes that the mode of criticism lends itself to being captured in terms of a distinction—one discussed earlier in this book in reference to John Searle's work (2.1.iv) that is frequently associated with the work of Paul Grice. At issue is a distinction between, on the one hand, "sentence-meaning" (spelled out in terms of both the meanings of the individual words of which a sentence is composed and the rules of the language) and, on the other, "intended meaning" or "speaker-meaning" (spelled out in terms of the practical, human point of coming out with a meaningful sentence).[14] Conant's point is that Wittgenstein's objection to Moore, as it is understood on the widely accepted reading of *On Certainty* under consideration here, can be described as concerned exclusively with the latter of these two Gricean categories of meaning. It has to do with the alleged impossibility of figuring out what intelligible point Moore might be making in coming out with knowledge-claims involving certain independently— or (as we might also put it) literally—meaningful sentences.

If it is right to represent Wittgenstein's critique of Moore, in a manner that thus suggests Gricean categories of sentence-meaning and speaker-meaning, as grounded in a use-theory of meaning, then, as we just saw, it must be the case that the many remarks in which Wittgenstein discusses *Sätze* to which Moore prefixes "I know" are properly understood as remarks not about sentences but about propositions. And at this point it might appear that we encounter powerful evidence in favor of ascribing a use-theory to Wittgenstein.

While it's clear that Wittgenstein is critical of Moore's anti-skeptical procedures, it's no less clear that his critical engagement is at bottom

13. James Conant, "Wittgenstein on Meaning and Use," *Philosophical Investigations*, vol. 21, no. 3, July 1988, pp. 222–250.

14. For Grice's introduction and discussion of this distinction, see *Studies in the Way of Words* (Cambridge, MA: Harvard University Press, 1989), esp. chapters 5, 6 and 18.

driven by a measure of real admiration. Wittgenstein takes Moore's "Defense of Common Sense" to contain an important insight. What Wittgenstein finds compelling is Moore's idea that certain empirical judgments play a special role in our modes of thought and speech. In *On Certainty* Wittgenstein returns again and again to different expressions of this idea. He talks about empirical propositions *(Erfahrungssätze)* and judgments *(Urteile)* which "stand fast for us" or which are "like the axis around which a body rotates" (e.g., §150–153); he compares the role certain empirical propositions play in our language to the stable but not permanent channels in a riverbed (§96); and he tells us that these propositions are like "hinges" on which our various questions, doubts, investigations, etc., turn (§§341–343).[15]

Insofar as these passages seem to support an understanding of remarks in which Wittgenstein talks about the *Sätze* to which Moore prefixes "I know" as remarks about a special set of empirical propositions, they may be—and, indeed, often are—taken to speak for attributing a use-theory of meaning to Wittgenstein. Further, insofar as they are taken to speak for attributing such a theory to Wittgenstein, they may be—and, indeed, often are—taken to speak directly for reading all of *On Certainty* along inviolability lines. The pertinent passages represent some empirical judgments as fundamental for our linguistic practices. So to the extent that Wittgenstein is taken to be arguing, in accordance with a use-theory, that it is impossible to question, doubt, investigate, advance knowledge-claims about, etc., certain judgments, and to the extent that he is also taken to be referring to precisely *these* judgments (viz., those that are fundamental for our linguistic practices), he appears to hold the view that there is a significant respect in which our linguistic practices are immune to rational scrutiny.

15. There is evidence of Wittgenstein's admiration for Moore's article not only in the text of *On Certainty* but also in various biographical sources. In an editor's preface to *On Certainty*, G. E. M. Anscombe and G. H. von Wright write that "Wittgenstein had long been interested in [Moore's "A Defense of Common Sense"] and had said to Moore that this was his best article" (p. vi). Norman Malcolm disputes Anscombe and von Wright's suggestion that Wittgenstein's interest in Moore's article predates conversations Wittgenstein had with Malcolm in the summer of 1949 (see "Moore and Wittgenstein on the Sense of 'I Know,'" in *Thought and Knowledge*, pp. 170–198, p. 172, n. 9), but nevertheless confirms their suggestion that Wittgenstein's interest—setting aside the question of when it was sparked—was grounded in sincere admiration for Moore. For Malcolm's account of his conversations with Wittgenstein about Moore's paper, see Norman Malcolm, *Ludwig Wittgenstein: A Memoir*, 2nd ed. (Oxford: Oxford University Press, 1984), pp. 70–75.

This gives us a rough sketch of the sort of inviolability interpretation that gets traced out within some of the most influential accounts of *On Certainty*.[16] For a clear and *prima facie* plausible version of such an interpretation, we might turn to Marie McGinn's 1989 book *Sense and Certainty*. According to the interpretation McGinn develops here, Wittgenstein's main ambition in *On Certainty* is to show both that Moore's anti-skeptical procedures isolate a class of judgments that play a special, framing role in our language game and that there can be no question of standing in epistemic relations to these judgments. The pertinent judgments might be thought of as composing, she writes:

> the completely unquestioned background against which all en-quiry, description of the world, confirmation and disconfirmation of belief, etc., goes on: they are all the judgments that are either "flamingly obvious" or which may be spoken with authority, which will be accepted without doubt, and which may be taken for granted in the justifications that we give for the knowledge claims or more interesting judgments we advance.[17]

On McGinn's reading, a central concern of *On Certainty* is showing that these "framework judgments" (as she calls them) can't be made to fit with the circumstances in which we ordinarily advance knowledge-claims, or, in her words, that "there is an implication carried by the use of "I know" that cannot be met by claims involving [these judg-ments]."[18] McGinn argues—in a manner that presupposes some ver-sion of a use-theory—that Wittgenstein's criticism of Moore turns for its force on the identification of just this sort of misfit. The alleged problem is that, as a result of the misfit, it is unclear what intelligible human point Moore might be making in trying to say that he has

---

16. The kinds of readings of *On Certainty* I am calling inviolability interpretations are fre-quently described, in the secondary literature, as readings on which Wittgenstein endorses a "theory of framework judgments" or a "theory of hinge propositions." The point of the ter-minology is that here Wittgenstein holds that certain special ("framework") judgments or ("hinge") propositions are immune to criticism.

17. McGinn, *Sense and Certainty*, p. 103. For a discussion of McGinn's reading of *On Cer-tainty* in *Sense and Certainty* that is both more detailed than my discussion here and congenial to it, see James Conant, "Wittgenstein on Meaning and Use."

18. Ibid., p. 106.

knowledge of certain "framework judgments."[19] McGinn thus invites us to understand Wittgenstein as championing the view that the judgments that make up the "framework" of our language cannot be submitted to rational scrutiny. She describes a full-blown inviolability interpretation of *On Certainty* on which the book's central intended moral is, as she puts it, that the application of all "questions of evidence and justification" is "restricted to propositions that are advanced *within* the framework of judgments which together constitute our view of the world."[20]

McGinn doesn't address the question of whether her interpretation has relativistic implications. But other readers have gone on from similar interpretations to attribute to Wittgenstein various forms of cultural relativism. The passages from *On Certainty* that typically get accented in this context contain descriptions—they are in every case highly schematic ones—of encounters between people with very different worldviews. Thus, to mention some central remarks, we are asked to envision ourselves confronted with people who consult oracles instead of physics (§609) and also with people who believe that human beings sometimes go to the moon (§§106 and 108),[21] and we are invited to imagine Moore disputing with a king who is brought up to believe the world started with him (§92). In his commentary on these encounters, Wittgenstein tells us that although we may "convert" others to our way of thinking, "it [will] be a conversion of a special kind" (§92). And he adds that, in contrast to what we may be inclined to assume, we are sometimes forced to pin our hopes for cross-cultural understanding not on reasons or proofs but on methods designed to shape our own or others' responses—i.e., on what he calls methods of "persuasion" (§§262, 612 and 669).

19. Ibid., pp. 85–86.

20. Ibid., pp. 120, 119. McGinn's isn't the only well-received interpretation of *On Certainty* that proceeds along these lines. One of the earliest readings of this sort is Malcolm's. (See "The Groundlessness of Belief" and "Moore and Wittgenstein on the Sense of 'I Know.'") And in a book-length study of *On Certainty*, Avrum Stroll, despite disagreeing with McGinn and Malcolm over various relatively minor exegetical issues, offers a similar description of the book's larger significance. Stroll declares that Wittgenstein's aim is to show that "some propositions—that the earth exists, that the earth is very old—are beyond any doubt; their certitude is absolute" (*Moore and Wittgenstein on Certainty* [Oxford: Oxford University Press, 1994], p. 138).

21. Here one has to bear in mind that Wittgenstein penned his remarks a couple of decades before anyone traveled to the moon.

I want to emphasize that it is not written into these remarks that they express a relativistic outlook. The remarks only seem to express such an outlook given the assumption that the persuasive methods Wittgenstein mentions here are properly understood as *non-rational* modes of communication. This assumption, in turn, seems reasonable if we take it for granted that Wittgenstein is maintaining, in accordance with an inviolability interpretation, that "framework judgments" are immune to rational assessment—and if we take it for granted, further, that he is suggesting that different linguistic communities may have different sets of such judgments. Against this background, it seems natural to suppose that what Wittgenstein is doing in his remarks on cross-cultural encounters is describing a relativistic creed on which it is impossible to overcome divergences between members of different linguistic communities by rational means and on which we should therefore place our hopes for convergence in the application of merely persuasive, non-rational methods.[22] Nevertheless, since an inviolability approach is built into the background that makes this supposition seem natural, it follows that there's a sense in which an account of Wittgenstein as a relativist stands or falls with such an approach.[23]

### 3.2.ii Meaning, Judgment and Limits of Sense

> Instead of saying that Moore's statement "I know that this is a tree"
> is a misuse of language, it is better to say that it has no clear meaning,
> and that Moore himself doesn't know how he is using it.
>
> ~ *Wittgenstein, as reported in Norman Malcolm,*
> Ludwig Wittgenstein: A Memoir *(1984), p. 72.*

If not in accordance with the sort of inviolability interpretation that McGinn and others elaborate, how should we understand Wittgenstein's charge that Moore's utterances are meaningless? According to

---

22. It is accordingly not unusual for commentators who favor this basic interpretative approach to explicitly argue that when Wittgenstein speaks of persuasive methods "he must mean non-rational persuasion" (James Klagge, "When Are Ideologies Irreconcilable? Case Studies in Diachronic Anthropology," *Philosophical Investigations* 21, no. 3, [July 1998]: 268–279, 270).

23. It was no part of my aim in this section to suggest that we need to turn to interpretation of *On Certainty* to find accounts of Wittgenstein's thought that proceed along inviolability lines. Many commentaries on Wittgenstein's later writings that lack any special emphasis on *On Certainty* likewise proceed along these lines.

inviolability interpretations, when Wittgenstein speaks of nonsense in connection with Moore's utterances of "I know that such-and-such," he is identifying a problem not with what "such-and-such" expresses but rather with Moore's efforts to assert *that*; Wittgenstein is complaining that there is no way for Moore to get his claim to know the particular judgments in question to dovetail with the circumstances in which we ordinarily say we know things. This observation about inviolability interpretations brings me to another point Conant makes in the paper of his touched on in the last section. Conant claims that it is a signal defect of this basic interpretative approach that it places philosophical weight on a distinction between kinds of meaninglessness that is one of Wittgenstein's central critical targets.[24] Conant develops this claim in connection with McGinn's work, noting that McGinn assumes both that Wittgenstein is primarily concerned with a type of nonsense that afflicts judgments (or 'literally meaningful' sentences) when used in unsuitable circumstances and that Wittgenstein brackets questions about a type of nonsense that occurs at the level of the sentence. Conant brings out how McGinn by and large reserves talk of "unintelligibility" for the former (and, by her lights, textually more significant) type of nonsense and speaks of "meaninglessness" and "failures of sense" in connection with the latter. Thus McGinn writes:

> The attempt to show that the knowledge claims that the philosopher investigates are illegitimate or unintelligible is thus an attempt to show, not that the words that the philosopher utters in introducing these claims are themselves meaningless, but that, given the context in which he utters them, we cannot see what *he* means by them, we cannot construe his utterance of them as an intelligible act of assertion.[25]

Abstracting for the moment from the question of whether it is possible to defend McGinn's distinction between two types of nonsense (i.e., meaninglessness and unintelligibility), it is worth stressing that there is in any case no trace of it in *On Certainty*. Wittgenstein uses "unintelligible" (*unverständlich*) only once, and even in this one case he employs

---

24. Conant, "Wittgenstein on Meaning and Use," p. 228.

25. McGinn, *Sense and Certainty*, p. 85; stress in the original. See Conant's commentary on this passage in "Wittgenstein on Meaning and Use," p. 228.

it in a context in which he elsewhere talks about things being "non-sense" (*Unsinn* or *unsinnig*) or, alternately, "failing to make sense" (*keinen Sinn haben*).[26] His attitude toward these terms is, quite plainly, that they are interchangeable.

This isn't a matter of sloppiness. Wittgenstein is happy to use these terms interchangeably because he wants to collapse the very distinction between kinds of meaninglessness that McGinn's more specialized terminology serves to mark. When Wittgenstein declares that Moore-type utterances are nonsense, he is not suggesting that the utterances involve judgments such that no claim to know them can be squared with the conditions of knowledge. He is suggesting instead that it's not clear what judgments are at issue at all. For instance, he occasionally glosses his references to Moore's *Sätze* as references to his *words* and, in doing so, invites us to greet his interest in these *Sätze* as interest not in items that already possess a determinate logical character (i.e., judgments or propositions) but in items that can only be characterized in grammatical terms.[27] He thus expresses sympathy for the view that, until we understand what intelligible act of speech Moore is performing with his sentences, we're not yet in a position to say what those sentences mean (even though, as Wittgenstein puts it, they are "extremely simple sentence[s] of the most ordinary kind" [§347] and we "can fairly easily imagine a situation to fit" them [§10]). Or, to put it in other words, he expresses sympathy for the view that there is something confused about the philosophical idea of literal sentence-meaning that Austin also attacks and that I discussed at length in the last chapter.

The hostility that Wittgenstein here expresses to the idea of literal sentence-meaning is of a piece with things he says, in both his early and later writings, about the limits of sense. Wittgenstein repeatedly says things to the effect that logic is internal to (or constitutive of) thought

---

26. The one occurrence of "unintelligible" comes at the end of *On Certainty*, §10: "One thinks that the words 'I know that . . .' are always in place where there is no doubt, and hence even where the expression of doubt would be unintelligible *[unverständlich]*." In the numerous other remarks in *On Certainty* about whether certain doubts are transparent to understanding, Wittgenstein exchanges this talk of unintelligibility for talk of nonsense or the absence of sense. See, e.g., §138, where the response to an interlocutor's attempt to raise a doubt about whether the earth has existed for a hundred years is "Nonsense *[Unsinn]*." See also, e.g., §372, where Wittgenstein writes, "'I doubt whether that is really my (or a) hand' makes no sense *[hat keinen Sinn]*."

27. See, e.g., *On Certainty*, §§348–351.

and that there is therefore no such thing as recognizing something both as a thought and as lacking logical structure.[28] He develops this view by attacking the suggestion that a combination of signs, or an utterance, might fail to make sense because of what it—in virtue of what we might confusedly slide into thinking of as its 'illogical logic'—tries but fails to convey. In the *Tractatus*, he puts it this way: "We cannot think anything illogical for then we would have to think illogically" (3.03).[29] In later writings, Wittgenstein's approach to these issues is inflected by the way in which he takes context to contribute to the content or logical character of an utterance. Now Wittgenstein expresses his hostility to the notion of 'illogical thought' by suggesting that there is no such thing as a linguistically impermissible move in a "language game."[30] He attempts to distance himself from the idea of a combination of words-and-context that fails to make sense because of what it—in virtue of what we might confusedly slide into thinking of as its "senseless sense"—tries but fails to convey.[31]

28. See, e.g., *Tractatus* (C. K. Ogden, trans., London: Routledge & Kegan Paul, 1985) 3.0: "The logical picture of facts is the thought."

29. Immediately following this remark, Wittgenstein goes on to write:

It used to be said that God could create everything, except what was contrary to the laws of logic—But we couldn't *say* of an "unlogical" world how it would look (3.031; I have revised Ogden's translation slightly here).

To present in language anything which "contradicts logic" is as impossible as in geometry to present by its coordinates a figure which contradicts the laws of space; or to give the coordinates of a point which does not exist. (3.032)

See, e.g., also the opening sections of Wittgenstein, "Notes Dictated to G. E. Moore in Norway," in *Notebooks, 1914–1916*, 2nd. ed., ed. G. H. von Wright and G. E. M. Anscombe, trans. G. E. M. Anscombe (Chicago: University of Chicago Press, 1979).

30. See, e.g., *Philosophical Investigations* (3rd. ed., trans. G. E. M. Anscombe (New York: Macmillan Publishing Co., Inc., 1958), §§499–500. *Philosophical Grammar*, ed. Rush Rhees, trans. Anthony Kenny (Berkeley, CA: University of California Press, 1974), p. 130 and *Wittgenstein's Lectures, Cambridge, 1932–35*, ed. Alice Ambrose (Chicago, IL: University of Chicago Press, 1979), pp. 63–64.

31. Although I point out in this paragraph that the later Wittgenstein holds that circumstances of use contribute to the meaning of expressions, I do not mean to deny that the early Wittgenstein already held a version of this view. The *Tractatus*, as I read it, describes a form of *inferentialism* on which grasping the proposition expressed by a combination of signs is a matter of appreciating both propositions from which it can be inferred and also inferences that it in turn licenses. Here the exercise of situating a string of signs within an inferential context eliminates alternate logical possibilities left open by the signs themselves (see, e.g., 3.323), and inferential context accordingly makes a direct contribution to content. It is in this respect that the *Tractatus* can be understood as anticipating Wittgenstein's later emphasis on

What is unsatisfactory about the roughly Gricean analysis of Wittgenstein's criticism of Moore that McGinn and other fans of inviolability interpretations favor is, we might now say, that it encodes this idea. According to the analysis, Wittgenstein is supposed to be assuming both that Moore's utterances of "I know that such-and-such" are nonsense and that it is nevertheless possible to identify the meanings of the sentences to which Moore prefixes "I know"—at least well enough to inquire whether they can be made to 'fit' with "I know." The upshot is that Wittgenstein appears to be describing the discovery of logical 'misfits' between the meanings of Moore's sentences and the contexts in which Moore produces them or, in other words, that Wittgenstein appears to be claiming that Moore's utterances are unintelligible on account of the particular (at least barely intelligible) things that they try, unsuccessfully, to say.

Consider the analysis of Wittgenstein's criticism of Moore suggested by an interpretation of *On Certainty* that, in contrast to inviolability interpretations, takes into consideration Wittgenstein's view of the limits of sense. On this alternative interpretation, Wittgenstein is claiming that there is no such thing as a clash between sentence-meaning and circumstances that results in the expression of a "senseless sense." So we should expect that when Wittgenstein describes Moore's utterance of "I know that such-and-such" as nonsense, his point is not that there is something discordant or ill fitting about what we may be inclined to

---

use. To be sure, there are significant differences between the ways in which Wittgenstein approaches these issues in his early and later writings. At the time of the *Tractatus*, he assumes that logical or inferential relations are exclusively truth-functional and that truth-functional connectives determine the "logical space" in which inferences get made in a quasi-mechanical manner. (See, e.g., the discussion of what follows from the introduction of a logical connective at *Tractatus*, 5.44–5.4541.) In later writings, Wittgenstein abandons this exclusive focus on truth-functionality and criticizes the picture of logical consistency or regularity he once championed in connection with it. Now he insists that our ability to understand a judgment depends on our appreciation of the importance of similarities and differences among other judgments that make up the language game to which the new judgment belongs. These are the kinds of textual observations that underlie the distinction I draw between Wittgenstein's early and later views of meaning. My aim is not to make the categorical (and, I believe, false) suggestion that it is only in his later writings that Wittgenstein takes a serious interest in how we use expressions but rather to make the more modest suggestion that there are philosophically significant differences between the kind of importance he places on use early and late.

think of as the sense Moore's words do have; his point is, rather, that we reject Moore's words because here they lack any clear meaning at all.[32] Notice that this analysis is directly at odds with tenets of inviolability interpretations. Since Wittgenstein isn't suggesting that any judgments are at play in Moore's anti-skeptical practice, it follows that he isn't suggesting that there are some judgments that are immune to criticism.

*But wouldn't it be too hasty at this point to conclude that inviolability interpretations of* On Certainty *are bankrupt? What about Wittgenstein's claim that some judgments "stand fast for us"? Doesn't the fact that Wittgenstein associates such judgments with Moore's anti-skeptical maneuvers show that he thinks certain very basic judgments figure in those maneuvers? And doesn't this fact speak (in a manner that conflicts with the above observations about Wittgenstein's remarks on the limits of sense) for an understanding of Wittgenstein as claiming that certain very basic judgments are inviolable?* Despite whatever initial plausibility it possesses, the protest traced out in this series of questions cannot be sustained. Wittgenstein's remarks about judgments "standing fast for us" do not speak for an inviolability interpretation. In making them, Wittgenstein is not claiming that certain judgments lie beyond the reach of critical assessment. Rather, he is discussing ramifications of a view of judgment that is the conceptual counterpart of his view of the limits of sense.

If we help ourselves to an understanding of a "judgment" as a move in a language game, we can reformulate the later Wittgenstein's view of the limits of sense in terms of the idea of the *priority of judgment.*[33] Wittgenstein rejects the assumption that we can somehow identify the logical character of expressions or features of speech-situations outside the context of complete judgments. This assumption is consistent with the possibility that some utterances are nonsense because they employ expressions in contexts with which they are supposedly incompatible. And the mark of Wittgenstein's view of the limits of sense just is the thought that there is at best the appearance of a possibility here. So to endorse the later Wittgenstein's view of the limits of sense is to suggest that if we want to identify the logical character of expressions or features of speech situations we need to *start with complete judgments* and

32. See the epigraph to this section.

33. For an account of the significance I am attaching to a distinction between Wittgenstein's early and later views of meaning and the limits of sense, see note 31.

ask what logical contributions the pertinent expressions or features make to the judgments in question.

One of the later Wittgenstein's strategies for defending the idea that judgments are logically privileged in this sense involves attacking pictures of language acquisition on which we originally learn how to judge by appealing to the guidance of prior logical categories or rules. Wittgenstein repeatedly observes that learning to judge is ultimately a matter of nothing more than cottoning on to, or developing a sense for, what different judgments have in common. He attempts to show that as learners we are called upon to manifest an appreciation of which of the similarities among judgments presented to us are important.[34] In one section of *On Certainty*, he puts it this way: "We do not learn the practice of making empirical judgments by learning rules: we are taught *judgments* and their connection with other judgments. A *totality* of judgments is made plausible to us" (§140, stress in the original). In another section, Wittgenstein sums up his view of judgment with these words: "We use judgments as principles of judgment" (§124; see also §§128–131).

There is a straightforward connection between the passages from *On Certainty* that culminate in this view of judgment and the passages from the *Philosophical Investigations* that I considered in section 1.2 (i.e., passages that criticize the assumption that conceptual competence is aptly spelled out in terms of, or in a manner suggestive of, the image of an infinitely long, ideally rigid rail). In discussing these passages from the *Investigations*, I brought out how they attack the idea of what I am calling an abstraction requirement,[35] and what I want to add here is that the passages from *On Certainty* just touched on likewise attack this idea. A central critical target of the passages from *On Certainty* is the idea of literal sentence-meaning and, more specifically, the particular idea of such meaning that I discussed in reference to Austin's work in Chapter 2. When Wittgenstein insists, as he does in the passages just touched on, that the minimal unit of language is the complete judgment, he is straightforwardly rejecting this idea. This is significant because, as I

34. This would, e.g., be a way of describing a central ambition of the opening seventy or so sections of the *Investigations*.

35. I.e., a requirement to the effect that we abstract from all our subjective endowments on the ground that it is only by doing so that we can assure ourselves of having our minds around more than mere appearance.

pointed out in section 2.2.i, rejecting this idea is tantmount to rejecting the view that it is possible to grasp what a set of words means independently of a sense of the practical point of using it on a particular occasion—and hence tantamount to rejecting an understanding of language as governed by an abstraction requirement. So, insofar as they develop a criticism of a familiar philosophical idea of literal sentence-meaning, the passages from *On Certainty* that I have been discussing are rightly taken to complement those from the *Investigations* discussed in 1.2 in bringing into question the idea of such a requirement. I return to this point in a moment, after first saying something about the importance that Wittgenstein attaches to the view of judgment developed in *On Certainty*.

This view of judgment forms the backdrop against which Wittgenstein talks about some judgments "standing fast" for us. Since, according to this view, our "judgments themselves characterize . . . what it is to judge" (*On Certainty*, §149), it follows that in order to recognize an utterance as a judgment we need to incorporate it into the pattern of things we recognize as judgments. This leaves room for the possibility of situations in which, although it at first appears that a person is judging very differently, we fail to locate her utterance or inscription within a nexus of judgments—and, as a result, fail to recognize her as judging at all. The author of *On Certainty* repeatedly describes cases in which, although we may be inclined to respond to a person's words by saying that she is wildly mistaken (e.g., when a man comes out with "I'm a woman"), it would—he thinks—be more correct to speak not of a mistake in judgment but of something like a mental disturbance.[36] One of the suggestions he is making here is that in these cases there is no smooth or natural connection between the new utterance or inscription we encounter and judgments we already recognize. Another suggestion is that our experience of not being able to make sense of a new utterance or inscription reveals our reliance on certain other judgments that, at least for the time being, don't come into question for us. *This* is what Wittgenstein has in mind when he claims that "we discover the judgments that stand fast for us."[37]

36. The parenthetical example is from *On Certainty*, §79. See also, e.g., §§71–74, 80–81, 138, 155, 420, 474, 494, 624, 628, 630, 645, 659 and 674.

37. This account of Wittgenstein's claim differs from the accounts given by advocates of inviolability interpretations in its incorporation of the view of judgment I've been ascribing to

Although there is, as I mentioned above (3.2.i), a sense in which Wittgenstein credits Moore (and, in particular, the Moore of "A Defense of Common Sense") with the insight that some empirical judgments thus play a special role in our language, what deserves emphasis at this juncture is that there's also a sense in which Wittgenstein charges Moore with betraying his own insight. In the part of his work in question here, Moore is attempting to refute skepticism about the external world by first listing sentences that (as Moore sees it) express commonsensical judgments and then prefixing "I know" to them. Moore recognizes that his verbal performances are irregular, but he doesn't think he needs to worry about their relationship to ordinary verbal performances.[38] Wittgenstein, in contrast, thinks Moore needs to worry. Wittgenstein holds that there's no such thing as recognizing something as a judgment in a manner that doesn't draw on our sense of how it fits into a larger pattern of judgments we already make. When Wittgenstein speaks, in a manner suggestive of indebtedness to Moore, of certain empirical judgments playing a special role in our language, it is precisely in reference to the idea of such a pattern. It follows that, from Wittgenstein's perspective, Moore's anti-skeptical procedures are unfaithful to the very insight on which they are founded. What Wittgenstein wishes to get us to see is that when Moore produces his utterances of "I know that such-and-such" (utterances that are supposed to involve certain special empirical judgments), there's not enough continuity with what "stands fast for us" for us to recognize the utterances as (even improper) assertions of knowledge—and hence not enough continuity for us to recognize them as involving any judgments at all.

---

Wittgenstein (i.e., the view that our ability to recognize judgments essentially presupposes our appreciation of the importance of similarities constitutive of a network of judgments). Inviolability interpretations at least tacitly assume that it's possible to recognize utterances (e.g., Moore's utterances of "I know that such-and-such") as concerned with particular ("framework") judgments even if we haven't yet appreciated them as intelligible moves in a language game. In making this assumption, these interpretations effectively represent us—in a manner unfaithful to Wittgenstein's view of judgment—as capable of surveying judgments from outside the sensibilities we possess as judgers.

38. Moore is happy to acknowledge that, as he once put it in a letter to Norman Malcolm, he is using *I know* "under circumstances under which [this expression] would not ordinarily be used." Moore defends his practice by insisting that although he is not using his words "under any ordinary circumstances," he is nevertheless using them "in the ordinary *sense*." (These passages from Moore's correspondence are cited in Malcolm, "Moore and Wittgenstein on the Sense of 'I know,'" pp. 173–174.)

At this point, it seems clear both that Wittgenstein's rejoinder to Moore does not take the form of an argument to the effect that certain special judgments (say, those that "stand fast for us") are inviolable and that Wittgenstein is therefore not an inviolability theorist. In addition, it seems clear that Wittgenstein is not a relativist. Wittgenstein only appears to be a relativist if his remarks about how certain cultural gulfs need to be bridged by *persuasive* methods are construed as remarks about how certain such gulfs can only be bridged by *non-rational* means. And Wittgenstein's view of judgment speaks directly against this construal of his remarks.

As I have noted, this view stands opposed to a familiar philosophical idea of literal sentence-meaning and, by the same token, to the idea of an abstraction requirement. Where, in sections 1.2 and 2.2.i, I argued that if we straightforwardly repudiate the idea of such a requirement we commit ourselves to exchanging the narrower conception of objectivity for a "wider" alternative, I now want to add that our willingness to reject the idea also has consequences for how we render the concept of rationality.

Suppose we speak of the *concept* of rationality both in reference to our concept of truth-preserving or valid inferences and in reference to our concept of capacities required for making such inferences.[39] And suppose we speak of different *conceptions* of rationality in reference to different specifications of what falls under these two intimately related concepts. This allows us to say that the criticism of the idea of an abstraction requirement developed in the opening chapters of this book, in addition to speaking against the traditional philosophical conception of objectivity that I am describing as "narrower," speaks against a traditional philosophical conception of rationality. The traditional philosophical conception that comes into question is one on which a person's ability to make the connections constitutive of a rational line of thought is taken to be essentially independent of her possession of any particular sensitivities or affective endowments. The point here is that in repudiating the idea of an abstraction requirement, and with it the idea that it is somehow possible to get our minds around how things are independently of the possession of any sensitivities, we at the same time repudiate this conception of rationality and make room for an alterna-

---

39. Admittedly it is possible to use "rationality" to pick out other concepts (e.g., the concept of a pattern of thought and behavior that is conducive to self-interest). My choice of terms is dictated by the concerns of this book.

tive conception on which the exercise of rationality necessarily presupposes the possession of certain sensitivities.

It is possible to capture part of what is striking about this alternative conception of rationality by noting that it makes room for us to enrich our inventory of modes of discourse that are capable of directly contributing to rational understanding. The conception accommodates the possibility that what, following Wittgenstein, we might call *persuasive* modes of discourse (i.e., modes of discourse that aim to elicit affective responses) can as such make direct contributions to such understanding. In section 2.3, I touched on this possibility in criticizing Austin's treatment of the perlocutionary, and in Chapter 4 I discuss it at significantly greater length in reference to various works of literature. Here it suffices to observe that, in accommodating the possibility, the conception of rationality that is at play in *On Certainty* deprives us of any need to insist that persuasive modes of discourse are as such incapable of serving as points of genuinely rational contact between people with very different cultural backgrounds.

To say that persuasive modes of discourse may serve as a point of rational contact between people is neither to say that they invariably do nor to absolve ourselves of the responsibility, when confronted with them, to critically reflect on whether things they seem to reveal to us are more than mere appearances. But the point I want to make now is simply that Wittgenstein's receptivity to an idea of rational persuasion is noteworthy given that he appears to be the relativist that some inviolability interpreters take him to be *only* if his remarks about persuasive methods are construed as remarks about non-rational methods. It follows that there is, in the end, no good reason to believe that he is a relativist.

## 3.3  Wittgenstein, Ethics and a New Direction

> You could attach prices to thoughts. Some cost a lot, some a little. And how does one pay for thought? The answer, I think, is: with courage.
>> ∼ *Wittgenstein*, Culture and Value *(1980), p. 52.*

> Work on philosophy is . . . actually more of a kind of work on oneself.
>> ∼ *Wittgenstein, "Philosophy," in*
>> Philosophical Occasions *(1993), p. 161.*

Thus far in this chapter I have been discussing how certain flawed interpretations of Wittgenstein's account of language obscure our understanding of his ethical preoccupations. Now I turn to discussing how the (in my terms) pragmatic account of language that Wittgenstein in fact defends in *On Certainty* and elsewhere animates many of his reflections on ethics. The reflections I have in mind take the form not of a separate and sustained treatment of ethics but rather of a set of remarks, scattered throughout his writings, that it seems natural to describe as bearing on 'ethical topics.'[40] In some of these remarks, Wittgenstein gives expression to an ethical view that represents the concerns of ethics as extending to individuals' entire sensibilities and that does so in a manner informed by concerns of his preferred pragmatic account of language. My thought here is that, when Wittgenstein thus evokes the ethical view in question, he in significant respects anticipates the view of ethics that I am defending in these pages.

Consider in this connection a couple of prominent themes in the relevant remarks of Wittgenstein's. One of these is that ethics is in some sense a condition of the very possibility of contentful thought or, in Wittgenstein's words, that "ethics is transcendental."[41] Wittgenstein's mature strategy for developing this theme takes for granted a pragmatic account of language, like the one presented in *On Certainty*, on which certain acquired sensitivities are internal to all our linguistic capacities. Wittgenstein in effect appeals to the account in pointing out that there is a sense in which all thought imposes a demand for an active or spontaneous contribution and is therefore something one cannot help but do for oneself. ("No one can think a thought for me," he writes in one passage, "in the way that no one can don my hat for me" [Culture and Value, 2].) Further, he in effect appeals to it in pointing out that thinking for oneself involves relying on and perhaps refining one's sense of salience and significance, and in this respect requires some sort of self-mastery. ("No one can speak the truth," he writes in another passage, "if he has still not mastered himself.")[42] In these and other passages, Wittgenstein is rightly seen as suggesting that the account of language he favors supports the idea that we cannot help but

40. *Culture and Value*, ed. G. H. Von Wright, trans. Peter Winch (Chicago: University of Chicago Press, 1980), is the collection of Wittgenstein's writings that goes furthest toward assembling Wittgenstein's remarks on 'ethical matters.'

41. *Tractatus*, 6.421. See also *Notebooks, 1914–1916*, p. 77, *Culture and Value*, p. 3 and this chapter's opening epigraph.

42. *Culture anad Value*, p. 35. There are other remarks, some of them likewise collected in *Culture and Value*, in which Wittgenstein claims that thinking imposes a demand for self-

"pay for" all our thoughts with a certain ethical effort.[43] And, insofar as, in making this suggestion, he connects the idea of an ethical cost with what he sees as the necessary reliance of language on acquired sensitivities, he expresses sympathy for a view, of the sort that interests me, on which ethics is concerned with the full array of sensitivities that individuals possess as language-users.

Consider a second, closely related theme of Wittgenstein's remarks on 'ethical topics.' In many of these remarks, Wittgenstein insists that his own philosophical practice is properly characterized in ethical terms.[44] The point of remarks in which he sounds this theme is not simply to apply the view that ethical demands are internal to all thought to the case of philosophical thought. For Wittgenstein, the task of underlining the ethical dimension of language, where this is conceived as the task of underlining how we draw on acquired sensitivities in every linguistic operation, is central to philosophy. An organizing preoccupation of his later writings is criticizing approaches to language that presuppose that we can survey and assess judgments, or moves in a language game, without relying on sensitivities we acquired in learning to judge. Wittgenstein consistently represents our tendency to make this presup-

---

mastery. See, e.g., Wittgenstein's claim that "you cannot write anything about yourself that is more truthful than you yourself are" (p. 33) and also his claim that "that man will be revolutionary who can revolutionize himself" (p. 45). Rush Rhees also records a number of Wittgenstein's remarks about how serious thought requires self-mastery in *Recollections of Wittgenstein*, ed. Rush Rhees (Oxford: Oxford University Press, 1984). For example, Rhees quotes the following remarks of Wittgenstein's from 1937:

If you are *unwilling* to know what you are, your writing is a form of deceit.

If anyone is unwilling to descend into himself, because this is too painful, he will remain superficial in his writing. (p. 174; stress in the original)

43. See the first epigraph to this section. See also, e.g., *Culture and Value*, p. 35 ("There is no more light in a genius than in any other honest man—but he has a particular kind of lens to concentrate this light into a burning point") and p. 38 ("Genius is *talent exercised with courage*" [stress in the original]).

44. Wittgenstein's conception of philosophy as an intrinsically ethical endeavor gets expressed not only in various (published and unpublished) remarks but also in various biographical anecdotes and letters. Rush Rhees reports that Wittgenstein used to try to impress on students what he saw as the ethical demands of philosophizing by urging them to go "the bloody *hard* way in philosophy." See Rush Rhees, "The Study of Philosophy," in *Without Answers* (New York: Schocken Books, 1969), p. 169. (I am indebted to James Conant for drawing my attention to this comment of Rhees'.) See also Wittgenstein's comments, in letters to Malcolm, about the ethical challenge of *teaching* philosophy (see Malcolm, *Ludwig Wittgenstein: A Memoir*, esp. pp. 33–34).

position as driving us into philosophical confusions about language. He also consistently discourages us from conceiving the project of working through such confusions as a merely intellectual enterprise directed toward convincing ourselves of the correctness of a new theoretical approach to language. He urges us to conceive it instead as an ethical enterprise directed toward bringing us face-to-face with our responsibility for what we say and think.[45] This is what Wittgenstein has in mind when he writes, for example, that philosophy calls for "a kind of work on oneself" and that it involves a peculiarly ethical type of "difficulty, having to do with the will, rather than with the intellect."[46] The point here is that, insofar as he thus speaks of a kind of ethical difficulty in reference to what he understands as the necessary reliance of language on accquired sensitivities, he is—again—expressing sympathy for the view that ethics is preoccupied with all of the sensitivities that individuals have as language-users.[47]

In the two sets of remarks just considered, Wittgenstein moves from a pragmatic account of language to a view of ethics as concerned with

45. Wittgenstein's remarks on the ethical point of his philosophical procedures shed light on his notoriously perplexing claims about how his ambition in philosophy is not to "advance theses" (*Philosophical Investigations*, §128) or to get us "to agree with [him] in particular opinions" (quoted by Rush Rhees, *Discussions of Wittgenstein* [New York: Schocken Books, 1970], pp. 42–43). These remarks also shed light on his claims about how he intends to leave to his reader "anything [his] reader can do for himself" (*Culture and Value*, p. 77; see also *Philosophical Investigations*, p. vi).

46. See the second epigraph to this section and *Culture and Value*, p. 17. See also "Philosophy" (or §§86–93 of the so-called "Big Typescript"), reprinted in *Philosophical Occasions*, eds. James Klagge and Alfred Nordmann (Indianapolis, IN: Hackett Publishing Company, 1993), p. 161.

47. *On Certainty* resembles Wittgenstein's other writings in exemplifying his conception of philosophy's ethical difficulty. Wittgenstein's guiding concern here is criticizing our tendency to imagine that we can turn on and investigate the credentials of our most basic beliefs from a standpoint independent of modes of response acquired in learning language. Wittgenstein thinks this tendency is what underlies our willingness to assume—in a manner he takes to be characteristic of both the skeptic and the skeptic's dogmatic, Moorean interlocutor—that there is no need to reflect on whether the circumstances in which we want to utter our (allegedly investigative) words bear any affinity to circumstances in which we ordinarily utter those words. So it is with an eye to getting us to repudiate the idea of a standpoint independent of our modes of response that he asks us to compare the utterances we produce in our philosophical endeavors with our ordinary modes of thought and speech. His goal is to get us to acknowledge that, to the extent that we fail to perceive any smooth and natural connection, we fail to attach any meaning to the words that we ourselves insistently produce. This is the respect in which the project of *On Certainty* is conceived as an ethical one. By redirecting attention back to sensibilities we possess as speakers, Wittgenstein hopes to get us to confront our responsibility for what we say and think.

sensibilities individuals possess as linguistic beings. I am making an analogous move in this book, and my suggestion here is that there is a straightforward sense in which Wittgenstein's work provides a model for the book's larger project.

But there are, in addition to analogies, also real differences. When Wittgenstein moves from a pragmatic account of language to a view of ethics as concerned with the sensibilities we have as speakers, his animating thought seems to be that, to the extent that the account represents certain sensitivities as internal to all of our linguistic capacities, and to the extent that it thereby suggests that we are ourselves implicated in everything we say and think, it licenses us to treat the concerns of ethics as thus extending to a dimension of all of language. When I make a similar move in this book, I am guided by certain additional considerations. I am starting from an understanding of ethics as essentially preoccupied with moral thought, and I am insisting on a question—one that does not come up in Wittgenstein's work—about how best to demarcate the domain of such thought.

Taking this question as my point of departure, I have been suggesting that the pragmatic account of language I favor equips us to revise a more traditional inventory of forms of moral thought so that it now includes more than moral judgments. Further, I have been arguing that the account both invites us to see sensitivities that it takes to be internal to language as composing individuals' moral outlooks and positions us to recognize that all episodes of moral thought (i.e., without regard to whether they take the form of moral judgments) are distinguished by the way in which they express the moral outlooks that these sensitivities thus compose. Given that this is what I have in mind in championing a view on which the concerns of ethics extend beyond moral judgments to the full array of sensitivities that individuals possess as language-users, it is appropriate to say that the case that I am making for this view—while indeed descended from and consistent with Wittgenstein's—is nevertheless distinctive. And right now I turn from arguing for the view and exploring its lineage to providing illustrations of the different forms of moral thought that come under its aegis.

~ II

ILLUSTRATIONS

# ~ 4

## Moral Thought beyond
## Moral Judgment:
## The Case of Literature

> Dorothea smiled, and Celia looked rather meditative.
> Presently she said, "I cannot think how it all came about."
> Celia thought it would be pleasant to hear the story.
> "I daresay not," said Dorothea, pinching her sister's chin. "If you
> knew how it came about, it would not seem wonderful to you."
> "Can't you tell me?" said Celia, settling her arms cozily.
> "No, dear, you would have to feel with me,
> else you would never know."
> ~ *George Eliot*, Middlemarch *(1994), pp. 821–822.*

FOLLOWING UP ON the three chapters in Part I of this book, which lay out and elaborate an argument for an inventory of forms of moral thought that is striking and unusual for its inclusion of more than moral judgments, the next two chapters provide illustrations of the different forms of moral thought that are in question. I begin in this chapter with the episodes of moral thought apart from moral judgments described in section 1.4. Then, in the next chapter, I show that conceiving moral judgments in accordance with the philosophically irregular view presented in section 1.3 does justice to actual practices of moral judgment-making. Since all of the current chapter's illustrations of moral thought apart from moral judgments are drawn from literary works, I open my discussion with a comment about why it makes sense to turn to literature in this context.

The pragmatic account of language in which my preferred view of ethics is grounded, in addition to incorporating the philosophically unorthodox conception of objectivity that I am referring to as "narrower" (1.2), incorporates a philosophically unorthodox conception of rationality—specifically, a conception on which a person's ability to make the connections constitutive of a rational line of thought necessarily presupposes sensitivities characteristic of her as a possessor of a language and on which modes of discourse that cultivate a person's sensitivities may therefore make direct contributions to rational understanding in virtue of doing so (3.2.ii). This conception of rationality provides the backdrop against which literature can be seen as a fertile source of examples of the kind of moral thinking, apart from moral judgment-making, that I want to consider. It is characteristic of literary works to engage us emotionally, and the conception leaves open the possibility that these works may directly contribute to rational understanding—of either 'moral' or 'non-moral' topics—insofar as they do so. This is noteworthy because, within the context of the pragmatic account of language that I am championing, the sorts of emotional responses that literary works elicit, in addition to thus being capable of making direct contributions to rational understanding of even 'non-moral topics', are capable of qualifying as developments of our moral outlooks. It follows that here we are right to represent literary works as capable of inviting thought that, while it plays the kind of role in expressing a person's moral outlook that establishes it as moral, nevertheless does not concern itself with 'moral topics'. This, very generally, is what I have in mind in claiming that literature is a promising source of examples of moral thought that does not take the form of moral judgment.

I preface my treatment of a set of literary examples by first saying a word about how the philosophically unorthodox conception of rationality that the examples depend on for their significance is foreign both to conversations in ethics quite generally (4.1) and to those that are specifically concerned with the relationship between moral philosophy and literature (4.2). I then turn to the examples themselves, arguing that they illustrate the existence of moral thinking apart from moral judgment-making (4.3 and 4.4).

## 4.1 Rationality, Argument and the Case of Literature

> However pivotal it may be to the notion of a proper human being
> that he has some capacity, however slight, to produce and follow
> proofs of propositions; or to give and accept reasons for propositions;
> or to draw and concur in inferences from propositions to

propositions; still surely it is not only for his puny, modest or glorious accomplishments in this dry and chilly propositional arena that we grade his life as a man's life as distinct from a brute's life, an infant's life or an idiot's life . . . Surely men differ from lions and infants in being liable to sillinesses, stupidities and wrong-headednesses other than scholastic ones, and in being capable of being judicious in other ways than judicial ways.

> ⌐ *Gilbert Ryle, "A Rational Animal," in*
> Collected Essays, 1929–1968, *vol. 2 (1990), pp. 416–417.*

A helpful place to start is with a conception of rationality that has been taken for granted in recent work in ethics. The conception I have in mind is one on which any stretch of discourse capable of making a direct contribution to understanding must be recognizable as such prior to and independently of any emotional engagement with it, and on which a person's ability to grasp the connections constitutive of a rational line of thought therefore cannot essentially depend on her possession of any particular emotional capacities. What count as rational on the terms of this conception are *arguments*, where an argument is understood as a bit of reasoning in which one judgment or set of judgments (i.e., a premise or set of premises) permits a further concluding judgment to be made in such a way that there is no room for the fact that it does so to depend on any tendency of the judgments in question, either individually or together, to elicit emotional responses. We sometimes speak of argument in a broader (some would say "looser") sense in connection with bits of discourse or texts that appeal to our hearts in various ways—as Milton, for example, speaks of "the argument" of the individual books of *Paradise Lost*[1]—but it is argument in this narrower sense that is taken to be the hallmark of the rational on the conception of rationality that dominates contemporary moral philosophy.[2]

---

1. See, e.g., John Milton, *Paradise Lost*, 2nd ed., ed. Scott Elledge (London: W. W. Norton, 1993), p. 7.

2. Notice that this narrower construal of argument is broad enough to accommodate, in addition to *formal* inferences, also what philosophers sometimes call *material* inferences—i.e., inferences taken to depend for their validity on the content of their premises and conclusions (e.g., "It's raining; I'll get wet"). The thinker who embraces a conception of rationality in terms of argument in the narrower sense need not be any sort of formalist. She need only hold that any bit of discourse containing a rational form of instruction, without regard to whether the inferences it licenses are formally or materially valid, must be recognizable as such independently of any emotional engagement with it.

It is a good measure of the extent to which this conception is engrained in ongoing discussions in ethics that moral philosophers not only for the most part at least tacitly rule out the possibility that a bit of discourse that educates the heart can, insofar as it does so, present us with rational instruction concerning views that it expresses but also by and large greet with a certain degree of perplexity the work of thinkers who are inclined toward the view that this possibility might be a real one. Intelligent attempts to begin a conversation about whether the conception furnishes us with an accurate picture of what rationality in moral discourse comes to are often represented as no more than muddled proposals to treat bits of thought that fall short of the strictly rational as fully legitimate.[3]

In what follows, I am concerned with the clash between this conception of rationality and the philosophically unorthodox conception touched on in this chapter's opening. More specifically, I am concerned with this clash insofar as it informs discussions about the relationship between moral philosophy and literature. For the sake of clarity in discussing these matters, I use the following terminology. I speak of *arguments* in connection with what a moment ago I called argument in the narrower sense. I refer to the philosophically unorthodox conception of

3. For a representative illustration, see Onora O'Neill, "The Power of Example," reprinted in *Constructions of Reason: Explorations of Kant's Practical Philosophy* (Cambridge: Cambridge University Press, 1989), pp. 165–186. Here O'Neill examines the work of a group of thinkers who give a central place in their ethical writings to a consideration of literary examples. Although several of the thinkers O'Neill mentions—e.g., Cora Diamond and Peter Winch—in fact turn to such examples because they take them to present us with rational forms of instruction that cannot accurately be captured in narrowly rational terms (for comments on relevant parts of Diamond's work, see below notes 15 and 17 and the associated text), O'Neill overlooks this aspect of their work. She claims, wrongly, that they take an interest in literary examples because they hold that telling stories represents a viable *non-rational* strategy for resuscitating rational moral communication after it has broken down, and she presents herself, again wrongly, as directly engaging their work in worrying that such examples are therefore equally likely to lead to ignorant and pernicious outlooks as they are to lead to more enlightened ones (p. 173). O'Neill concludes by recommending that treatments of literary examples be supplemented with *principles*—principles "which indicate or suggest which *sorts* of correspondence between example and actual case are important and which trivial" (p. 176; stress in the original)—so that they will count as fully rational contributions to moral reflection. This recommendation, whatever value or interest it possesses on its own terms, simply takes for granted the narrower conception of rationality that some of O'Neill's interlocutors hope to challenge and thus begs one of the main philosophical questions that their literary investigations are supposed to raise, namely, the question of whether this conception captures all that rationality in moral thought comes to.

rationality that represents rational discourse as swinging wide of argument in this sense—and that, as I observed in section 3.2.ii, is the conceptual counterpart of the wider conception of objectivity—as *the wider conception of rationality*. And I refer to the philosophically more traditional conception that represents the realm of rational discourse as no wider than the realm of argument—and that, as I observed in section 3.2.ii, is the conceptual counterpart of the narrower conception of objectivity—as *the narrower conception of rationality*. Taking seriously the challenge that the wider conception of rationality poses to work in ethics informed by its narrower counterpart means taking seriously the possibility that the domain of rational moral reflection is broader than the domain of argument. By the same token, taking this challenge seriously in connection with questions about the relation between moral philosophy and literature means taking seriously the possibility that some stretches of literary discourse are rightly credited with containing rational modes of moral instruction not because they contain moral arguments but because they engage our feelings in various ways.

It is not an exaggeration to say that this possibility is rarely contemplated within ongoing conversations about moral philosophy and literature. The narrower conception of rationality is simply taken for granted within a prevalent view of the relation between literature and moral philosophy. The view I have in mind is not one that is held only by members of the small group of philosophers who explicitly concern themselves with questions about the value of literature as a tool of moral instruction. It is at least implicit in the practice of a great number of moral philosophers—in ways in which they take literature to have a bearing on their investigations of moral thought. An advocate of this view who undertook to spell out its basic features might express herself as follows:

> We must start from the recognition that it is possible to capture a rational defense of a moral doctrine or a conception of the moral life in the form of an (implicit or explicit) argument or set of arguments. If we take seriously the thought that reflection about the moral life as such, when it is fully developed, consists in arguments, we will represent the ways in which literature can contribute to moral reflection as a function of ways in which it can contribute to arguments about features of the moral life: literature

may develop ideas that can be elaborated into arguments; it may it-self contain full-blown arguments; and, perhaps most importantly, it may provide us with detailed and nuanced descriptions of actions, traits of characters, etc., that can serve as illustrations of points we make in developing insightful arguments in moral philosophy.

This view of how literature can teach us about the moral life—which I refer to here as *the prevalent view*—respects the logic of the narrower conception of rationality insofar as it presupposes that a literary work can contribute to moral understanding only by making a contribution to a stretch of reasoning that can be expressed as a fully explicit argu-ment. One of my aims in what follows is to show that the prevalent view, to the extent that it rests on this presupposition, places an artifi-cial restriction on the kind of reflection on the moral life that literature can contain and, further, that an approach to studying literature that frees itself from this presupposition—thus helping itself to the wider conception of rationality—does more justice to ways in which literature can inform moral thought. My larger aim is to show that once we rec-ognize that the moral interest of certain literary works needs to be un-derstood in widely rational terms, we position ourselves to see that literary works are frequently in the business of eliciting moral thinking that, while rationally fully legitimate, does not take the form of moral judgment-making.

## 4.2  A Representative Version of the Prevalent View

> In literature style is so little the mere clothing of thought—need it be insisted on at this late date?—that we may say that from the earth of the novelist's prose spring his characters, his ideas and even his story itself.
>
> ⟶ *Lionel Trilling, "Reality in America," in*
> The Moral Obligation to Be Intelligent *(2000), p. 82.*

Before we turn to examples, it will be helpful to have before us a more de-tailed description of the prevalent view of the relation between literature and moral philosophy. For a representative version of this view, we might consider D. D. Raphael's "Can Literature Be Moral Philosophy?"[4]

4. D. D. Raphael, "Can Literature Be Moral Philosophy?" *New Literary History* 15 (1983): 1–12. Raphael's paper appears in a special issue of *New Literary History* devoted to "Literature

In this paper, Raphael formulates his view of the relation between literature and moral philosophy against the backdrop of the assumption that a fully developed instance of moral philosophy is moral doctrine "presented as the outcome of a carefully structured argument."[5] He claims that while a work need not contain explicit argument to teach us about features of the moral life—it may instead contain what he calls "rational forms of persuasion"—the question of whether its methods of persuasion are rational is answered by considering their relation to explicit argument. The methods a work employs to persuade us to adopt a new perspective on our moral lives are only rational if they appeal to "common experience" that could serve as evidence in an argument for that perspective or if they develop ideas that can serve as the basis for an argument for it.[6]

Drawing on this conception of moral philosophy as aspiring to arguments, Raphael describes three basic respects in which texts with literary features can qualify as moral philosophy or inform it in useful ways.[7] First, works that have literary features can qualify as moral philosophy in an entirely straightforward sense if they themselves contain explicit arguments in favor of moral doctrines or conceptions of the moral life. With reference to this class of works, Raphael distinguishes,

---

and/as Moral Philosophy." In this chapter, I will refer to several other papers that appear in the issue: Cora Diamond, "Having a Rough Story about What Moral Philosophy Is," pp. 155–169, reprinted in *The Realistic Spirit: Wittgenstein, Philosophy and the Mind* (Cambridge, MA: MIT Press, 1990), pp. 367–381; Martha Nussbaum, "Flawed Crystals: James' *The Golden Bowl* and Literature as Moral Philosophy," pp. 25–50, reprinted in *Love's Knowledge: Essays on Philosophy and Literature* (Oxford: Oxford University Press, 1990), pp. 125–147; Richard Wollheim, "Flawed Crystals: James' *The Golden Bowl* and the Plausibility of Literature as Moral Philosophy," pp. 185–191; and a response to Cora Diamond by D. D. Raphael entitled "Philosophy and Rationality: A Response to Cora Diamond," pp. 171–177. All page references to these papers will be to the versions included in this volume of *New Literary History*.

5. Raphael, "Can Literature Be Moral Philosophy?" p. 4.

6. There are some thinkers Raphael takes to rely on non-rational methods of persuasion whom he is nevertheless willing—albeit reluctantly—to represent as in the business of producing moral philosophy. (He places Nietzsche and Kierkegaard, e.g., in this category. See "Can Literature Be Moral Philosophy," pp. 4–5.) But his grounds for crediting these thinkers with a concern with moral philosophy is simply that they rely on what he regards as rational methods of persuasion in at least some of their works. (See "Philosophy and Rationality," p. 173.)

7. Passages in which Raphael describes the rational character of moral philosophy in terms of *argument*—such as those touched on in the last paragraph—do not by themselves demonstrate that he takes for granted the narrower conception of rationality, since, as I have noted, it is possible to speak of "argument" in a wider sense. But an examination of his essay plainly reveals that he is operating with the logic of the narrower conception of rationality.

on the one hand, texts that are "primarily work[s] of philosophy" but that "have merit as work[s] of literature" (here he discusses the *Phaedo*) and, on the other, literary works that he takes to contain, in addition to their literary elements, arguments for getting us to adopt a fresh perspective on our moral lives (here he discusses Samuel Butler's *Erewhon*).[8]

Second, literary works can qualify as moral philosophy if they develop ideas that could, when further elaborated, assume the form of fully explicit arguments in favor of moral doctrines or conceptions of the moral life. Raphael mentions the *Oresteia* as a representative member of this class of works.[9] Within the drama, we are presented with two different conceptions of justice and encouraged to embrace one of them—namely, justice by legal process. Raphael thinks the drama earns the label "moral philosophy" because its comparison between two conceptions of justice could be developed into an argument in favor of one of the two conceptions. (He points out that a utilitarian might argue in favor of choosing the conception which maximizes happiness.)[10] His willingness to count the *Oresteia* as moral philosophy is a compliment he pays to a work that he thinks approximates, without yet fully attaining, the form of genuine moral philosophy. However, since he does not take the *Oresteia* to contain "philosophy full blown," he is ready to sympathize with those philosophers who refuse to regard it as itself an instance of moral philosophy.[11]

Third and last, we come to what Raphael takes to be "the most obvious, the richest, and the most satisfying way in which literature and moral philosophy are connected." Literary works can "feed" moral philosophy in productive ways insofar as they present us with detailed descriptions of particular actions, traits of character, etc.[12] Raphael takes this to be "the most obvious and most satisfying" connection between literature and moral philosophy because it bespeaks a way in which literary discourse is *as such* suited to make a contribution to moral philosophy. His thought is that, to the extent that literature can inform moral philosophy in this way, appeals to literature have an important place in the practice of all moral philosophers. As moral philosophers we can

8. Raphael, "Can Literature be Moral Philosophy?", pp. 2–4 and 10–13.
9. Ibid., pp. 6–9.
10. Ibid., p. 8.
11. Ibid., pp. 8–9.
12. Ibid., p. 1.

turn to literature when we are trying to understand some aspect of human conduct or character. The rich depictions of human life that works of literature contain may then help us to understand what perplexed us or bring us to the realization that the question we were asking didn't take into account certain subtleties or complexities of human life—and they may in these ways facilitate progress in moral philosophy.

In thus describing the respects in which he thinks literature can contribute to arguments in moral philosophy, Raphael distinguishes the ideas, descriptions, etc., he thinks can be extracted from literary works and used within such arguments from the features of those works in virtue of which they have a tendency to engage our feelings. We might speak here of a distinction between *descriptive* and *emotive* (or *expressive*) features of literary texts. Now, although when Raphael speaks of literary features of a text, he generally has in mind both descriptive features and emotive features, it is a central and pivotal tenet of his view that it is always in principle possible to separate any descriptive features a text contains from its emotive features.[13]

This emerges clearly in passages in which he suggests that although "literary art" may contribute to the tendency of the ideas or descriptions a work contains to engage our sympathies it is those ideas or descriptions by themselves—in isolation from any specifically emotive features—that matter with regard to any bearing the work has on moral reflection.[14] Literary art does not matter insofar as it endows a text with expressive qualities because (as Raphael sees it) this part of literary art contributes only to the force with which the moral thought a work contains is conveyed and not to the integrity of that thought. This means that a work must be regarded as employing methods of persuasion that are less than fully rational to the extent that its ability to persuade us to embrace a moral doctrine or a conception of the moral life is a function, not of any arguments (or compressed or elliptical arguments) that it contains, but rather of its emotive features.

13. It would be possible to capture one of my aims in this chapter by saying that I hope to cast doubt on the assumption that it is invariably possible to perform this feat of separation. It follows that there is an important sense in which talk of descriptive and emotive features of texts represents for me a merely transitional vocabulary. In so far as such talk carries the suggestion that descriptive and emotive elements of texts are always in principle distinct and separable, it should, I hope to show, ultimately be given up.

14. Raphael, "Can Literature Be Moral Philosophy," esp. pp. 2–3.

Raphael's assumption that emotive features of a text can be skimmed off its descriptive features as a sort of expressive extra is faithful to the logic of the narrower conception of rationality. Within the framework of this conception, it appears that the features of a work that engage our feelings cannot be internal to the moral thought it contains and, further, that it must in principle be possible to strip away any such features from the moral thinking within it. The view of the relation between literature and moral philosophy that Raphael develops is therefore properly understood as a straightforward version of the prevalent view. To the extent that he relies on the narrower conception of rationality, Raphael's willingness to describe arguments as exhausting the realm of the rational shows that he is concerned with arguments in the narrower sense. And to the extent that he thus uses "argument" narrowly, his insistence on characterizing ways in which literature can inform moral philosophy in terms of ways in which it can contribute to arguments about the moral life is properly understood as an expression of the prevalent view.

One distinction of this view is the presupposition that literary works are incapable of making an internal contribution to moral understanding in virtue of ways in which they appeal to our hearts. Raphael himself never even recognizes the possibility of challenging this presupposition, and his response to efforts to contest it is a sort of puzzlement.[15] Since he assumes that the emotive features of a text can't essentially add to any rational moral instruction it contains, he can only hear proposals to regard emotive features of a text as internal to its philosophical interest as absurd calls for doing away with rationality as one of the marks of the philosophical.[16] But, against the backdrop of the kinds of doubts about the merits of this conception that I am here exploring, it seems clear that a more charitable interpretation is available. Moreover—and this is the point that I particularly want to emphasize—we need to see that a more charitable interpretation is available if we are to make room for the possibility that some literary texts are designed to elicit modes of moral thinking that are not a matter of moral judgment-making.

---

15. In "Having a Rough Story about What Moral Philosophy Is," Cora Diamond asks, in reference to Raphael's work, whether "the response demanded or invited by [a] work as a work of literature [can contribute] to what we may learn from it as moral philosophers" (p. 159). In "Philosophy and Rationality," Raphael treats Diamond's question as unintelligible: "I am not clear that I understand the question" (p. 174).

16. Raphael, "Philosophy and Rationality," pp. 171–172.

## 4.3  Moral Thought beyond Moral Judgment: Three Literary Examples

> How then are we to attack the novel . . . ? Not with any elaborate apparatus. Principles and systems may suit other forms of art, but they cannot be applicable here—or if applied their results must be subjected to re-examination. And who is the re-examiner? Well, I am afraid it will be the human heart, it will be this man-to-man business, justly suspect in its cruder forms.
>
> ~ *E. M. Forster*, Aspects of the Novel *(1955), p. 23.*

What might a philosopher have in mind in proposing that the affective responses demanded by, for instance, a novel as a novel can contribute to what we learn from it as moral philosophers? A novel may draw us into more intimate relations with some characters than others, give us discordant accounts of a specific situation through the eyes of some characters and leave us with ambiguous accounts of central events in the lives of others. And, in doing these things, it may elicit a variety of emotional responses. It may lead us to empathize with and love some characters and despise or pity others, to find certain aspects of a state of affairs funny and others boring, to find some features of a mode of life important and others unimportant, and so on. In making a proposal along these lines, a philosopher might be asking us to consider the possibility that a novel, in virtue of its tendency thus to invite a distinctive pattern of affective reactions, may enable us to recognize features of the fictional lives it describes, and also of our own lives, that aren't neutrally available.[17] If this possibility were realized, it would mean that novels (and something similar might be said about other literary works) were capable both of containing modes of moral instruction that can only be understood in terms of the wider conception of rationality and of eliciting moral thought that is not composed of moral judgments.

My ambition in this section is to show that this possibility is indeed a real one and that we are justified in representing some stories and novels as inviting moral reflections that do not have the form of moral

---

17. Three of the contributors to the special issue "Literature and/as Moral Philosophy" of *New Literary History* mentioned in note 4, e.g., make such a proposal with an eye toward getting us to consider this basic possibility: Martha Nussbaum (see also esp. chapter 1 of *Love's Knowledge*, "Introduction: Form and Content, Philosophy and Literature"), Cora Diamond (see esp. chapter 11 of *The Realistic Spirit*, "Anything But Argument?") and Richard Wollheim, "Flawed Crystals."

judgments. I consider three literary examples—the novels of Jane Austen, the novels of E. M. Forster and the stories and novels of Leo Tolstoy—with an eye to showing these things. Since my initial goal is demonstrating that what the works in question can teach about the moral life is essentially a function of narrative strategies that appeal to our hearts in various ways, I should acknowledge that some critics will want to protest that such examples cannot help but be philosophically irrelevant in the sense that, even if they succeed in illustrating that we sometimes take stretches of literary discourse to contain rational instruction in virtue of the fact that they engage our feelings, they nevertheless cannot provide support for the conclusion that we are warranted in doing so. I am inclined to think that the arguments presented in earlier chapters against the idea of an abstraction requirement (see 1.2 and 2.2; see also 3.2.ii) discredit this sort of prior blanket dismissal of apparent counterexamples to the narrower conception of rationality, and I explicitly return to this topic at the chapter's close (4.4). But first I illustrate that some literary works engage us in ways that, taken at face value, demand to be understood in widely rational terms, and I use my illustrations to make the case that some literary works are properly understood as eliciting moral reflections that do not take the form of moral judgments.

### 4.3.i  The Novels of Jane Austen

> I have claimed to detect an incongruity . . . in the idea of a man's recognizing, without being appreciative of, the excellences of Jane Austen.
>
> ~ Gilbert Ryle, "On Forgetting the Difference Between Right and Wrong," in Collected Essays, 1929–1968, vol. 2 (1990), p. 389.

A good way to approach some of the things I want to say about Jane Austen's novels is via a consideration of claims that Gilbert Ryle once made about them. In a 1966 paper, Ryle argues that Austen's moral ideas are fundamentally Aristotelian.[18] What he means is that Austen's moral vocabulary reflects a conception of human cognitive capacities

---

18. Gilbert Ryle, "Jane Austen and the Moralists," *Collected Papers*, vol.1: *Critical Essays* (Bristol: Thoemmes Press, 1990), pp. 266–291. Ryle made no secret of his admiration for Jane Austen. When once asked whether he read novels, he replied, "All six, every year."

and capacities for feeling as essentially tied together.[19] Thus, for instance, he points out that many of the personal qualities Austen refers to when she describes characters in her novels represent capacities that are simultaneously affective and cognitive.[20] And in a passage in which he floats the suggestion that Austen encounters Aristotelian ideas by reading Shaftesbury, he proposes that she inherits an Aristotelian moment in Shaftesbury's thought when, like him, she uses the word *mind* "without the definite or indefinite article, to stand not just for intellect or intelligence, but for the whole complex unity of a conscious, thinking, feeling and acting person."[21]

Ryle argues that Jane Austen's conception of human understanding leaves room for the possibility of forms of instruction that persuade in that they engage our feelings and that contribute directly to understanding in so far as they do so. Further, he attempts to show that the moral thought her novels contain is tied to various elements of their narrative form—to ways in which they elicit emotional responses from us specifically as novels. He claims that her novels provide us with rational tutelage about the outlooks on human conduct expressed within them by presenting us, not with arguments, but rather with narratives that shape our emotional responses in a carefully orchestrated manner. And he suggests that the mode of moral education to which they aspire takes for granted the Aristotelian conception of moral rationality expressed in their descriptive vocabulary. This Rylean suggestion is of particular interest here. For it serves to underwrite an understanding of

19. Anyone familiar with the larger drift of Ryle's own writings will be aware that Ryle presents his own moral ideas as Aristotelian in this sense. A central theme of Ryle's work—one that he develops in his famous discussions of "knowing-how" and "knowing-that"—is that competence in a discursive practice invariably involves certain responsive capacities and that training that cultivates such capacities can therefore as such be productive of "intelligent powers." At various points in his opus Ryle ties this theme to what he regards as an Aristotelian thought to the effect that the habituation of feeling plays an essential role in the growth of moral understanding. See, e.g., "Knowing How and Knowing That," in *Collected Papers*, vol.2: *Collected Essays, 1929–1968* (Bristol: Thoemmes Press, 1990), pp. 212–225, esp. pp. 223–224, "Teaching and Training," in *Collected Essays*, pp. 451–464, esp. p. 455; see also "Forgetting the Difference Between Right and Wrong," *Collected Essays*, pp. 381–390, and "Conscience and Moral Convictions," *Collected Essays*, pp. 185–193.

20. See esp. Ryle, "Jane Austen and the Moralists," pp. 284–286 and 289.

21. Ibid., p. 290. Ryle points out that in *Emma* Austen speaks of "the elegancies of mind" and of "delicacy of mind," and in *Sense and Sensibility* she speaks of "rectitude and integrity of mind."

Austen's novels as eliciting moral reflections that do not take the form of moral judgments.

Ryle approaches a defense of his suggestion by observing that Austen's novels are centrally concerned with specific theoretical moral questions. He points out that the abstract nouns in the titles of three of them— *Sense and Sensibility*, *Pride and Prejudice* and *Persuasion*—are descriptive of some of their central concerns:

> *Sense and Sensibility* really is about the relations between Sense and Sensibility or, as we might put it, between Head and Heart, Thought and Feeling, Judgment and Emotion, or Sensibleness and Sensitiveness. *Pride and Prejudice* really is about pride and about misjudgments that stem from baseless pride, excessive pride, deficient pride, pride in trivial objects, and so on. *Persuasion* really is or rather does set out to be about persuadability, unpersuadability and over-persuadability.[22]

Ryle's account of how these themes are developed in Austen's novels centers on one feature of her narrative technique. She conducts investigations into particular personal qualities within her novels using what he describes as a technique like that of a "wine-taster." She studies a particular quality of character not by developing it within a single character but rather by "matching it against the same quality in different degrees, against simulations of that quality, against deficiencies of it, against qualities which, though different, are brothers or sisters of that selected quality."[23] Thus, for example, in *Pride and Prejudice* we are not merely presented with characterizations of Elizabeth Bennett and Mr. Darcy as moving toward pride of the right sort (the former initially lodging too much confidence in her own assessments, the latter initially too haughtily conscious of his own merits). We are given accounts of nearly every character in terms of the type of pride they possess ("pride of a bad or silly sort or pride of a good sort, sham pride or genuine pride"), its amount and the appropriateness of its object. Ryle writes:

22. Ibid., pp. 276–277. Further, Ryle claims here that, although their titles aren't similarly suggestive, *Emma* and *Mansfield Park*, like these first three novels, are centrally concerned with specific theoretical moral questions. *Emma* is about the question of when the exercise of influence becomes interference (ibid., p. 280), and *Mansfield Park* is about the proper relation between fraternal and conjugal relationships (p. 282). Only *Northanger Abbey* is said to lack "an abstract ethical theme for its backbone" (ibid., p. 283).

23. Ibid., p. 278.

Elizabeth Bennett combines a dangerous cocksureness in her assessments of people with a proper sense of her own worth. Jane is
quite uncocksure. She is too diffident. She does not resent being put
upon or even realize that she is being put upon. There is no proper
pride, and so no fight in her. Their mother is so stupid and vulgar
that she has no sense of dignity at all, only silly vanities about her
dishes and her daughters' conquests. Mr. Bennett has genuine pride.
He does despise the despicable. But it is inert, unexecutive pride.
He voices his just contempt in witty words, but he does nothing to
prevent or repair what he condemns. It is the pride of a mere don,
though a good don. Bingley has no special pride, and so, though a
nice man, spinelessly lets himself be managed by others where he
should not. His sisters are proud in the sense of being vain and
snobbish. Darcy is, to start with, haughty and snobbish, a true
nephew of Lady Catherine de Burgh. His early love for Elizabeth
is vitiated by condescension. He reforms into a man with pride of
the right sort. He is proud to be able to help Elizabeth with her socially embarrassing family. He now knows what is due from him as
well as what is due to him. Mr. Collins is the incarnation of vacu-
ous complacency. He glories in what are mere reflections from the
rank of his titled patroness and from his own status as a clergyman.
He is a soap-bubble with nothing at all inside him and only bulging
refractions from other things on his rotund surface.[24]

Similarly, in *Persuasion* we receive not only a characterization of Anne
Elliot in terms of persuadability (she grows from a dutifully persuadable girl into a woman who exhibits appropriate firmness of mind), but
also characterizations of her acquaintances and family members in
terms of the extent of their persuadability and the types of considerations that persuade them.[25]

How is this "wine-tasting technique" supposed to help us to better
understand what it is to possess in their proper proportions the personal qualities with which the specific novels are concerned? In speaking of such a technique, Ryle is claiming that Jane Austen's novels elicit
emotional responses to ways in which different characters exemplify
specific personal qualities and that they invite us to compare and contrast those responses—just as we might sample different wines and

24. Ibid., pp. 278–279.
25. Ibid., p. 279. I return to a discussion of *Persuasion* below.

compare and contrast them in terms of their bouquet and body. Further, he is claiming that what we can learn from the novels is not separable from the fact that they do these things. He believes that the pedagogical strategy of the novels reflects the Aristotelian view of moral understanding encoded in Jane Austen's descriptive terminology. The idea is that it is impossible to disentangle what the novels aspire to teach about certain personal qualities from ways in which they engage our feelings. This means that we run the risk of obscuring what the novels can teach if we insist that it must be possible to capture that teaching in a plain form—say, by extracting from them descriptions of the different personal qualities and then taking those descriptions, ranked in some plausible way, to constitute the moral doctrines of the novels.[26] And it also means, as Ryle puts it in another context, that there is an incongruity in "the idea of a man's recognizing, without being appreciative of, the excellences of Jane Austen."[27]

Consider what this talk of "wine-tasting" comes to in the case of *Pride and Prejudice*. Ryle is claiming that what we can learn about proper pride cannot be prized apart from the way in which the narrative asks us to respond to the foolish and pompous sermonizing of Mr. Collins, to Jane Bennett's excessive diffidence, to Mr. Bennett's self-confident intelligence and his failure to act on it, to Mrs. Bennett's displays of silly pride in her dishes and the prospects of her daughters for marrying, and so on; and he is also claiming that what we can learn about proper pride cannot be prized apart from the way in which the novel calls upon us to compare and contrast the finely grained distinctions it draws among ways in which these different species of pride manifest themselves in the different characters' gestures, manners, turns of phrase, and so on. His thought is that to the extent that the novel elicits a range of different emotional responses it invites us to place value on certain specific modes of conduct and forms of accomplishment as worthy of pride and to disparage others as unworthy of it—and that the novel thereby calls on us to trace out a set of patterns in our practical lives that only come into view from the perspective of the particular emotional responses elicited from us. The contribution the novel makes to our understand-

---

26. Any such plain rankings would be the sorts of doctrines that, as we might put it, a Mr. Collins could without loss include in one of his impromptu sermons or a Mary Bennett could without loss rehearse at the dinner table.

27. See the epigraph to this section.

ing of proper pride, as Ryle sees it, comes through our recognition that the patterns those emotional responses enable us to trace out help us to make better sense both of the fictional world of the novel and of our own life—and in this way lead us to the sort of moment of self-recognition at which we may find that we can say, with Elizabeth Bennett, "Till this moment I never knew myself!"[28]

I just credited Ryle with bringing out how *Pride and Prejudice* contains moral instruction that needs to be understood in widely rational terms. While Ryle himself does not make this additional point, his treatment of the novel also positions us to recognize that the novel imparts such moral instruction in large part by eliciting moral thought that does not take the form of moral judgments. We can see this if we note that Ryle represents the novel as to a significant extent preoccupied with quite ordinary and—as we might think of it—'non-moral' features of the fictional world that it depicts (e.g., Mrs. Bennett's culinary arrangments, the prospects of her daughters for marrying, Mr. Collins' social habits, etc.). The Rylean insight is that the novel tries to bring us to a good understanding of these things by getting us to reflect on them in a manner informed by the shift in our modes of responsiveness that it seeks to foster (i.e., the shift that, as Ryle puts it, is internal to an appreciation of what proper pride is like) and, further, that this shift constitutes the novel's central moral teaching. It is on the basis of this insight that we are justified in representing *Pride and Prejudice* as in the business of eliciting thought that, while dedicated to 'non-moral topics', and while accordingly lacking the form of moral judgments, is nevertheless rightly classified as moral.

---

28. Ryle's suggestion that Jane Austen's moral outlook is basically Aristotelian was anticipated by some of her contemporaries. Thus, e.g., in an 1821 review of *Northanger Abbey* and *Persuasion*, Richard Whately wrote, "We know not whether Miss Austen ever had access to the precepts of Aristotle; but there are few, if any, writers of fiction who have illustrated them more successfully" (cited in B. C. Southam, ed., *Jane Austen: The Critical Heritage* [London: Routledge and Kegan Paul, 1968], p. 96). And many readers of Jane Austen since Ryle have taken up the suggestion of Austen's Aristotelianism. See, e.g., Alisdair MacIntyre's discussion of her novels in *After Virtue: A Study in Moral Theory* (Notre Dame, IN: University of Notre Dame Press, 1984). (Interestingly MacIntyre also follows Ryle in claiming that Jane Austen's moral ideas are given expression in the form of her writing. In MacIntyre's words, "Jane Austen's moral point of view and the narrative form of her novels coincide" [p. 243].) See also Anne Ruderman, *The Pleasures of Virtue: Political Thought in the Novels of Jane Austen* (London: Rowman and Littlefield, 1995), and David Gallop "Jane Austen and the Aristotelian Ethic," *Philosophy and Literature* 23 (1999): 96–109.

Something similar could be said about Austen's last complete novel, *Persuasion*. In order to see this it is, however, necessary to depart from Ryle's assessment of this work. Where Ryle is critical of *Persuasion*—he tells us that the theme of persuadability is "too boring to repay [Austen's] selection of it"[29]—I believe that this novel contains Austen's most comprehensive attempt to grapple with the very moral themes that Ryle highlights in his treatment of her authorship. Following in Ryle's footsteps, we have already registered Austen's concern—it is a concern that is consistently expressed in her choice of both vocabulary and narrative design—with the possibility that explorations of new routes of feeling may be capable of contributing essentially to the growth of moral understanding. To leave open this possibility is to allow that we may need to permit our feelings to be engaged in various ways—or, in other words, that we may need to be receptive to various forms of *persuasion*—in order to further develop such understanding. We might accordingly speak, in reference to Austen's different literary productions, of interest in a theme of "rational methods of persuasion."[30]

Let me preface my specific comments about how this theme is addressed in *Persuasion* with some general remarks about Jane Austen's work. The characters in Jane Austen's novels who win her purest admiration are those who rely firmly (but, for the most part, not flawlessly) on their own judgment: they are self-reliant individuals.[31] The topic of the self-reliant individual is dramatized, in the case of Austen's hero-

---

29. Ryle's comment continues as follows:

I believe that she herself found that her story tended to break away from its rather flimsy ethical frame. Certainly, when Anne and Wentworth at last came together again, their talk does duly turn on the justification of Anne's original yielding to Lady Russell's persuasion and on the unfairness of Wentworth's resentment of her so yielding. But we, and I think Jane Austen herself, are happy to hear the last of this particular theme. We are greatly interested in Anne, but not because she had been dutifully docile as a girl. We think only fairly well of Lydia [Louisa] Musgrove, but her deafness to counsels of prudence is not what makes our esteem so tepid. Some of the solidest characters in the novel, namely the naval characters, are not described in terms of their persuadability or unpersuadability at all, and we are not sorry ("Jane Austen and the Moralists," p. 279).

30. I am speaking here of "rational methods of persuasion" in a different sense than Raphael does. (See the second paragraph of section 4.2.) Whereas in Raphael's work, the question of whether a method of persuasion is rational is answered by considering its relation to argument, here no appeal to argument is called for.

31. There is a fine irony in the fact that Emerson—the philosopher who champions self-reliance as the mark of a genuine individual—is so mean in his estimate of the merits of Jane Austen. In a well-known passage in his journals, Emerson confides:

ines, by their lack of sound mentoring. They are without exception deprived of any effective parental authority. Their mothers have died (Lady Elliot and Mrs. Woodhouse) or are distracted and unavailable (Mrs. Morland) or are too indolent to guide them (Lady Bertram) or are too foolish to do so (Mrs. Bennett) or are, in any case, not firm enough in their own judgments (Mrs. Dashwood); their fathers are simply weak and uninvolved (Mr. Morland) or are foolish and unfit to command respect (Mr. Woodhouse) or have relinquished the authority properly invested in them (Mr. Bennett) or neglect the duties their authority confers on them (Sir Thomas Bertram) or positively abuse their authority (Sir Walter Elliot).

It is not hard to see that the absence of any genuinely authoritative parental figures is, in some of Austen's later novels—and in *Persuasion* in particular—intended to indicate a more general social decay. Nevertheless, since this claim is in tension with the once widely accepted view that Austen writes about the homely and private details of manor life in a manner that insulates them from changes wrought by significant social and political events, it will be helpful to discuss how one other novel of Austen's supports the claim (as, indeed, all do) before considering it specifically in reference to *Persuasion*.[32]

---

I am at a loss to understand why people hold Miss Austen's novels at so high a rate, which seem to me vulgar in tone, sterile in artistic invention, imprisoned in the wretched conventions of English society, without genuine wit, or knowledge of the world. Never was life so pinched and narrow. The one problem in the mind of the writer . . . is marriageableness. All that interests in any character introduced is still this one, Has he (or she) the money to marry with, and conditions conforming? . . . Suicide is more respectable. (*The Journals and Miscellaneous Notebooks of Ralph Waldo Emerson*, ed. Linda Allardt and David Hill [Cambridge: HUP, 1982], vol. 25, p. 146)

32. A classic statement of the view that Jane Austen the novelist repudiates any serious concern with larger social and political events is in Raymond Williams, *The Country and the City* (London, Chatto and Windus, 1973). Echoing one of the most famous sentences in Austen's opus in an (in my view, failed) attempt at satire, Williams writes, "It is a truth universally acknowledged, that Jane Austen chose to ignore the decisive historical events of her time" (p. 113). In a similar vein, Henry James once disparaged what he describes as "the narrowness of Miss Austen's social horizon" (*The Critical Muse* [London: Penguin, 1987], p. 173). And Edward Said revives the view that Jane Austen fails to engage broader social concerns in "Jane Austen and Empire," *Culture and Imperialism* (New York: Alfred A. Knopf, 1993), pp. 80–96, esp. pp. 81–82. But this view of Jane Austen no longer enjoys the favor it once did. Two particularly insightful pieces of contemporary commentary that challenge it are Lionel Trilling, *Sincerity and Authenticity* (Cambridge, MA: Harvard University Press, 1972), chapters 3 and 4, and Tony Tanner, *Jane Austen* (London: Macmillan, 1986). I draw significantly on Tanner's work in the next few paragraphs.

In *Mansfield Park*, Sir Thomas leaves home, neglecting his duties as a landowner and father, to look after the financial welfare of his Antigua business (which presumably involves the use of slaves or forced labor). In his absence, the Crawfords come to Mansfield. The Crawfords are a young brother and sister from the new, urban world of London—a world whose rapid growth is, we are invited to believe, connected to financial harvests of colonialism of the sort that Sir Thomas is reaping.[33] The presence of the Crawfords is instrumental in bringing about events that threaten the core values of Mansfield. Sir Thomas's failure to attend to his responsibilities betokens the social decay represented by the growth of London and the disintegration of the values of landholders.

In *Persuasion*, social disintegration once again threatens the traditional values of landholding society, and it is represented most vividly in the character of Sir Walter Elliot. Sir Walter is vain, and he sees his position as a landowner as valuable only insofar as it flatters his sense of self-importance. A claim to property does not, in his eyes, confer duties and obligations. Landed possessions are, for him, simply an occasion for self-indulgence. When it becomes clear that he can no longer afford to live in Kellynch Hall, the seat of the family estate, in a style that suits his vanity, he prefers renting it to living in it more modestly. Sir Walter retains some of the forms of the landholding society into which he was born (deference to rank, aristocratic manners, etc.) without cherishing the values that those forms once signified. In the novel, his attachment to empty form is portrayed as representative of a more general abandonment of the values of landholding society.[34]

While the social decay that threatens Mansfield can be contained— Fanny Price, in her unwavering commitment to the values of Mansfield, ultimately succeeds in restoring its proper order—the social disintegration surrounding Kellynch Hall has advanced too far and received too much external reinforcement to be halted. Anne Elliot, Sir Walter's second daughter, recognizes her father's degradation but is in-

33. Throughout the novel, London represents moral laxity. It is home to the Crawfords, and it is also the scene of Tom Bertram's dissipation, Maria Bertram's disgrace and Julia Bertram's elopement.

34. Thus, for instance, young Mr. Elliot cares about the baronetcy he is to inherit (which he once despised for its lack of monetary value) only on account of the social status it confers; Mrs. Clay is attentive to distinctions of rank, but her attentiveness is grounded not in respect but in zeal for advancing her private interests; and Lady Dalrymple is, we are given to think, as vulgarly and hypocritically self-important as Sir Walter is.

capable of checking him in vices in which he has much company and en-couragement. In terms of narrative, this means that Anne must look be-yond the landed gentry to a new social order if she is to preserve hope of the company of people of good understanding.[35] Thematically, it means that the question of her self-reliance is a particularly pressing one. Cut off for the most part from the companionship of people of good under-standing, she is baldly confronted with the need to rely on herself.

The central events of *Persuasion* concern a mature Anne, but at the novel's opening we are given a glimpse of Anne as a very young woman. One of the novel's main concerns is the question of how a young person—such as an Anne Elliot—becomes self-reliant, and the theme of persuadability figures prominently in the answer that gets returned.

Anne falls in love with and becomes engaged to Frederick Went-worth—a nobody in the world of her father, since Wentworth is with-out rank, connections, property or wealth—when she is nineteen. Soon afterwards she allows herself to be persuaded by Lady Russell, a friend of her deceased mother and her own most trusted friend and counselor, to break off the engagement. Lady Russell sways Anne by telling her that ending the engagement is not only in her own best interest but also in his. Anne dutifully follows the advice but soon comes to suspect that it was misguided. She is encouraged in her suspicions by the gradual re-alization that Lady Russell is inclined to place too much importance on rank and to overlook the virtues and strengths of those who lack it. (In this regard, Lady Russell, although in other respects a sensible woman, bears some resemblance to Sir Walter and his cronies.) But even though many years later Anne still is not inclined to think that Lady Russell gave her good advice, she believes that she herself was right to allow herself to be persuaded.

This brings us to the question that forms the thematic backbone of the novel (i.e., the question that Ryle finds too dull to contain its interest): was Anne right to allow herself to be persuaded by Lady Russell? The novel gives its affirmative answer through an application of what Ryle calls Jane Austen's wine-tasting technique. It invites us to compare and contrast our responses to the different ways in which—and the different extents to which—its various characters are persuadable. As Ryle puts it:

35. She is the only one of Austen's heroines whose marriage doesn't tie her to property and the social world of landowners: when she marries Captain Wentworth, she in effect becomes a member of a new, naval society.

Anne had suffered from having dutifully taken the bad advice of the over-cautious Lady Russell. Her father and sister Elizabeth can be persuaded to live within their means only by the solicitor's shrewd appeals to quite unworthy considerations. Her sister Mary is so full of self-pity that she can be prevailed on only by dexterous coaxings. Lydia [Louisa] Musgrove is too headstrong to listen to advice, so she cracks her skull. Her sister Henrietta is so over-persuadable that she is a mere weathercock. Mr. Elliot, after his suspect youth, is apparently eminently rational. But it turns out that he is amenable to reason only so long as reason is on the side of self-interest.[36]

Insofar as the novel invites us to respond in a certain manner to an array of different forms of persuadability, it encourages us to trace out a distinctive set of patterns in the moral world the novel portrays. The novel is successful in contributing to our understanding of what it is to be properly persuaded to the extent that the relevant patterns enable us to make better sense of our moral lives. It is in this way that it tries to show us that Anne was right to allow herself to be persuaded—and, further, that her having been persuaded in the way in which she was is non-accidentally related to her growth into a person of good understanding.

Given these reflections about Austen's novel, it is not obvious that we have good grounds for following Ryle in asserting that the novel ultimately breaks away from this ethical frame.[37] For the solution to the problem of Anne Elliot's need for self-reliance is, simultaneously, the solution to the larger problem of social change with which the novel grapples. With her mature understanding, Anne can see not only what is ugly about her father's mode of life but also what is correct in the manners and forms of conduct characteristic of naval society. (Although Louisa Musgrove is, like Anne, an admirer of naval life—bursting into "raptures of admiration and delight on the character of the navy"—and although the book by and large upholds Louisa's assessment of sailors, we are not invited to regard her enthusiastic outburst as grounded in a good understanding. We are to credit Louisa with having found some-

36. Ryle, "Jane Austen and the Moralists," p. 279.
37. See note 29.

thing congenial in the spirit of the navy but not with having genuine insight into its value.) Within the context of the novel, we need to rely on Anne's insight to see in the navy the possibility of a new, morally sound social world.

Now we are in a position to see how *Persuasion* demands moral thinking that does not take the form of moral judgment-making. We need to bear in mind that Austen's novel is to a significant extent preoccupied with various 'non-moral' features of the lives of its characters (e.g., the social constraints of Anne's life, the financial conditions and habits of her father, the marital circumstances of the different women in the book, etc.). Further, we need to bear in mind both that the emotional responses that the novel is designed to produce (i.e., responses internal to an appreciation of "proper persuadability") are intended to contribute directly to a genuine, fully rational understanding of these features and that, taken together, these responses represent the change in moral outlook that constitutes the novel's primary moral lesson. It is in the light of these observations that we are justified in describing the novel as inviting thought that, while engaged with 'non-moral topics', has the kind of relation to our moral outlook that establishes it as moral.

### 4.3.ii  *The Novels of E. M. Forster*

> The driver [Dante] replied, "I am the means and not the end. I am the food and not the life. Stand by yourself, as that boy has stood. I cannot save you. For poetry is a spirit; and they that would worship it must worship in spirit and in truth."
>
> ∼ *E. M. Forster, "The Celestial Omnibus,"*
> The Celestial Omnibus and Other Stories *(1976), p. 73.*

The world that E. M. Forster's fictional and non-fictional writings describe is, to use some of his characteristic terms, a place of "richness and subtlety," the mysteries of which only people with "developed hearts" can begin to fathom.[38] Forster's wonted vocabulary reflects his view, a view perhaps shaped by his immersion in ancient Greek ethics at Cambridge, that the acquisition of a mature moral understanding is essentially tied to emotional development. Within Forster's fiction, it is only

---

38. The inset quotes here are from E. M. Forster, "Notes on the English Character," in *Abinger Harvest* (London: Harcourt Brace Jovanovich, 1964), pp. 3–15.

characters endowed with generous sympathies—or "developed hearts"—
who are equipped to understand complexities of the world. The characters whose moral understandings are limited in one way or another and
who are prone to finding themselves in (to use another characteristi-
cally Forsterian term) "muddles" are for the most part characters whose
minds and emotional lives have been shaped by the values and institutions of the British middle class—values and institutions that Forster
typically portrays as hindering the expression of feeling and the growth
of imagination.[39]

When we turn specifically to Forster's novels, we find an intimate relation, of the kind present in Austen's novels, between the conception
of moral understanding given expression in his descriptive vocabulary
and elements of his narrative technique. The approach to the task of
moral edification characteristic of his novels centers on engaging readers' sympathies in various ways. The specific methods he uses for appealing to our sympathies, here again resembling what we find in Austen,
include different sorts of mild irony. His novels are designed to instruct
by provoking responses through the use of an amused and sympathetic
narrative voice, and they depend for their success—yet another similarity to Austen's works—on eliciting moral thinking that is not a matter
of moral judgment-making.[40]

For an illustration of these features of Forster's literary productions,
we might turn, for example, to *Howards End*. To begin with, it is important to note that in this novel the question of the cognitive significance
of imagination and emotional depth represents a dominant thematic
preoccupation. A central motif is the clash between the Schlegel and
Wilcox families. The Schlegels, partly of German extraction, are the
family of "Literature and Art," and the Wilcoxes, solidly English, are
the family of hard facts and business. While the Schlegels are high-
spirited, affectionate and sometimes "sloppy," the Wilcoxes are moder-

---

39. These motifs enjoy the same kind of prominence (without the same kind of sophisticated treatment) in Forster's short stories, collected in *The Celestial Omnibus* and *The Eternal
Moment*, as in his novels. Again and again, the stories suggest that there is no such thing as understanding various aspects of our lives apart from the possession of sympathies cultivated by,
say, the pathos of age, unprejudiced communion with literature or natural beauty.

40. The parallel between Austen and Forster described in this paragraph is not accidental.
Forster once declared himself to be an enthusiastic "Jane Austenite," declaring, "She is my favorite author!" ("Jane Austen," in *Abinger Harvest*, pp. 148–164, 148).

ate, restrained and "practical." Now, it would be wrong to suggest that the novel invites an entirely unqualified endorsement of either Schlegelian or Wilcoxian styles of life. The plot is driven by a crisis that, while given a tragic twist by one of the Wilcoxes, is the product of Schlegelian romantic blindness as well as Wilcoxian obtuseness. Nevertheless, an important aim of the novel is to get us to see that there is a sense in which the unimaginative modes of response characteristic of members of the Wilcox family are flawed and in which the warm and amused modes of responses characteristic of members of the Schlegel family are more appropriate. The novel attempts to achieve this aim in part by presenting us with sympathetic and gently ironic depictions of the social world of the Wilcoxes—depictions designed to elicit the kinds of emotional responses that are characteristic of the Schlegels. These depictions are intended to put us in a position in which we can make more sense of the lives of the Wilcoxes than the Wilcoxes (who lack propensities toward the sorts of responses the depictions aim to elicit) can themselves.[41]

Consider the novel's treatment of Mr. Wilcox. Mr. Wilcox is a successful middle-aged businessman who, although he doesn't have a bad heart, strives to streamline its impulses—stifling any that threaten to introduce complications into the neat social space in which he attends to professional obligations and personal duties. The novel shows us various people and events in his life in a different light from that in which he sees them. We are, for instance, given a portrait of Leonard Bast, a young clerk in an insurance company, who is an acquaintance of Helen and Margaret Schlegel's and whom Mr. Wilcox meets through the Schlegels. Mr. Wilcox mostly thinks of Mr. Bast quite impersonally—

41. It is not an accident that Forster gives the emotionally more responsive family in his novel the name of some of the most prominent German romantics. (Compare his choice of "Schlegel" here with his choice of "Emerson" in *A Room with a View* as the name of the family whose worldview most closely resembles that of the novel.) Moreover, the European connection that this tie to German romanticism bespeaks is itself thematically important for Forster. In his novels, England often figures thematically as the site of emotional restraint in contrast to Europe, which figures as the site of relative emotional freedom. (Europe and, more specifically, Italy plays this role within *A Room with a View*, *Where Angels Fear to Tread* and, in a slightly less developed manner, *The Longest Journey*.) There is an interesting parallel between Forster's thematizing of a contrast between England's emotional stiltedness and Europe's emotional freedom and Henry James' thematizing of a contrast between America's puritanism and Europe's aestheticism. (Think of, e.g., *The Ambassadors*, *The Europeans* and *The American*.) See my discussion of James in section 6.3.ii.

as a person of a lower social station with such-and-such a position in the world of business. But as readers we are invited to share in the more sympathetic interest that the Schlegels take in this young man. We are asked to place importance on Leonard Bast's romantic dreams and to see both comedy and pathos in the crudeness of his methods for pursuing them.

Or, further, we are at various points led to regard Mr. Wilcox's own manner of life with a more humorous eye than he does himself. One thing we learn early in the narrative is that he has a great fondness for motor-cars. On an occasion on which he is showing Margaret Schlegel the room in his house where "we fellows smoke"—a room that prominently displays several maroon leather chairs resembling the big, comfortable and somewhat tasteless seats of new automobiles—the narrator, betraying a hint of Margaret's amused perspective on the scene, tells us that "it was as if a motor-car had spawned." We are in this way asked to take part in Margaret's amusement. At the same time, we are shown that, in contrast to Margaret, Mr. Wilcox barely (if at all) notices that his enthusiasm for motor-cars and all things efficient and powerful is reflected in his personal habits and domestic arrangements and, moreover, that if someone insisted on trying to draw his attention to the connection he would fail to see its significance.

How are the affective responses the novel thus elicits from us supposed to enable us to understand Mr. Wilcox's life better than he does himself? Toward the close of the novel, we are presented with two momentous episodes in Mr. Wilcox's life: one in which he is confronted with his fiancée's—Margaret Schlegel's—knowledge of an affair he had when married to his first wife, another in which he is forced to deal with his son's conviction on manslaughter charges. On neither occasion is he fully able to make sense of the situation in which he finds himself or of the extent to which he himself is responsible for it. He is, to use the novel's most famous slogan, unable to "connect" aspects of the situations he now confronts with features of his experience that would render them transparent to understanding. The responses the novel elicits from us are supposed to lead us to the conviction that Mr. Wilcox's modes of response to the world suffer from severe shortcomings, in part by enabling us to make the connections he can't make.

The responses demanded from us lead us to place importance on aspects of Mr. Wilcox's life that he dismisses as insignificant (for instance, aspects of his life that highlight its commonalities with the life of Leonard Bast and aspects of his life which bring into relief links between his passion for motor-cars, on the one hand, and the manner in which he organizes his personal life, on the other). The novel is successful in at least one of its larger aims to the extent that, by thus giving us a sense of what is important in his life that is very different from his own sense, the novel puts us in a position in which we can recognize patterns in his life that he can't see and in which we can make sense of the situations in his life that leave him in a muddle. It is in this way, by directing our sympathies in various ways, that *Howards End* attempts to offer a rational mode of instruction about an amused and compassionate view of human life.

This brings me to the point that primarily interests me—namely, that Forster's novel presents us with modes of moral instruction that, in addition to thus demanding to be understood in widely rational terms, invite moral thought that does not take the form of moral judgment. The novel for the most part draws attention to everyday, 'non-moral' features of the social world it presents (e.g., the Wilcox's and Schlegel's characteristic ways of organizing their households, Leonard Bast's characteristic hopes and fears, etc.). It tries to get us to bring such features properly into focus by inviting us to reflect on them in the sympathetic and mildly humorous manner that it seeks to cultivate. Moreover, it is to the extent that we reflect on these features in the relevant manner, and to the extent that we thus arrive at a better understanding of them, that we imbibe the moral lesson that the novel seeks to impart. This is what justifies us in representing the novel as eliciting moral thought that does not take the form of moral judgment.

Similar claims can be made about Forster's other novels. To appreciate this, we need to see that it is not by presenting us with arguments that *A Room with a View* endeavors to get us to see things that Charlotte Bartlett, with her prudish and unadventuresome way of reacting to the sights of Italy, can't bring into focus; and we need to see that it is not by presenting us with arguments that *Maurice* tries to get us to understand things that Maurice, equipped only with the narrowly conventional modes of thinking and acting drilled into him in the public schools, cannot understand; or that *A Passage to India* tries to help us to comprehend the events surrounding the excursion to the Marabar Caves— events that leave Miss Quested, with her frigid manner, in a muddle until it is almost too late; and it is not by presenting us with arguments that *Where Angels Fear to Tread* attempts to lead us to recognize things that the Herritons of Sawston, with their characteristic emotional detachment, can't recognize and that Gino Carella of Monteriano, for all his crudity, intuits; or that *The Longest Journey* attempts to bring us to appreciate things that the rigidly conventional and repressed Agnes and Herbert Pembroke are blind to and that the wild Stephen Wonham, for all his brutishness, grasps. The kind of rational moral instruction characteristic of Forster's novels does not center on the presenting of arguments but rather on the eliciting of emotional responses. Moreover, like *Howards End*, the other novels present us with such instruction in large part by asking us to contemplate 'non-moral' elements of their fictional worlds. They try to lead us to a good understanding of these elements by getting us to contemplate the elements in a style informed by the modes of response that the novels aim to produce. This is noteworthy because we only properly assimilate the moral lessons that the novels impart if we thus come to contemplate the elements in the appropriate style, while at the same time progressing toward a better understanding of them. These are the kinds of considerations that warrant us in describing all of Forster's novels, and not only *Howards End*, as calling for episodes of thought that, while genuinely moral, do not come in the form of moral judgments.

### 4.3.iii  Tolstoy's Stories and Novels

> Knowledge has no answer to the question of life.
> ～ *Tolstoy, "A Confession," in* A Confession and
> Other Writings *(1987), p. 34.*

> All of us . . . must have personal experience of all of the nonsense of life, in order to get back to life itself; the evidence of other people is no good.
> ～ *Sergey Mikhaylych in Tolstoy, "Family Happiness," in*
> The Death of Ivan Ilych and Other Stories *(1960), p. 90.*

One prominent theme of Leo Tolstoy's fiction has to do with the difficulty of understanding the conditions of our lives. Tolstoy repeatedly suggests that there is a kind of understanding of human life that neither comes in the form of nor is reducible to knowledge of plain doctrines.

He also repeatedly suggests that the relevant kind of understanding is not only prior to and more important than knowledge of plain doctrines but is also something that we are inclined to neglect in favor of the pursuit of such knowledge. There are some very familiar expressions of this theme in Tolstoy's opus: Tolstoy tends to be preoccupied both with educated characters, like *Anna Karenina*'s Levin, whose scholarly pursuits fail to bring them spiritual fulfillment, and also with uneducated peasant characters, like *War and Peace*'s Platon, whose tranquility and wisdom remain essentially unqualified by their ignorance.

In addition to shaping his descriptive practice in these familiar ways, Tolstoy's concern with this theme also shapes his narrative strategies. A number of his works have narrative structures that are designed to combat our tendency to try to satisfy our hankering for understanding of our lives by equipping ourselves with plain doctrines. Appreciating this fit between Tolstoy's thematic concerns and his narrative technique is necessary for appreciating that, as I want to show here, his literary writings are designed to invite moral thought apart from moral judgments. This fit is, however, generally harder to demonstrate than the analogous fit in the writings of Austen and Forster. One reason for this is that Tolstoy's presentations of characters tend to be multifaceted in ways that prevent them from furnishing simple narrative clues. Bearing this in mind, I turn here, for an illustration of the alignment between Tolstoy's thematic preoccupations and his narrative techniques, to the relatively simple context of one his stories, "The Death of Ivan Ilych."[42]

This story attempts to get us to look at death (and our lives as beings who will die) in a more appropriate way by attacking a style of thinking and talking about death that Tolstoy portrays as characteristic of a certain segment of Russian society. In the story it is signaled unambiguously that what we need to learn about our relation to death cannot be formulated in plain language—say, as a set of plain moral doctrines. We are shown that Ivan's mastery of various facts about human mortality (e.g., his appropriation of the syllogism "Caius is a man, men are mor-

---

42. Leo Tolstoy, *The Death of Ivan Ilych and Other Stories* (New York: Penguin, 1960), pp. 93–152. It might seem reasonable to protest that this story is characterized by a didacticism that defeats the very aim that I am maintaining it pursues in an especially clear manner (viz., combating our tendency to seek understanding of our lives in the form of doctrines). Although I am receptive to the thought that this story is relatively didactic, compared to certain longer works of Tolstoy's that pursue the same aim, I believe that it attains its aim.

tal, therefore Caius is mortal," his appropriation of this or that bit of information about his illness, etc.) does not bring him closer to a true understanding of his condition.[43]

In thus indicating that the kind of understanding Ivan craves eludes him as long as he insists on finding it in doctrinal form, the story asks us to question the assumption that what *it itself* has to teach us about our relation to death can be captured in doctrinal form. It asks us to question the assumption that we will have done justice to its moral insight when we have extracted from it, for example (to mention a slogan not infrequently associated with the story), the doctrine that it is wrong to represent death as something that doesn't pertain to our own case and to console ourselves with the reflection, as Ivan Ilych's intimate friend Peter Ivanovich does, that what happened to Ivan "should not and could not happen to [us]."[44]

If we represent this doctrine—or any other plain doctrine—as fully capturing the moral content of the story, we will have distorted what it aspires to teach us about death. The story doesn't aim to provide information about death that we are lacking. It assumes that we know, as Ivan does, the sorts of things that everyone knows about death. Nor does the story aim to provide us with some further piece of information about how, even though we know everything there is to know about death, the way in which we live doesn't reflect that knowledge. This bit of information would be something that we could recite along with other facts we know about death. To suggest that this is what can be learned from the story would still be to give the impression that what the story aims to teach us about death can be conveyed, without distortion, in the form of a plain doctrine.

So how does the story aspire to teach us about death, if not by imparting doctrines? The story pursues its edifying aims in significant part through a narrative technique that is designed to invite identifications of different sorts with its various characters. As readers, we are asked to respond emotionally in specific ways to the characters and forms of human social life with which the story is concerned. We are asked to feel repugnance for the empty life that Ivan leads with his wife and for the similarly empty lives their relatives and acquaintances lead, to feel a sort of horrified exasperation with Ivan's doctors and friends who lie to him while he is dying, to feel relief at the simple solicitousness of the

43. Ibid., p. 129.
44. Ibid., p. 100.

peasant Gerasim. Our ability to take from the story the kind of under-standing of death it seeks to impart is not independent of our capacity to respond in these ways. We imbibe the moral message of the story to the extent that the ways it calls on us to respond enable us to make sense of certain features of Ivan's life that he has somehow forgotten or obscured—and to the extent that these modes of response at the same time enable us to make sense of analogous features of our own mortal lives. And, because we are here largely concerned with features of Ivan's life that we ordinarily classify as 'non-moral,' we can rightly say that we imbibe the moral message of the story to the extent that we are led by it to undertake some reflections that, while directly pertinent to our moral outlook, do not take the form of moral judgments.[45]

### 4.3.iv  An Aside about the Notion of Vividness

> Everything [the pseudo-scholar] says may be accurate but all is useless because he is moving round books instead of through them, he either has not read them or cannot read them properly. Books have to be read (worse luck, for it takes a long time); it is the only way of discovering what they contain . . . The reader must sit down alone and struggle with the writer.
>
>         ∼ *E. M. Forster,* Aspects of the Novel *(1955), p. 13.*

45. There is a respect in which my account of the kind of moral instruction contained in the literary works discussed in the last three sections might be misunderstood. Someone might take it that in saying the sorts of things I said about *how* these works endeavor to teach what they aim to teach, I was myself endeavoring to impart *what* they aim to teach. The idea would be that I was implying that it is possible to grasp what the works try to impart in the absence of any particular emotional responsiveness, simply by assimilating the argument of a book chapter (like this one) that describes some of their narrative mechanisms. If this were true, it would mean that my discussion of these works embodied a straightforward inconsistency. Consider, e.g., what I just said about Tolstoy's story. I claimed that the story tries to teach us about life and death using a strategy that itself reflects a conception of moral under-standing as essentially tied to emotional depth and that its teaching therefore cannot be isolated from ways in which it engages our feelings. If I were also suggesting that we can arrive at the sort of understanding the story hopes to convey simply by grasping the nature of its narrative strategy, I would be contradicting myself by denying this very claim. And something similar might be alleged about my discussions of Austen's and Forster's novels. But the allegations misfire. My discussion of these works is not intended to supply the sort of moral understanding that I claim it is possible to derive from reading them. My descriptions of the narrative strategies of the works are intended not to convey (now in a form more familiar to philosophers) the sorts of moral reflections the works elicit but only to serve as a reminder that we do take some literary works to contain rational instruction in virtue of ways in which they appeal to our hearts.

The examples in this section put pressure on the assumption, at play in most versions of the prevalent view, that it must be possible to isolate descriptive features of a text from any emotive features it possesses by illustrating that we sometimes take literary works to contain forms of moral instruction that are internally connected to ways in which they engage our feelings.[46] If we don't simply assume (in a manner that we might wrongly take to be dictated by the narrower conception of rationality) that the fact that we sometimes take ourselves to derive such forms of instruction from literature must be a sign of philosophical confusion, then we may interpret this fact (as I believe we should) as supporting a "widely rational" view of the moral instruction literary works can contain. Indeed, as I have been stressing, we *must* interpret it in this manner if we are to represent ourselves as entitled to claim that some literary works elicit moral thinking that does not take the form of moral judgment-making. Given that a widely rational interpretation of our reception of certain literary works is thus necessary to support the central claim I am making in this section, it is worth closing the section by considering one objection that such an interpretation may well encounter.

There is a sense in which it may seem possible to take at face value what the above examples reveal about how we sometimes take descriptive and emotive features of literary texts to be essentially wedded together without conceding that we are here confronted with widely rational modes of moral instruction. It may seem possible to develop an alternative version of the prevalent view that, although elaborated within a narrowly rational problem-space, nevertheless allows that the descriptions of actions, traits of character, etc., we encounter in literary works may have an essential tendency to engage our feelings.

The narrower conception of rationality excludes the possibility of forging a necessary link between descriptions and affective reactions by claiming that the kind of cognitive exercise required for grasping certain descriptions is itself a mode of emotional engagement with them.

---

46. Claiming that emotive features cannot always be disentangled from descriptive features does *not* commit us to denying that it is sometimes useful to extract descriptions of actions, traits of character and so forth from literary texts and to employ them in arguments. It only commits us to allowing that when we do extract literary descriptions and employ them in arguments we may fail fully to capture the contribution the relevant stretches of discourse make to the moral thought of the works from which they are drawn.

But it may appear to leave open the possibility of forging such a link by appealing to the quality of *vividness* characteristic of literary descriptions. The idea would be that the vividness of a description enjoys the sort of independence from emotional responses that enables it to play a role in explaining them. This would mean that while, on the one hand, this quality has an essential tendency to elicit emotional responses, on the other, it is nevertheless still possible fully to grasp any description in which it inheres, in a manner respectful of the constraints of the narrower conception of rationality, without drawing on any particular capacities of emotional response.

The assumption that the notion of vividness is independent—and explanatory—of emotional responses seems reasonable in the context of a conception of an image or an idea as a sort of inner mental picture. Now it appears that we can construe the vividness of an idea or image as independent of any responses it elicits—by appealing to various of its intrinsic features (e.g., the clarity of its lines, the brilliance of its colors, the sharpness of its sounds, etc.). But this conception of an idea or image is subject to familiar philosophical objections, and it ultimately frustrates efforts to make sense of the notion of vividness.

Consider a case in which two people have been told about an event and are trying to form visual images of it and in which the first of the two, but not the second, claims to have before her mind's eye a picture with bold and clear lines and brilliant colors. Would we be warranted in concluding that the first of the two has the more vivid image of the event? The first person, in spite of everything she says about the brilliance and clarity of her mental picture, may lack awareness of how features of the image she has connect with aspects of the event (or even of how it is an image of that event as opposed to some other, either real or invented). In the absence of the sort of intentional awareness that would underwrite such connections, it is not clear what sense it makes to say that she has an image of the event, much less a vivid one. The second person, in contrast, may be aware of—and may even be able to give an account of—how the elements of her image are connected to details of the event. What is vivid about this person's image, we might say, is that it leads her to organize various features of the event represented, to see some as similar, and others as different.

To speak of the vividness of someone's idea or image is not to speak of features it possesses apart from her engagement with it but rather to speak of the intensity of that engagement itself—where its intensity is a matter of the quantity and quality of the connections it leads her to make. So there is a confusion inherent in attempts to represent the vividness of an idea or image, in the style suggested by a conception of an idea or image as an inner mental picture, as independent of the various things it provokes the mind to do.[47]

This conclusion upsets the prospects for the alternative version of the prevalent view that I just sketched. In order successfully to defend this alternative, we would need to show that the vividness of certain literary descriptions is independent of emotional responses they elicit. And what emerges here is that we have no reasonable hope of showing this.

It is, however, yet possible within the narrower confines of the prevalent view to characterize the notion of vividness in terms of certain kinds of non-emotional mental responses—in particular, mental responses that qualify by the lights of the narrower conception as genuinely cognitive. We might construe various features of the form of vivid literary descriptions (say, various stylistic and narrative features) as calling for certain not specifically emotional responses. And we might then construe the tendency of vivid descriptions to impress us as a function of the fact that there may be no such thing as fully grasping them apart from responding in these non-affective ways.[48]

But this construal of the notion of vividness, whatever merits it is taken to have on its own terms, does not provide the thinker committed to respecting the narrowly rational constraints of the prevalent view with means for representing descriptive and emotive features of literary texts as essentially yoked together. There is no way for such a thinker to avoid being committed to the view that it is in principle possible to isolate descriptive features of literary texts from emotive ones. The only way this thinker can consistently respond to examples, like those discussed in the last section, that are suggestive of an essential tie between the descriptive and the emotive is by insisting that such examples must

47. For a helpful treatment of these topics, see Richard Moran, "The Expression of Feeling in Imagination," *Philosophical Review* 103 (1994), 75–106, esp. 86*ff*.

48. There would be a straightforward analogy between the vividness of a literary description, conceived in this way, and, e.g., the *elegance* of a proof. The elegance of a proof lies—roughly—in its directing us in an economical and perspicuous manner to make the connections on which it depends for its validity. We may be unable to recognize that a particularly elegant proof is a valid one unless, in inspecting it, we are led to make certain connections—unless, that is, we are led to respond in various ways.

be misleading. And such a response, although internally consistent, is not warranted.

## 4.4  Conclusion: Literature and the Concerns of Ethics

> "She's a very nice woman, extraordinarily well-behaved, upright and clever and with a tremendous lot of good sense about a good many matters. Yet her conception of a novel—she has explained it to me once or twice, and she doesn't do it badly as exposition—is a thing so false that it makes me blush. It's a thing so hollow, so dishonest, so lying, in which life is so blinked and blinded, so dodged and disfigured, that it makes my ears burn . . . There's a hatred of art, there's a hatred of literature—I mean of the genuine kinds. Oh the shams—*those* they'll swallow up by the bucket!"
>
> ∼ *Mark Ambient in Henry James,*
> The Author of Beltraffio *(1922), p. 41.*

One of my concerns in this chapter has been to demonstrate that we naturally understand some literary works as presenting us with rational modes of moral instruction in virtue of ways in which they address our feelings. A second and more general concern has been to argue that, if we are in fact right to understand some literary works as thus presenting us with rational modes of moral instruction, we are entitled to take seriously the possibility that some of these works are in the business of eliciting rational moral thought that doesn't take the form of moral judgment. The demonstration in which this argument is grounded will, as I noted earlier (see the opening of 4.3), appear inadequate to moral philosophers who take for granted the authority of the narrower conception of rationality. To the extent that they draw on the logic of this conception, these moral philosophers in effect assume that any stretch of discourse that contributes to moral understanding by engaging our feelings must do so in a manner that is non-rational in the sense of being accidentally related to the content of what is understood. In the light of this assumption, it appears that anything we uncover about how we ordinarily take some considerations that engage our feelings to constitute rational modes of moral instruction needs to be understood as showing that we are ourselves confused about what genuine, rational instruction is like.

The idea that there must be a confusion here, however compelling it

appears when the narrower conception rationality is presumed authoritative, is brought into question by the kinds of doubts about the cogency of an abstraction requirement explored earlier in this book (1.2
and 2.2; see also 3.2.ii). The appropriate response to these doubts is to
leave open the possibility that emotional growth of the sort that some
literary works seek to promote may make an internal contribution to
rational understanding. To be sure, we have no a priori grounds for denying that, in a given case, we might successfully challenge the appearance
that the sensitivities a given work instills are necessary for understanding significant features of our lives. There are, after all, unintelligent,
manipulative, sentimental, irresponsible and even corrupt works of literature.[49] The point here is that we also have no a priori grounds for
insisting that sensitivities a literary work instills must in every case be
vulnerable to challenge and, furthermore, that we are accordingly
obliged to acknowledge that, if we antecedently reject any tutelage they
offer, we run the risk of finding ourselves in a position (like that of the
emotionally handicapped and muddled Mr. Wilcox) in which we are incapable of grasping connections that are partly constitutive of the fabric of our lives.

Since we lack good a priori reasons to exclude the possibility that literary works that engage us emotionally may sometimes contain fully
rational modes of moral instruction insofar as they do so, we are on
solid ground in taking this chapter's examples to show that some literary works in fact realize this possibility. And, since allowing that literary works may realize this possibility commits us to leaving open the

---

49. It is not difficult to find works that use strategies for engaging us emotionally that depend for whatever success they enjoy on flawed or corrupt systems of metaphor and imagery
and that thus call on us to reshape our sense of what is salient and significant about particular
situations in ways that hamper moral understanding. For one interesting and influential account of this phenomenon, see, e.g. Toni Morrison, *Playing in the Dark: Whiteness and the Literary Imagination* (Cambridge, MA: Harvard University Press, 1992). Morrison argues that central
works in the American literary canon—such as, e.g., Mark Twain's *Huckleberry Finn* and
Ernest Hemmingway's *To Have and Have Not*—rely on unacknowledged and indefensible
racial imagery and metaphoric systems in developing ideals central to their larger narrative
themes and that they thus effectively invite us to champion corrupt, racist renderings of these
ideals. For another interesting account of this phenomenon, see W. G. Sebald's description of
how the German postwar novelist Alfred Andersch uses literary strategies that bear the imprint of a social vision compromised by its participation in fascist modes of thought and
speech (W. G. Sebald, *On the Natural History of Destruction*, trans. Anthea Bell [New York:
Random House, 2003], pp. 105–142).

further possibility that such works may elicit rational moral thought that does not have the form of moral judgment, it follows that we are also on solid ground in taking this chapter's literary examples to support the conclusion that there is moral thinking beyond moral judgment-making.

In closing, let me stress that it is possible to accept this conclusion while also recognizing that moral judgments play an important role in moral thought. Taking my cue from this reflection, I turn now from offering illustrations of moral thought that does not take the form of moral judgment to offering illustrations of this book's irregular understanding of moral thought that does.

# Reclaiming Moral Judgment: The Case of Feminist Thought

"Learning what goodness is" is changing oneself.
~ *Iris Murdoch, personal journal, in Peter J. Conradi,*
Iris: The Life of Iris Murdoch *(2001), p. 272.*

ALTHOUGH WHAT IS most unusual about the inventory of possibilities for moral thought defended in this book is its inclusion of moral thinking that does not take the form of moral judgment-making, the inventory includes moral judgments as well. This inclusion would be unremarkable if not for the distinctive manner in which moral judgments are here understood. One of my guiding suggestions in the book has been that, if we want to do justice to what moral thought is like, we need to refashion more familiar images of moral judgments so that they reflect philosophical considerations in favor of recognizing that moral thought extends beyond such judgments.

Central to the case I made for a revised view of moral judgments is an account of language that derives its original impetus from an attack on the idea of an abstraction requirement. I argued that if we reject the idea of an abstraction requirement we make room for a conception of objectivity "wide" enough to include qualities such that an adequate conception of what it is for an object to possess them can only be developed in terms of the object's tendency to merit certain affective responses. I also claimed that, insofar as it equips us to depict these particular qualities as objective, the wider conception of objectivity positions us to take at face value our ordinary understanding of moral judgments as, at one and the same time, essentially a matter of sensitivity to how things objectively are and immediately pertinent to action and choice. My proposal was that a view of moral judgments as concerned with these qualities permits us to represent moral judgments as essentially preoccupied with how things objectively are without thereby disqualifying ourselves from also representing the judgments as standing in the sort of internal relation to affect that would allow them to be intrinsically practical (1.3.i).

The view that emerges is philosophically distinctive in that it depicts moral judgments as both objectively authoritative and concerned with patterns that are intelligible only in terms of certain evaluative perspectives (1.3.ii). Having already argued for this view, I now want to show that it contains a faithful image of actual practices of moral judgment-making and that, when we turn to these practices, we find that they invite description in its terms.

For the sake of simplicity, I focus here on two cases that are described in the work of contemporary feminist activists and writers in the United States. In both cases, we are presented with defensible moral claims whose authority is recognizable only to the person capable of occupying a certain evaluative perspective (5.1). Although to some extent my choice of illustrations simply reflects my own interests, there is a respect in which feminist thought is especially appropriate for the purposes of this discussion. Contemporary feminist thinking is accompanied by a theoretical corpus that aims to provide a second-order account of how it arrives at its insights, and there is a line of reasoning within this corpus that in important respects complements things I say, in reference to two episodes of feminist thinking, about the nature and difficulty of moral judgment. After discussing the examples, I briefly develop this line of reasoning with an eye to highlighting its fit with the account of moral judgment that is here in question (5.2).

## 5.1 Feminist Thought

> It is now possible to grasp one of the reasons why oppression can be hard to see and recognize: one can study the elements of an oppressive structure with great care and some good will without seeing the structure as a whole, and hence without seeing or being able to understand that one is looking at a cage and that there are people there who are caged, whose motion and mobility are restricted, whose lives are shaped and reduced.
>
> $\sim$ *Marilyn Frye*, The Politics of Reality Essays in
> Feminist Theory *(1983), p. 5.*

The examples of feminist thinking that I discuss have to do with (1) sexual harassment and (2) domestic violence, and in what follows I examine a central line of thought within feminist treatments of these topics. Each of the lines of thought, in addition to suggesting that the wrong with which it is concerned is a genuine (objective or non-relative) wrong, suggests that there is no such thing as fully grasping that wrong apart from a particular evaluative perspective—specifically, a perspective partly constituted by an appreciation of the injustice of sexism. What interests me here is following up on these suggestions in both cases and pointing out that the lines of thought in which they are at home resonate with and provide support for the view of moral judgment defended in this book.

### 5.1.i Sexual Harassment

> The concept of "sexual harassment" . . . performs a double function. It points out that certain experiences are indeed intrusive and coercive. But it also suggests a realignment of the concept of "harassment"—a reorganized perception of what sorts of things are intrusive or coercive. And it draws new analogies between different forms of human experience—between, for example, the experience of black young people of police harassment and the experience of a secretary in her office.
>
> ~ *Jean Grimshaw*, Philosophy and
> Feminist Thinking *(1986), p. 88.*

When, in the mid-nineteen seventies, feminist activists in the United States began talking about sexual harassment, one thing that they were doing was challenging received views about the extension of the concept of "harassment."[1] They were proposing to apply this concept to certain kinds of unwelcome sexual attention women receive that, far from having been previously taken to amount to harassment, were generally seen as at best innocuous and at worst distasteful. Many feminists went on from making proposals along these lines to offering detailed

---

1. Two of the most outspoken of these activists were Lin Farley, then a young teacher in an experimental Cornell University program on women and work, and Catharine MacKinnon, then a law school student. Farley initially presented her view of the problem represented by sexual harassment in *Sexual Shakedown: The Sexual Harassment of Women on the Job* (New York: McGraw-Hill, 1978). MacKinnon's first book, *The Sexual Harassment of Working Women: A Case of Sex Discrimination* (New Haven, CT: Yale University Press, 1979) was instrumental in getting sexual harassment to be treated as sex discrimination under the law. For a recent assessment of the legal impact of MacKinnon's work, see the essays in Catharine MacKinnon and Reva B. Siegel, eds., *Directions in Sexual Harassment Law* (New Haven, CT: Yale University Press, 2004).

defenses of their willingness to speak in this connection of "sexual harassment," and in this section I develop one set of considerations that
figures prominently within these defenses.[2]

My interest here lies strictly with these considerations and not with
the legal and regulatory concerns that have tended to frame discussions
of them. A guiding aim of many of the feminists who first spoke of sexual
harassment—including, most influentially, Catharine MacKinnon—was
establishing sexual harassment as a form of sex discrimination under existing U.S. law.[3] Although it is by no means part of my project to impugn this aim, I do not discuss it.[4] The considerations that I discuss do
not by themselves commit us to any particular views about how we
should in practice deal with the wrong of sexual harassment, and, given
how controversial such views invariably prove, it seems advisable to indicate clearly here at the outset that the force of these considerations
need not be tainted by any misgivings we have about particular laws or
policies, or their implementations.[5]

The argument that interests me has a bearing on any society in

2. It is important here to bear in mind that when feminists started to talk about "sexual harassment" they were not attempting to illuminate the character of every mode of conduct that
is both (1) sexual in content and (2) essentially similar to other conduct that counts as harassment. They were instead attempting to show that certain sexual modes of conduct that are directed at women and that have historically been discounted as relatively innocuous are in fact
rightly brought under the concept of "harassment." A case might be made for thinking that
"sexual harassment" is an overly general label for this relatively specific phenomenon, but I do
not examine the merits of this terminological question here.

3. See the references to MacKinnon's work in note 1.

4. The aim was very quickly achieved. By 1980, there was already good legal precedent
both for recognizing sexual harassment in the workplace as sex discrimination under Title VII
of the 1964 Civil Rights Act and also for recognizing sexual harassment in academic settings
as sex discrimination under Title IX of the Education Amendments Act of 1972.

5. There is another good reason to abstract here from questions about how the law should
deal with sexual harassment. Such questions are bound to introduce additional complicating
factors. Existing sex discrimination legislation is generally interpreted not only as including
under the heading of "sexual harassment" some modes of conduct that central feminist analyses effectively exclude but also as excluding others that they effectively include. Such legislation is generally interpreted as including not only the kinds of unwanted sexual attention *paid
to women* that are the main concern of feminists but also some kinds of unwanted sexual attention paid to men (see note 2, above). And while existing sex discrimination legislation is
generally interpreted as excluding unwanted sexual attention that gets paid to women outside
highly organized institutional settings such as the workplace and the classroom, central feminist reflections about sexual harassment have a straightforward bearing on some such attention in less structured settings such as, e.g., public streets, religious institutions and doctors'
and lawyers' offices (see, e.g., MacKinnon, "Afterword," in MacKinnon and Siegel, *Directions
in Sexual Harassment Law*, pp. 672–704, esp. 672–673).

which women have an inferior social status in virtue of their gender. Very generally, the point is that, within the context of gender inequality, there are circumstances in which *sexual* attention that women receive (i.e., attention that addresses or is concerned with those features of their makeups that are the basis of their social classification as women) is as such threatening. More specifically, the point is that, within this context, sexual attention that is (or ought to be) known to be unwanted, and that serves no legitimate purpose in a given situation, can, without regard to the intentions of the man who pays it, play the role of exploiting and reminding a woman of her socially inferior status as a woman and, by the same token, also of reinforcing that status. What gives this point its salience here is that conduct that thus affirms a woman's relative lack of social power is both alarming and intimidating and is, in these respects, essentially like other things that count as harassment. This is the basic argument underlying the feminist conclusion that certain kinds of unwanted sexual attention that women receive are properly brought under the concept of "harassment."[6]

A prominent concern of the feminist thinkers who first argued along these lines was addressing certain workplace cases in the United States, and for the sake of simplicity I here limit myself to a word about each of the two main work-related applications that get discussed. Since these applications are grounded in the assumption that American working women encounter significant forms of gender inequality, I preface my comments by noting that it is characteristic of members of the relevant group of feminist thinkers, both in their original writings about the United States in the seventies and in their updated writings about the United States today, to take as central signs of gender bias the familiar and well documented features of working women's lives that get placed under the headings of "the wage gap" and "occupational segregation and stratification."[7] Further, although I am anything but sympathetic to those who deny the existence of gender bias, I should add that

6. MacKinnon provides a concise summary of one of its main tenets when she declares that some kinds of unwanted sexual attention "use and help create women's structurally inferior status" and are accordingly "neither incidental nor tangential to women's inequality" (*Sexual Harassment of Working Women*, pp. 10 and xi).

7. It is customary to speak of the "wage gap" in connection with the observation that women get paid less than men for the same work. Although it has shrunk over the last four decades, this gap remains significant. In 1963, at the time of the passage of the Equal Pay Act, which prohibits unequal wages to women and men who have the same positions and job

doubts about whether these (and other) features of working women's lives need to be explained in terms of such bias do not destroy the interest of the exercise of applying feminist reflections about sexual harassment to work-related cases. It is open to the person who—by my lights, wrongly—insists on such doubts to talk about gender inequality in American women's experience in the workplace in reference to an earlier period of time.[8]

Bearing these observations in mind, consider the application of the above argument about sexual harassment to a widely discussed type of workplace case—one now generally described as involving "quid pro quo" sexual harassment—in which a male employer places sexual demands on a female subordinate as a condition of some employment benefit or as a term of employment altogether.[9] Notice, to begin with, that, according to the relevant line of thought, the justification for talk of sexual harassment in connection with this sort of quid pro quo case is not the wrong represented by an abuse of professional power for sexual ends. The justification for such talk is, rather, ways in which, within a sexist society, this wrong is aggravated by women's unequal social status. The aggravating factors are, not only ways in which the sexual demands in question exploit forms of gender inequality that (for instance) tend to deprive women of the authority to protest effectively and tend to make it economically less tolerable for them to risk doing so unsuccessfully, but also ways in which such demands, in virtue of their sexual nature, at the same time promote women's awareness of and perpetuate these forms of inequality. What thus emerges is that quid pro quo cases involve a species of harassment that has a necessary reference to gender inequality and is therefore aptly described as sexual.[10]

---

responsibilities, women across the professions earned 58 percent as much as men. By 1974 that percentage had risen to 60 percent, and in 2004 it stood at 77 percent. "Occupational segregation and stratification" refers to the fact that working women tend to be employed in jobs that mostly women do and to the fact that women tend to be men's subordinates on the job.

8. This person might choose the first years of the sixties before the passage of the Equal Pay Act of 1963 (see note 7) and the Civil Rights Act of 1964 (i.e., the act that prohibits sex discrimination in employment).

9. MacKinnon introduces talk of "quid pro quo" sexual harassment in *Sexual Harassment of Working Women* (see esp. p. 32).

10. For two of the earliest versions of this analysis of quid pro quo cases, see MacKinnon, *Sexual Harassment of Working Women*, pp. 32*ff.*, and Farley, *Sexual Shakedown*, pp. 23–24.

The feminists who first developed this basic line of thought wanted also to extend it beyond quid pro quo cases to workplace cases—now generally described as involving "hostile environment" sexual harassment—in which a female employee receives unwanted sexual attention (e.g., propositions, sexual epithets or insults, sexual gestures, pinches, slaps, etc.) from male co-workers with no direct control over the terms of her employment.[11] The line of thought bears on these further workplace cases in just the same way that it does to those involving a quid pro quo. The license for speaking of sexual harassment in connection with hostile environment cases is not simply the (in some cases perhaps relatively innocuous) wrong of imposing unwanted and inappropriate forms of sexual attention on a co-worker. What licenses us to speak of sexual harassment here is, instead, the manner in which within a sexist society this wrong is compounded by women's unequal social position. The point is that it is compounded both by ways in which the sexual attention in question is grounded in gender inequalities that (for instance) tend to deny women the social standing to protest effectively and tend to make it economically unreasonable or even intolerable for them to take the chance of failing and by ways in which such attention, because it is sexual in character, simultaneously fosters women's consciousness of and sustains these inequalities. The result is that, like quid pro quo cases, hostile environment cases involve a species of harassment that is internally related to gender inequality and is therefore usefully characterized as sexual.[12]

The feminist argument about sexual harassment that I just laid out has applications beyond these types of workplace cases. It also applies to some unwanted and inappropriate sexual attention that women in sexist societies receive in, for instance, educational institutions, doctors' and lawyers' offices, private homes and public streets. What primarily interests me here is not, however, the range and variety of its applications but rather the basic insight that unites them. The argument is at bottom driven by the idea that a society that systematically subjects

11. MacKinnon introduces talk of "hostile environment" sexual harassment in *Sexual Harassment of Working Women*. See esp. p. 40.

12. For two of the earliest versions of this analysis of "hostile environment" cases, see MacKinnon, *Sexual Harassment of Working Women*, pp. 40*ff.*, and Farley, *Sexual Shakedown*, pp. 55*ff.*

women creates conditions under which some unwanted and inappropriate interpersonal exchanges that (qua sexual) underline the social position
they occupy as women first rise to the level of harassment. And this—
quite intuitive—idea has a significant epistemological presupposition.[13]
It presupposes that an appreciation of the wickedness of particular
forms of gender inequality is a necessary precondition of recognizing
some bits of sexual behavior as cases of harassment.[14]

We would be justified in speaking in reference to this presupposition
of an understanding of the concept "harassment" on which our ability
to correctly project it is in some cases inseparable from the ability to
survey the world from a particular evaluative perspective. This understanding is suggestive of the view of moral concepts, and of the judgments in which they figure, that I developed in section 1.3. I say more

13. One measure of the intuitive character of the idea is its resemblance to ideas that animate familiar lines of thought about other types of harassment. A familiar line of thought
about, e.g., racial harassment turns on the idea that a society that systematically subjects those
individuals it identifies as members of a particular racial group creates conditions under which
some unwelcome and inappropriate interpersonal transactions that underline individuals'
racial identities (think, e.g., of the use in the U.S. of anti-black racial slurs like "nigger") qualify as harassment.

14. Although intuitive, the idea of a species harassment internally related to sexism comes
under attack in a number of well-known critiques of feminist treatments of sexual harassment.
One of the most famous of these critiques is Katie Roiphe's *The Morning After: Sex, Fear, and
Feminism on Campus* (Boston, MA: Little, Brown, 1993), pp. 51*ff.* While Roiphe's main critical target is university policies and programs inspired by feminist treatments of sexual harassment, she also directly attacks the idea, central to many of these treatments, of a kind of
harassment that contains a necessary reference to gender inequality. After first granting for
the sake of argument that "*in this society* men are simply much more powerful than women,"
Roiphe claims that it would be "dangerous" to conclude from this that some unwanted sexual
attention women receive is as such threatening (ibid., p. 89; stress in the original). Although
it is hard to locate an argument for this claim in Roiphe's highly polemical prose, she does tell
us that she takes the inference in question to be "dangerous" because it leaves room for the
possibility that some unreflective or "unconscious" sexual conduct might qualify as harassment (ibid., p. 91). But it is unclear why we should want to exclude this possibility wholesale.
A comparison with racial harassment sheds light on what is misguided about doing so. Imagine a case in which a white person repeatedly uses anti-black racial slurs (e.g., "nigger") and
then denies that she consciously intended to say anything threatening. It would be wrong to
take this person's denial, however sincere, as by itself grounds for concluding that her speech
didn't rise to the level of harassment. If we wanted a slogan for the specific mistake at play
here, we might say that it involves equating the actual social meaning of an act with what the
agent intended it to mean.

about this parallel in a moment. First I present one further example from the writings of contemporary feminists.

### 5.1.ii  Domestic Violence

> The basis of wife-beating is male-dominance—not superior physical strength or violent temperament . . . but social, economic, political and psychological power . . . It is male dominance that makes wife-beating a social rather than a personal problem. Wife-beating is not comparable to a drunken barroom assault or the hysterical attack of a jealous lover, which may be isolated incidents . . . Defining wife-beating as a social problem, not merely a phenomenon of particular violent individuals or relationships, was one of the great achievements of feminism.
>
> ⁓ *Linda Gordon*, Heroes of Their Own Lives:
> The Politics and History of Family Violence *(1988), p. 251.*

One of the central goals of the feminist thinkers who, toward the beginning of the second wave of the women's movement, began to talk about domestic violence was showing that there is an important sense in which abuse that women receive from men in intimate relationships—abuse that society and the law had traditionally treated as less pernicious than similarly violent episodes occurring in other settings—is in fact especially hateful.[15] These thinkers tended to suggest that the wrong represented by the pertinent type of abuse gets magnified by ways in which it contributes to social mechanisms that keep women as a group in a structurally inferior position. Several feminist thinkers went on to defend this suggestion at length, and in what follows I examine a line of reasoning central to many of their defenses.[16]

15. Although by the end of the nineteenth century U.S. law for the most part prohibited what had come to be called "wife-beating," in practice the police and the courts were inclined to treat abuse in marriage as a private matter that shouldn't be closely scrutinized or harshly penalized. For several historical studies of how the United States deals with violence against women, see Linda Gordon, *Heroes of Their Own Lives*, esp. pp. 256*ff.*; Elizabeth Pleck, *Domestic Tyranny: The Making of Social Policy Against Family Violence from Colonial Times to the Present* (New York: Oxford University Press, 1987), esp. p. 182; Elizabeth Schneider, *Battered Women and Feminist Law-Making* (New Haven, CT: Yale University Press, 2000), pp. 13*ff.*; and Reva B. Siegel, "'The Rule of Love': Wife Beating as Prerogative and Privacy," *Yale Law Journal* 105, no. 8 (June 1996) pp. 2117–2207.

16. When feminists began to speak of "domestic violence," their primary concern was violent attention that women receive from their male partners within the context of intimate

As in the last section, my interest lies exclusively with a particular line of feminist reasoning and not with legal and policy concerns that inform treatments of it. A central priority of the feminists who introduced talk of domestic violence was changing the way in which society and the law deal with abuse that women receive in intimate relationships, but I do not discuss any of these political projects in what follows.[17] The feminist reflections that I explore can be presented in isolation from specific views about how best to respond to domestic violence.

The line of thought that interests me resembles the argument about sexual harassment just discussed in that it bears on any society in which women have a structurally inferior position in virtue of their gender. It starts from the observation that attention a man pays to his female partner within the framework of an intimate heterosexual relationship, without regard to whether it is sexual in content, is attention paid to her as a woman.[18] The basic idea is that, under conditions of gender inequality, any wrong represented by violent, unwanted attention a man thus pays to his female partner can, without regard to his intentions, play the role of reminding her of her socially inferior status and, by the same token, of reinforcing that status. Moreover, conduct that thus presupposes and advances a woman's mindfulness of her structurally inferior social status is properly understood as making a direct contribu-

---

relationships. This is noteworthy both because violent attention of this kind can be paid to women outside domestic settings and because there are many types of violent interpersonal exchanges inside domestic settings that fall outside feminists' main area of concern. There has recently been some discussion about exchanging the label "domestic violence" for a label better suited to the particular modes of conduct feminists originally set out to isolate and illuminate (e.g., "intimate partner violence"), but I do not comment on this terminological dispute here.

17. It is difficult to find one project that is central to feminist political efforts surrounding domestic violence in the same way that the project of establishing different kinds of sexual harassment as actionable forms of sex discrimination is central to feminist political efforts surrounding sexual harassment. Feminists have worked for greater legal recognition of the wrong of domestic violence. (Their efforts met with significant success with the Violence Against Women Act of 1994, which was reauthorized in 2000 and 2005.) Another focus of feminist work in this area is developing battered women's shelters, to give women and their children a place to go when they leave violent homes and educating police officers, judges and doctors about the peculiar hardships battered women confront.

18. Domestic violence may involve conduct that is sexual in content (e.g., rape) but need not do so. To the extent that it does, a full analysis of the wrong it represents needs to refer not only to the line of thought about domestic violence that is my current concern but also to the line of thought about sexual harassment presented in the last section.

tion to gender-based forms of oppression. So, under conditions of gender inequality, domestic violence amounts to a problem with a necessary reference to sexism.

One of the most widely discussed applications of this line of thought is to the institution of marriage in the United States. The application takes for granted an understanding of U.S. society as characterized by significant forms of gender inequality, and the feminist thinkers who broach these topics tend to take as signs of gender bias not only the facts about working women's lives touched on in section 5.1.i, but also, for instance, facts about how women-headed households are disproportionately poor, about how U.S. courts penalize those assaults and murders in which men target their intimate female partners significantly less harshly than other assaults and murders, and so on. However, since the project of applying feminist reflections about domestic violence to marriage can be undertaken in connection with any society that is significantly sexist, the person who claims (unjustly, by my lights) that these facts can be explained without any reference to gender bias is not on that ground entitled to dismiss its interest.

Consider a case in which a woman is regularly beaten by her husband. According to these reflections, the wrong at play in such a case is not simply the wrong represented by a violent assault. A full specification of this wrong needs to mention ways in which within a sexist society this wrong is exacerbated by women's disadvantaged social situation. The wrong is magnified by ways in which the abuse preys on forms of gender inequality that (for instance) make it more difficult for women to protect themselves from violence or to muster the financial resources to leave a relationship in which they are exposed to it and, in addition, by ways in which such violence, insofar as it here targets women as women, at the same time contributes to cognizance of and preserves these forms of inequality. Domestic violence within marriage can thus be seen as involving a wrong that stands in an internal relationship to gender inequality.

The original impetus to these considerations about domestic violence is the idea that a society that systematically subjects women creates conditions under which abuse that is delivered within the context of an intimate heterosexual relationship, and that accordingly targets women as women, is more hateful than it would be otherwise. This intuitive idea is a close relative of the idea that drives the line of thought about sexual harassment considered in the last section, and it has simi-

lar epistemological interest.[19] It follows from this idea that an appreciation of the insidiousness of particular forms of gender inequality is a
necessary precondition of a full understanding of the wrong at issue in
domestic violence. Our ability to make accurate judgments involving
the concept "domestic violence" turns out to be inseparable from the
ability to adopt a particular evaluative perspective. This observation
brings me back to the account of moral judgment from which I began.[20]

## 5.1.iii  Feminist Thought and Moral Judgment

> Even those who acknowledge that sexual abuse is a serious
> problem often fail to see its connection to broader patterns of
> sexual inequality. Many Americans perceive sexual harassment
> [and] acquaintance rape . . . as issues of sex, or perhaps bad sex,
> but not of subordination. By contrast, serious domestic assaults
> [and] stranger rapes . . . are viewed as examples of violence, not
> sex. What falls through the cracks are issues of power.
>
> ⁓ *Deborah Rhode*, Speaking of Sex:
> The Denial of Gender Inequality *(1997), pp. 95–96.*

It is not strained to suggest that the two examples of feminist thinking just
presented invite description in terms congenial to the view of moral judgment defended in this book. This view is distinguished by the idea that

19. One measure of its intuitive character is its resemblance to ideas that animate familiar
lines of thought about anti-gay violence. A familiar line of thought turns on the idea that a society that systematically subjects those individuals it identifies as gay creates conditions under
which violence that targets them as such individuals ("gay bashing") is more hateful than it
would be otherwise.

20. The idea that domestic violence involves a wrong internally related to sexism gets criticized in a number of well-known critiques of feminist treatments of domestic violence. One of
the most famous of these critiques is Christina Hoff Sommers *Who Stole Feminism? How Women
Have Betrayed Women* (New York: Simon and Schuster, 1994), esp. chapter 9. While Sommers
never offers a rigorous argument for her resistance to understanding domestic violence as a
crime of gender bias, she presents herself as motivated by the observation that batterers are often "cowardly and often sadistic" criminals who abuse their partners in a brutish and thoughtless
manner (ibid., p. 208). The trouble is that this observation is entirely compatible with the idea
that domestic violence is a crime of gender bias. To see this, consider the in some respects
similar case of anti-gay violence. In a situation in which a straight man targets and beats up
gay men in a brutish and thoughtless manner, it would be a mistake to take the brutishness or
thoughtlessness of his crimes to show that he isn't guilty of gay bashing. The mistake here—and
also in Sommers's work on domestic violence—is that of equating the actual social meaning of
an act with what the agent intended it to mean. (Compare note 14.)

moral judgments apply concepts that, in addition to being genuine in the
sense of determining fully objective regularities, are such that considerations for applying them are accessible only in terms of particular evaluative perspectives. And there is a straightforward sense in which this idea
finds support in the examples at hand. Each example involves a case that is
naturally described as one in which, if we are to fully understand considerations for identifying a particular abuse that women are made to suffer,
we need to survey matters from a perspective informed by an appreciation
of the injustice of sexism. Further, each suggests that the person who is
unable or unwilling to adopt this perspective, and who denies that there
are any real abuses of the sort that the perspective equips us to pick out, is
doing something more suspect than simply rejecting a cognitively optional (or non-objective) way of looking at things. Both examples can thus
be seen as illustrating a view on which moral judgments bespeak modes of
contact with the world that, while fully objective, are only perspectivally
available.

We now have before us the illustrations that were this chapter's main
objective. Before closing my discussion, I consider a strand of thought
in feminist theory that lays claim to the features of feminist thinking
that these illustrations serve to highlight. The strand of thought I have
in mind attacks the idea of an abstraction requirement with an eye to
accommodating the philosophically heterodox conception of objectivity that I have been describing as "wider." My suggestion is that it is insofar as this strand of thought accommodates the wider conception of
objectivity that it resembles the view of moral judgment I favor in its
capacity to capture the features of feminist thinking that the above illustrations bring to light.

## 5.2  Feminist Theory

> One of the great powers of feminism is that it goes so far in making
> the experiences and lives of women intelligible. Trying to make sense
> of one's own feelings, motivations, desires, ambitions, actions and
> reactions without taking into account the forces which maintain the
> subordination of women to men is like trying to explain why a
> marble stops rolling without taking friction into account.
>
> ⁓ *Marilyn Frye*, The Politics of Reality *(1983), pp. xi–xii.*

The particular strand of thought that I am going to consider is characterized by a focus on epistemological questions, so it is worth observ-

ing, to begin with, that feminist theory's concern with epistemological questions is a natural extension of its distinctive aims. Feminist theory is devoted to making the lives of women intelligible, and it begins with the recognition that doing so requires shedding light on forces that contribute to the social subjection of women. Some of its most significant contributions to our understanding of women's lives take the form of descriptions of how established bodies and practices of knowledge harm women. Many of these descriptions are specifically concerned with ways in which women have been excluded from knowledge. Feminist theorists have, for instance, underlined ways in which women are excluded as objects of knowledge. Classic economic analyses of the relation between labor and capital neglect unpaid work that women do in the home;[21] standard historical narratives routinely ignore women's roles in social and political life;[22] biomedical research often fails to take women as subjects even for studies whose results are alleged to bear on the health of all people.[23] Feminist theorists have also underlined ways in which women are excluded as subjects of knowledge. Women have been deprived of education even concerning the conditions of their own lives;[24] women's perspectives and experiences have been ignored even when they are directly pertinent to the species of knowledge in

21. Feminist concern about such neglect is what drives the "domestic labor dispute" (i.e., the dispute about whether Marxian analysis is capable of providing an adequate account of women's domestic labor). For a classic discussion, see Heidi Hartman, "The Unhappy Marriage of Marxism and Feminism," in *Women and Revolution*, ed. Lydia Sargent (Boston: South End Press, 1981).

22. The resurgence of feminism since the 1960s has brought with it new interest in the historical study of women's lives. Feminist contributions to social history often call not for mere supplements to older histories but for corrective reworkings. Thus, e.g., Nancy Scott and Elizabeth Pleck open the introduction to their volume *A Heritage of Her Own* (New York: A Touchstone Book, 1979) with the declaration that "all readings of the past . . . are fatally defective if lacking women's outlook or failing to treat women's position" and that most written history therefore "compels a thorough re-viewing" (p. 9).

23. Feminist activism led to the creation, in 1991, of the Office of Research on Women's Health at the National Institute of Health and the inauguration, in 1992, of the Women's Health Initiative, a large-scale clinical intervention and prevention trial that takes women as research-subjects. Feminist publications such at the Boston Women's Health Collective's *Our Bodies Ourselves* (New York: Touchstone, 1998) also aim to supply needed health information about women.

24. See the discussion of feminist efforts, during the first wave of the women's movement, to improve women's access to education in Eleanor Flexner, "Early Steps Towards Equal Education," in *Century of Struggle: The Women's Rights Movement in the United States* (New York: Atheneum, 1971), pp. 23–40.

question;[25] women have been described as irrational and hence as unfit to
be knowers[26] and have had their claim to epistemic authority, their credibility, undermined even in cases in which they possess knowledge.[27]

Over the past several decades a central project of feminist theory has
been to give our concern with these and other ways in which women
are excluded from knowledge a specifically philosophical inflection. Feminist theorists have attempted to deepen our understanding of these
matters by arguing that there is an important sense in which received
renderings of our most basic logical ideals—or perhaps even these
ideals themselves—reinforce sexist (and also classist, racist and heterosexist) biases. They have focused a great deal of attention, in particular,
on questions about how to understand the notion of objectivity that is
partly constitutive of our image of knowledge.[28] The target of a signif-

25. Feminist memoirs from the 1960s and 1970s often emphasize women's sense of a misfit between their own experience and official accounts of what they went through. Thus, e.g.,
Sheila Rowbotham writes that she suffered a "sense of dislocation between [her] sense of self
inside and [her] behavior outside" (*Women's Consciousness, Man's World* [London: Penguin,
1973], pp. 20–21), and Adrienne Rich tells us that she felt "paralyzed by the sense that there
exists a mesh of relationships . . . which, if [she] could see it, make it valid, would give [her]
back [herself], make it possible to function lucidly and passionately" ("When We Dead
Awaken: Writing as Re-Vision," in *On Lies, Secrets and Silence: Selected Prose 1966–1978* [New
York: W. W. Norton, 1979], p. 44).

26. A classic feminist account of philosophical representations of reason as 'male' and
hence out of women's reach is Genevieve Lloyd, *The Man of Reason: "Male" and "Female" in
Western Philosophy*, 2nd ed. (Minneapolis: University of Minnesota Press, 1993).

27. See e.g., Lorraine Code, "Credibility: A Double Standard," chapter 6 of *What Can She
Know? Feminist Theory and the Construction of Knowledge* (New York: Cornell University Press,
1991).

28. Any satisfactory list of the most interesting and influential contributions to the vast
body of feminist literature on the nature of objectivity would have to include: Lorraine Code,
*What Can She Know?*; Donna Haraway, *Simians, Cyborgs, and Women: The Reinvention of Na-
ture* (New York: Routledge, 1991); Sandra Harding, *The Science Question in Feminism* (Ithaca,
NY: Cornell University Press), 1986, and *Whose Science? Whose Knowledge? Thinking from
Women's Lives* (Ithaca, NY: Cornell University Press, 1991); Nancy Hartsock, *The Feminist
Standpoint Revisited and Other Essays* (Boulder, CO: Westview Press, 1998); Sally Haslanger,
"On Being Objective and Being Objectified," in *A Mind of One's Own: Feminist Essays on Reason and Objectivity*, ed. Louise Antony and Charlotte Witt (Boulder, CO: Westview Press,
1993), pp. 85–126; bell hooks, *From Margin to Center* (Boston: South End Press, 1984); Eve-
lyn Fox Keller, *Reflections on Gender and Science* (New Haven, CT: Yale University Press,
1985); Elisabeth Lloyd, "Objectivity and the Double Standard for Feminist Epistemologies,"
*Synthese* 104 (1995): 351–381; Helen Longino, *Science as Social Knowledge: Values and Objectivity in Scientific Inquiry* (Princeton, NJ: Princeton University Press, 1990); Catharine MacKinnon, *Towards a Feminist Theory of the State* (Cambridge, MA: Harvard University Press, 1989);

icant number of these feminist discussions is the prevalent philosophical conception of objectivity that I have been describing as "narrower." Many feminist theorists attack the "abstraction requirement" that, as I have argued, is internal to this conception of objectivity, claiming that the assumption that glimpsing objective reality invariably requires a maximally abstract (i.e., dispassionate and dehumanized) vantage point is both philosophically and politically defective. Indeed, it is now difficult to find even one feminist theorist who undertakes wholeheartedly to defend this assumption.[29]

There has been a conspicuous shift in the kinds of claims feminist theorists are prepared to make about how constraints internal to the narrower conception of objectivity excludes women's voices. Twenty years ago it was not uncommon for feminist theorists to argue that objectivity, conceived as demanding an abstract stance, is a logical ideal that governs "male ways of thinking" and, further, that theoretical discourses that appeal to it therefore *essentially* exclude women's voices.[30] Somewhat more recently, however, many feminist theorists have claimed that these sorts of essentialist arguments (which typically insist on the need for new logical ideals to govern "female ways of thinking") threaten to deprive us of conceptual resources requisite for treating discoveries

---

and Naomi Scheman, *Engenderings: Constructions of Knowledge, Authority and Privilege* (New York: Routledge, 1993).

29. The point here is not that every recent feminist treatment of objectivity attacks the narrower conception of it but only that it is hard to find any treatment that specifically aims to preserve this conception. Some recent feminist projects are, however, concerned with the harm done to women by norms of objectivity that can be considered independently of the question of whether a view of how things objectively are requires detachment. See, e.g., Haslanger, "On Being Objective and Being Objectified."

30. Contributions to feminist epistemology that explicitly defend essentialist arguments about objectivity include Susan Bordo, *The Flight From Objectivity: Essays on Cartesianism and Culture* (Albany: State University of New York Press, 1987); Mary Daly, *Gyn/Ecology* (Boston: Beacon Press, 1978); Andrea Nye, *Words of Power* (New York: Routledge, 1990); Sheila Ruth, "Methodocracy, Misogyny and Bad Faith: The Response of Philosophy," in *Men's Studies Modified: The Impact of Feminism on Academic Disciplines*, ed. Dale Spender (New York: Pergamon Press, 1981); and Liz Stanley and Sue Wise, *Breaking Out: Feminist Consciousness and Feminist Research* (London: Routledge and Kegan Paul, 1983). It is possible to identify in addition a set of feminist arguments about objectivity that are characterized by an unacknowledged slide into essentialist modes of thought. Lorraine Code discusses how some feminist theorizing slides unwittingly into essentialism in "Knowledge and Subjectivity," chapter 2 of *What Can She Know?* I discuss this topic in my essay "A Question of Silence: Feminist Theory and Women's Voices," *Philosophy* 76, no. 96 (July 2001): 371–395.

of masculine bias as grounds for criticism of established bodies of knowledge and hence that, however laudable their original political motives, such arguments are ultimately both philosophically and politically problematic. Most feminist theorists who propose to defend the claim that the narrower conception of objectivity excludes women's voices now present themselves as doing so on non-essentialist grounds. Feminist theorists tend to agree in holding that the narrower conception describes an epistemic ideal that is illegitimate for all modes of thought (not merely for those we might once have thought of as "female") and that this conception contributes to the silencing of women's voices, not by means of any simple "essential" exclusion, but rather by obstructing efforts to reveal various forms of sexist bias in received discourses. They tend to agree, further, in wanting to support this view by arguing that, in contrast to what the conception implies, some morally significant features of the world (and, in particular, some with profound consequences for women's lives) are available only from perspectives afforded by social positions that women of different backgrounds have historically been made to occupy.

This agreement forms the backdrop for recent feminist conversations about objectivity. The central, ongoing feminist debate about this issue takes place between, on the one hand, theorists who criticize the narrower conception of objectivity as problematic and propose to revise it and, on the other, theorists who maintain that the very notion of objectivity (understood in narrower terms) is hopelessly tainted and that we must therefore reject it wholesale.

In order to arrive at a more precise description of this debate, we need to bear in mind that the conception of objectivity that is in question, in somewhat different ways, on both sides of it is characterized by the *ontological* assumption that no genuine feature of the world can be subjective in the sense that it cannot adequately be conceived except in terms of human subjective responses and also by the *epistemological* assumption that we approach a view of objective reality by abstracting from any local or subjective perspectives. Feminist theorists on both sides of the debate believe that we need to reject this pair of epistemological and ontological assumptions. But they differ over whether rejecting it undermines our very ability to offer an authoritative ontology or epistemology, or whether it instead suggests the need to broaden our ontology to include some subjective features of the world, while at the same time broadening our epistemology to include perspectival judgments capable of revealing such features.

Theorists on one side take the pair of assumptions to be essential to the notion of objectivity. They take it for granted that, if we reject the pair, we turn our backs on the very notion of objectivity and, by the same token, abandon the enterprises of ontology and epistemology as traditionally conceived. Theorists on the other side, in contrast, hold that this pair of assumptions fails to capture what objectivity is like. They maintain that, if we reject the pair, we find ourselves called on not to acknowledge the loss of the notion of objectivity but rather to re-fashion this notion in terms of broader, or more permissive, ontological and epistemological assumptions. Since the alternative conception of objectivity that members of this latter group of theorists champion qualifies, in virtue of its more permissive ontology and epistemology, as a version of what I am calling the wider conception of objectivity, and since the less permissive ontology and epistemology that their interlocutors champion is constitutive of the narrower conception, it follows that the ongoing feminist debate about objectivity might aptly be described as turning on the question of whether a consistent gesture of rejection of the narrower conception commits us to a form of skepticism about objectivity, or whether it instead commits us to making room for a wider conception of what objectivity is like.

The remainder of this chapter is dedicated to presenting central concerns of the participants in this debate who appeal to the wider conception of objectivity and, more specifically, to showing that their work provides theoretical underpinnings for the feminist reflections about sexual harassment and domestic violence discussed in the last section. Since some of the earliest feminist epistemologies to lay claim to the wider conception of objectivity were *feminist standpoint theories*, I start with an overview of these theories and of criticisms to which they have been subjected.

The label "feminist standpoint theory" derives from a line of thought in Marx's critique of capitalism, one commonly associated with Lukács's commentary, that represents the "standpoint" of the proletariat as conferring an epistemic privilege.[31] This line of thought starts with an account of consciousness as mediated by the material conditions in which

---

31. See esp. Georg Lukács, "Reification and the Standpoint of the Proletariat," *History and Class Consciousness* (Cambridge, MA: MIT Press, 1971), pp. 149–222.

we interact with others. Since material conditions thus structure consciousness in addition to behavior, it follows that, under capitalism, a
vision of social relations that is biased in favor of capitalists will appear
to be authoritative. For it will tend to capture the conduct of members
of both (capitalist and proletarian) social classes, and it will also tend to
be reflected in their judgment. However, although members of the proletariat will, like members of the dominant class, generally endorse the
received social vision and will in this way be complicit in their own oppression, their lives nevertheless furnish a standpoint from which class
relations under capitalism can be recognized as offensive to our natures. Investigations of proletarian lives reveal forms of unease or suffering that the received social vision cannot incorporate, and efforts to
occupy an evaluative perspective from which these anomalies disappear
move us toward an objectively more accurate account of society. This is
the conclusion of the relevant Marxian line of thought (viz., that if we
thus actively develop the "proletarian standpoint" we improve our understanding of objective reality). And because it presupposes that some
features of the objective social world come into view only from a particular evaluative perspective, it is properly understood as depending
for its cogency on the wider conception of objectivity.

Feminist standpoint theories set out to extract a basic epistemological insight from this Marxian line of thought and to apply it to the case
of the social subordination of women. The basic strategy is clearly worked
out in the writings of Nancy Hartsock, the first defender of feminist
standpoint theory.[32] Hartsock combines the Marxian view that "material life not only structures but sets limits on the understanding of social
relations" with the feminist observation that, in all historical societies,
material life varies in systematic ways with gender.[33] She claims that "the
vision of the ruling . . . gender . . . structures the material relations in
which all parties are forced to participate."[34] Her goal is to establish
that, despite the fact that women are thus made complicit in their own

32. Hartsock's article, "The Feminist Standpoint: Developing the Ground for a Specifically Feminist Historical Materialism," was originally published in Sandra Harding and Mer-
rill Hintikka, eds., *Discovering Reality: Feminist Perspectives on Epistemology, Metaphysics,
Methodology, and Philosophy of Science* (Dordrecht: D. Reidel Publishing, 1983), pp. 283–320. It
was reprinted in 1998 in Hartsock, *The Feminist Standpoint Revisited*, pp. 105–132. All citations
here are to the reprinted version.
33. Ibid., p. 107.
34. Ibid.

oppression, "women's lives make available a particular and privileged vantage point."[35] Although women (like men) tend to endorse received, sexist accounts of society and their own lives, they at the same time suffer in ways that don't fit within these accounts. We approach a more just and accurate understanding of social relations by trying to occupy a vantage point from which such suffering is intelligible. This vantage point, Hartsock writes, "exposes the real relations among human beings as inhuman, points beyond the present, and carries a historically liberatory role."[36]

The reception of feminist standpoint theories is marked by a widespread impression of *essentialism*. Early versions of the theories, including Hartsock's, were presented as resting on the assumption that it is possible to identify a vantage point, transcending all cultural differences, as distinctively or essentially that of women, and the most common criticisms of the theories are addressed to this assumption.[37] Critics charge that, insofar as feminist standpoint theories make this assumption, they suggest—wrongly—that women's subjectivity is untainted by oppressive social systems or, as one critic puts it, that women "are not in fundamental ways damaged by their social experience."[38] Further, critics also charge that, in making this assumption, the theories encourage us to artificially force all women into one restrictive model and to overlook politically decisive differences in the lives of individual women and groups of women.[39] These two charges are clearly merited by certain specific feminist standpoint theories. Nevertheless, it is worth noting that the assumption they target has no analogue in the Marxian line of the thought that the theories aspire to inherit and in

35. Ibid.

36. Ibid., p. 108.

37. In "The Feminist Standpoint Revisited," Hartsock catalogues the work of critics who charge feminist standpoint theory with essentialism (see, e.g., pp. 230–233). She defends her original discussion of feminist standpoint theory against this charge, while also claiming that some of her early formulations helped to invite it. I believe that there is more merit to the charge, directed at Hartsock's original piece, than she admits, but I cannot discuss this matter further here.

38. Jane Flax, "Postmodernism and Gender Relations in Feminist Theory," in *Feminism/ Postmodernism*, ed. Linda Nicholson (London: Routledge, 1990), p. 56.

39. For some clear statements of this charge, see Lorraine Code, *What Can She Know?*, p. 317, Donna Haraway, "Situated Knowledges," reprinted in Haraway, *Simians, Cyborgs, and Women*, and Nancy Bauer, *Simone de Beauvoir, Philosophy and Feminism* (New York: Columbia University Press, 2001), p. 35.

fact tends to subvert one of its central points. A central point of the Marxian line of thought is to describe a form of social criticism that, while distinctive in form, retains a claim to objective authority, and, when social criticism is conceived, in accordance with the targeted assumption, as informed by a perspective that is essentially and exclusively women's there can be no question of its laying claim to such authority.

It is for these reasons unsurprising that a number of feminist theorists have undertaken to argue that—setting aside flaws of some of the theories' particular elaborations—feminist standpoint theories are properly understood as lacking any essentialist dimension. The most influential theorist to attempt this project is Sandra Harding.[40] Harding describes her interest in feminist standpoint theory as driven by a preoccupation not with perspectives that are supposedly 'essentially those of women' but rather with the diverse "actual perspectives" that "actual women" occupy at different historical periods and in different social contexts.[41] She claims that women's (and men's) experience is "shaped by social relations" and hence tends to bear the imprint of the various sexist (and also classist, racist, heterosexist, etc.) social forces feminists want to resist. She argues that, although it follows that treating women's self-understanding as by itself "provid[ing] reliable grounds for knowledge claims about the nature of social relations" would threaten to reaffirm oppressive social forms, it is nevertheless also the case that successful, objectively valid criticism of these forms needs to include reflections that aim to account for certain of women's experiences that can't easily be made to fit within a sexist social vision.[42] This very general type of non-essentialist criticism is what Harding has in mind when she declares that "standpoints" from which certain of women's experiences become intelligible are necessary to an objectively accurate understanding of social reality.[43]

If we set aside for a moment Harding's efforts to preserve the label

---

40. Harding's most complete description of the version of a feminist standpoint theory she favors is in Harding, *Whose Science? Whose Knowledge?* For her repudiation of the suggestion of essentialism, see esp. pp. 49, 68, 134 and 173*ff.*

41. Ibid., p. 123.

42. Ibid.

43. Ibid. See also pp. 127*ff.* and 167. Harding describes the "wider" ideal of objectivity to which she believes such criticism is beholden as "strong" objectivity. See chapter 6 of esp. *Whose Science, Whose Knowledge.*

"feminist standpoint theory" and focus exclusively on her description of objective, non-essentialist modes of thought that are dedicated to making sense of anomalous elements in women's experience, then we can justly say that her work resonates with a well developed strand of thought in contemporary feminist theory. A significant number of feminist theorists likewise describe such modes of thought and criticism. They maintain that, if we are to account for what is anomalous in women's experience, we need to look at women's lives from a perspective informed by an appreciation of the injustice of structures that keep women as a group in an inferior social position. We need to avoid being "riveted upon the individual event in all its particularity" and to survey the features of women's lives in question in a manner that, insofar as it is informed by such an appreciation, allows us to "see the various elements of the situation as systematically related in larger schemes."[44] The point is that by surveying women's lives in this style, we position ourselves to make sense of painful elements of women's experience that are otherwise perplexing. Now we can see that certain things that get done to women, while generally regarded as relatively innocuous, in fact exploit sexist social structures in ways that causes real suffering.[45]

The strand of thought in feminist theory that proceeds along these lines turns on the idea that a good understanding of women's lives is unavailable apart from an appreciation of the insidiousness of sexism. The strand of thought thus resembles the view of moral judgment that is my larger concern in this chapter in finding confirmation in the two examples of section 5.1—examples of cases in which certain particular features of women's lives (viz., the abuses that get described as sexual harassment and domestic violence) are unavailable apart from an appreciation of the insidiousness of sexism. I say more about this resemblance in just a moment, after first briefly considering two of the most common criticisms of the strand of thought in question.

I start with a terminological observation. Whatever the merits of the efforts of Harding and others to reclaim "feminist standpoint theory" for their preferred, non-essentialist project in feminist theory, most

---

44. Marilyn Frye, *Politics of Reality*, pp. 5 and 6.

45. A classic feminist account of this basic strand of thought is developed in *Frye, Politics of Reality*, esp. the essays entitled "Oppression" and "Sexism," pp. 1–16 and 17–40. See also Elisabeth Lloyd, "Objectivity and the Double Standard for Feminist Epistemologies," Helen Longino, *Science as Social Knowledge*, and Naomi Scheman, *Engenderings*.

feminist theorists continue to associate the label with a philosophically and politically troubling essentialism. This includes, significantly, many feminist theorists who are likewise convinced of the epistemic value of widely objective, non-essentialist modes of feminist thought.[46] There is thus a residual problem with the proposal to use "feminist standpoint theory" as a label for theories that aim to illuminate such modes of thought—a problem that I sidestep here by referring to members of this class of theories as *feminist objectivisms*.[47]

It is no secret that feminist objectivisms come under attack within feminist theory. Their critics typically sympathize with the call for rejecting constraints of the narrower conception of objectivity but think that to reject such constraints just is to relinquish the notion of objectivity. The most prominent current of feminist thought characterized by this inference is concerned primarily with its bearing on identity categories such as "woman." A recent, widely influential strain of feminist thought proceeds from the claim that there are no transcendent truths determining the correctness of applications of identity categories (such as "woman") in a way that satisfies the narrower ideal of objectivity to the conclusion that these categories, far from admitting the sorts of objective applications that feminist objectivists invite us to envision, are fundamentally unstable.[48]

This criticism of feminist objectivism is often placed under the heading of "feminist postmodernism."[49] But this way of talking, although

46. See, e.g., Lorraine Code's discussion of feminist standpoint theory in *What Can She Know?* and *Rhetorical Spaces: Essays on Gendered Locations* (New York: Routledge, 1995), pp. 180–181.

47. I am grateful to Nancy Bauer, Hilde Nelson, and Peg O'Connor for helpful discussion about this issue. Let me add that, in speaking of "feminist objectivism" in connection with the wider conception of objectivity, I am not denying that some thinkers whose political inclinations are decidedly feminist are committed to defending "narrower" objectivisms. (I discuss the work of such thinkers later in this section.) I am simply taking advantage, for the purposes of a perspicuous terminology, of the fact that within feminist theory almost all defenses of objectivism lay claim to the wider conception.

48. The classic elaboration of this—now familiar—position is Judith Butler, *Gender Trouble: Feminism and the Subversion of Identity* (New York: Routledge, 1990). For an additional comment about relevant aspects of Butler's work, see Chapter 2, note 69, above, as well as the associated text.

49. This terminology is used both by many feminist defenders of and by many feminist detractors from the relevant form of skepticism about objectivity. For a representative defender who speaks in these terms, see Jane Flax, *Thinking Fragments: Psychoanalysis, Feminism and*

widespread, is misleading. It is not unusual to speak of the "modern" in reference to the cultural and intellectual tradition to which the narrower conception of objectivity belongs and to speak of the "postmodern" in reference to cultural and intellectual movements that aspire to free themselves from this tradition. Indeed, some feminist objectivists, adopting this terminology, present themselves as "postmodernists."[50] Given the terminology, we can see that our willingness to understand "feminist postmodernism" in terms of the form of skepticism about objectivity described in the last paragraph will seem to imply sympathy for the view that our claim to objectivity stands or falls with the narrower conception. And it will thus seem to commit us to prejudging the very issue that separates feminist objectivists from their critics. Moreover, even if, while adopting this way of talking about "feminist postmodernism," we explicitly leave room for the possibility of a wider conception of objectivity, we run the risk of obscuring the fact, just noted, that some self-avowed "feminist postmodernists" likewise insist on this possibility.[51] In order to avoid these risks, I refer to the relevant set of critics of feminist objectivisms (i.e., those who assume that in relinquishing the narrower conception we lose our very entitlement to objectivity) simply as "feminist skeptics."[52]

---

*Postmodernism in the Contemporary West* (Berkeley, CA: University of California Press, 1990). For a representative detractor who does so, see Seyla Benhabib, "Feminism and Postmodernism: An Uneasy Alliance," in *Feminist Contentions: A Philosophical Exchange*, ed. Seyla Benhabib et al. (London: Routledge, 1995).

50. Thus, e.g., Sandra Harding describes her own work in these terms (see esp. *Whose Science? Whose Knowledge?* pp. 47ff.). See also Nancy Fraser and Linda Nicholson, "Social Criticism with Philosophy: Feminism and Postmodernism" in *Feminism/Postmodernism*, ed. Linda Nicholson (London: Routledge, 1990), pp. 19–38, esp. pp. 34–35. This Nicholson anthology, the classic source for discussions of the relation between feminism and postmodernism, contains both essays such as this one of Fraser's and Nicholson's that interpret "postmodernism" to include the wider conception of objectivity and also essays that associate "postmodernism" with skepticism about objectivity (see, e.g., the essay by Jane Flax).

51. This is not an idle worry. Many feminist critiques of "feminist postmodernism" that understand it in terms of a certain skepticism about objectivity obscure fundamental epistemological differences among thinkers who call themselves "feminist postmodernists." For a clear and relatively recent illustration of the problem, see Miranda Fricker, "Feminism in Epistemology: Pluralism Without Postmodernism," *The Cambridge Companion to Feminism in Philosophy*, ed. Miranda Fricker and Jennifer Hornsby (Cambridge: Cambridge University Press, 2000), pp. 146–165.

52. Skeptical critics of feminist objectivisms are sometimes referred to as "anti-epistemologists" in virtue of their hostility to the very ideal of objectivity that is partly constitutive of

A feminist skeptic might express her worries about feminist objectivisms in the following terms:

> What is troubling about feminist objectivisms is simply their attachment to the notion of objectivity. Advocates of these theories are plainly right to point out that the narrowly objective ideal of "point-of-viewlessness" functions, illegitimately and in a manner harmful to women, to make it seem as though there is nothing to be learned from perspectival investigations of women's lives. They are also right to insist that any politically viable feminist theory must rely on perspectival modes of thought. The problem is that these theorists try to combine these insights with an aspiration to objectivity with which the insights are deeply in tension. Admittedly, they don't intend to put themselves in this conflicted position. They assume that there are modes of thought tied to particular cultural perspectives that are as such capable of revealing how things objectively are. But this assumption is simply false. In their concern with objective reality, feminist objectivists undermine their own, politically decisive efforts to legitimize the perspectival. The upshot is that if we want a theoretical or epistemological outlook that truly serves feminist political purposes, we need to describe one that, unlike feminist objectivisms, is free from any lingering attachment to the notion of objectivity.

The feminist skeptic who presents this criticism need not have any interest in attacking the political motives of feminist theorists who insist on preserving our entitlement to full-blooded objectivity. Feminist skeptics often acknowledge that the prospect of having "no objective basis for distinguishing between true and false beliefs" and of being in a position in which "power alone will determine the outcome of competing truth claims" is a genuinely frightening one, especially for those who "are oppressed by the power of others."[53] Their main goal is to

---

the object of epistemological research, as traditionally conceived. But this terminology is no more transparent than talk of "postmodernism." This is because feminist objectivists are also sometimes referred to as "anti-epistemologists"—now in virtue of their hostility to the idea of a point of view external to responses and reactions we learn in learning language from which we can advance a philosophical theory about the structure of knowledge.

53. Jane Flax, "Postmodernism and Gender Relations," p. 42.

discredit the presupposition, distinctive of feminist objectivism, that it is possible consistently to combine an attachment to objectivity (however well motivated) with a commitment to including perspectival modes of thought.[54]

This brings me to a second criticism of feminist objectivists. Since it is unusual for feminist theorists to defend the narrower conception of objectivity, it is rare for feminist objectivists to be criticized within feminist theory for attacking this conception. But outside feminist theory this criticism is anything but rare. Indeed, the most frequently recited external criticism of contemporary feminist theory is that it betrays an allegedly thoughtless and irresponsible tendency to depart from our logical ideals, when these ideals are understood in narrower terms.[55] This criticism is sometimes given a specifically feminist twist. The idea is that the "perspectival" innovations of feminist theorists, including those who defend wider objectivisms, make it impossible for feminists to present themselves as concerned with purging our discourses of sexist bias and approaching an objectively more accurate account of social reality. This criticism of feminist objectivism is an expression of a "narrow," philosophically more orthodox objectivism—or, as I will put it, of a *traditional objectivism*.[56]

---

54. The tendency of thought distinctive of feminist skeptics (i.e., the tendency to move from rejecting the narrower conception of objectivity to insisting on some qualification of our entitlement to objectivity) tacitly informs the work of some feminist objectivists. Consider in this connection the writings of Lorraine Code. Although one of the central claims of Code's work is that feminists should refashion objectivity along wider lines (see, e.g., *What Can She Know?* pp. 4–5), she repeatedly characterizes her attack on the narrower conception as a departure from "a perfect, ideal objectivity" (ibid., p. 215). Code differs from feminist skeptics in resisting the conclusion that we should give up the pursuit of objectivity, encouraging us to try "to occupy as objective a standpoint as possible" (ibid.). Nonetheless, she maintains that our best efforts in this pursuit won't take us farther than a "mitigated relativism" (ibid., pp. 251, 264 and 320).

55. The enthusiasm with which this patronizing criticism of feminist theory is rehearsed reveals what one feminist theorist, Elisabeth Lloyd, describes as a "double standard" for feminist research ("Objectivity and the Double Standard"). Although *non*-feminist critiques of "narrower" metaphysics are often discussed within mainstream philosophical circles, they are rarely assessed in the same patronizing terms.

56. More familiar names for members of the group of feminist intellectuals who endorse what I am calling traditional objectivisms include "feminist empiricists" (see, e.g., Harding, *Whose Science? Whose Knowledge?* p. 111*ff.*) and "liberal feminists." I prefer to avoid these more familiar names because I believe that it is possible to be an empiricist or a liberal without insisting on the narrower conception of objectivity.

A traditional objectivist might express her worries about feminist objectivisms as follows:

> What is troubling about feminist objectivisms is that they forfeit their entitlement to the notion of objectivity. This forfeiture is, admittedly, not an aim of the theories' advocates. These theorists assume that there are modes of thought tied to particular cultural perspectives that are capable of revealing how things objectively are. But this assumption is simply false. In relying on perspectival modes of thought, feminist objectivists—in spite of any comforting rhetoric about "wider" conceptions of objectivity—effectively give up any claim to be concerned with objective reality. This is worrisome because it places us, as feminists, in a position in which we can no longer represent accounts of the social world that we devise as genuinely, objectively superior to any competing sexist (or classist or racist or heterosexist, etc.) descriptions we hope to discredit. The upshot is that if we want a theoretical or epistemological outlook that truly serves feminist political purposes, we need to describe one that, unlike feminist objectivisms, is free from any necessary reliance on perspectival modes of thought.

Comparison of this criticism of feminist objectivism with the kinds of criticisms leveled by feminist skeptics reveals a striking parallel. Although the two criticisms disagree about whether an unqualified commitment to objectively authoritative modes of social criticism is something feminist objectivists ought to want, they nevertheless agree that a thinker's willingness to rely essentially on perspectival modes of thought invariably represents a qualification of her commitment to the ideal of objectivity. And this agreement plainly expresses the internal logic of the narrower conception of objectivity. The narrower conception is partly composed of an epistemological assumption from which it follows that any evaluative perspective has an intrinsic tendency to interfere with access to objective reality. So there is a basic respect in which feminist skeptics and traditional objectivists agree with each other in putting forth criticisms of feminist objectivism that bear the narrower conception's imprint.

This brings to a close my discussion of the strand of thought in feminist theory that I have placed under the heading of "feminist objectivism." I turned to this strand of thought here both because, like the view of moral judgment central to this chapter, it draws on the logic of the wider conception of objectivity and because, also like this view, it finds confirmation in the examples of feminist thinking presented in section 5.1. Where, within the view of moral judgment, the wider conception underwrites a representation of moral concepts as concerned with objective features of the world that are unavailable apart from particular evaluative perspectives, within feminist objectivism, it underwrites an understanding of feminist thought as uncovering objective forms of gender bias that are likewise unavailable apart from particular evaluative perspectives—specifically, perspectives informed by an appreciation of the injustice of sexism. Feminist objectivism thus resembles this view of moral judgment in encountering illustrative support in feminist social criticism that depicts some abuses women are made to suffer as first coming properly into view from perspectives shaped by a sense of the wrongness of sexist social structures.

These remarks conclude my illustrations of the different forms of moral thought that inform the view of ethics defended in this book. Equipped with further support for my argument for this view, I now proceed to a consideration of moral consequences of its adoption.

~ *III*

*A MORAL*

# ～ 6

## Moralism as a
## Central Moral Problem

I know I've been wrong—often, continually. But yet, sometimes
when I have done wrong, it has been because I have feelings that you
would be the better for if you had them. . . . You thank God for
nothing but your own virtues—you think they are great enough to
win you everything else. You have not even a vision of feelings by the
side of which your shining virtues are mere darkness!
～ *Maggie Tulliver to Tom in George Eliot,*
Mill on the Floss *(1979), p. 50.*

HAVING IN EARLIER CHAPTERS made a case for the non-
traditional view of ethics central to this book's ambitions—a view that represents moral thought as including more than moral judgments—I turn
in this chapter to a specifically moral criticism the view implies of the
more traditional, moral judgment-centered approaches in ethics it aims
to supplant. One of the marks of the view is a conception of demands of
moral reflection on which, in order to avoid antecedently limiting the
development of our rational moral capacities, we need to attend not
merely to individuals' moral judgments but to all of their ways of responding to the world, to the entire patterns of their lives (1.4, 2.3, 3.3
and 4.3). This conception of demands of moral reflection drives the
moral criticism that I investigate in this chapter. With the conception
in place, it appears morally risky for an individual to assume, in accordance with moral judgment-centered views of ethics, that it must in
principle be possible for her to understand the circumstances of her life
in the absence of the kinds of refinements of sensibility that explorations of different modes of responses to the world promise to foster.
The risk is that of committing herself to simply retaining certain biases

or forms of moral ignorance, and the trouble is that, if she commits herself to preserving these biases, then, however mild and non-judgmental she otherwise is, she can't help but veer toward a kind of moral presumptuousness.

In this chapter, I claim that this kind of moral presumptuousness is aptly understood as a species of *moralism*. Since there is a danger that the charge of moralism that interests me will be confused with other moral criticisms that get placed under the same heading, and since the charge that I want to examine is particularly likely to be conflated with one that gets leveled in recent debates about "impartiality in ethics," I approach the task of isolating it by first outlining these debates (6.1) and distinguishing the charge of moralism that they are taken to fund from the fundamentally different charge that I claim bears directly on traditional moral judgment-centered views of ethics (6.2). One noteworthy feature of the latter charge is that it concerns moral differences, of the sort suggested by this book's description of forms of moral thought apart from the employment of moral concepts, that are not a matter of disagreements about how or whether to apply particular moral concepts. I bring out the familiarity of the kinds of moral differences at play by following up my discussion of the bearing of this charge of moralism on more traditional approaches in ethics with additional examples of moralism. I turn for examples to classic and notably coincident treatments of moralism in the novels of Theodor Fontane and Henry James (6.3). I then conclude with a comment about the bearing of this distinctive conception of moralism on the project of this book as a whole (6.4).

## 6.1 Competing Conceptions of Impartiality

> They always say, "Love is blind," but it makes us see clearly and off into the future, too.
>
> ~ *Lene to Botho in Theodor Fontane,*
> Delusions, Confusions *(1989), p. 29.*

The last several decades witnessed the emergence within Anglo-American moral philosophy of a family of criticisms that, cutting across the familiar divide between consequentialist and deontological theories, attack the enormously influential idea that the point of view distinctive of moral reflection is *impartial* in a sense that includes an abstraction

from all feelings.[1] The central line of reasoning common to these criticisms starts from the thought that particular emotional attachments
may be essential to who we are in the most fundamental sense, that they
may be what give our lives meaning and make them worth living at all.[2]
It then tries to establish that an understanding of morality as impartial
is inseparable from a certain dislocation between our emotional attachments or the things we care about—our values—and our practices of
moral reflection. The idea is that, since moral considerations conceived
as impartially available must be intelligible independently of any standpoints that we occupy as people with particular emotional attachments,
it follows that, given an understanding of morality as impartial, our attachments cannot directly inform moral reflection. This is taken to
show that within the framework of an impartial morality there is an important sense in which moral reflection requires us to distance ourselves from our emotional attachments and to regard them as parts of
our makeup from which we can detach ourselves. The result is that we
are prevented from treating such attachments as essential to who we are
in the most fundamental sense. So it appears that any ethical theory
that embodies an understanding of morality as impartial cannot help
but fail to respect necessary conditions of our moral identity.

The point of criticisms that proceed along these lines is not that,
within the framework of an impartial morality, we are prohibited from
endorsing moral considerations that are available to us from perspectives afforded by particular emotional attachments. The point is, rather,
that within this framework the rightness or appropriateness of such
considerations, setting aside the question of how we in fact arrive at
them in particular cases, can be confirmed only from a neutral stand-

---

1. The original contributions to this—now dauntingly large—body of critical literature include Lawrence Blum, *Friendship, Altruism and Morality* (London: Routledge and Kegan Paul,
1980); John Kekes, "Morality and Impartiality," *American Philosophical Quarterly* 18 (1981):
295–303; Michael Stocker, "The Schizophrenia of Modern Ethical Theories," *Journal of Philosophy* 73 (1976): 453–466; and Bernard Williams, "Morality and the Emotions," in *Problems
of the Self: Philosophical Papers, 1956–1972* (Cambridge: Cambridge University Press, 1973),
pp. 207–229, "A Critique of Utilitarianism," in *Utilitarianism: For and Against*, ed. J. J. C.
Smart and B. Williams (Cambridge: Cambridge University Press, 1973), pp. 77–150, and
"Persons, Character and Morality," in *Moral Luck: Philosophical Papers 1973–1980* (Cambridge: Cambridge University Press, 1981), pp. 1–19.

2. In "Persons, Character and Morality," Williams speaks in connection with this thought
of "ground projects" and "categorical desires."

point that we occupy by reflectively dissociating ourselves from any such attachments. Thus, although we are endorsing considerations supplied by our emotional attachments, we are at the same time dissociating ourselves from those attachments by adopting a reflective point of view from which they are treated as inessential to who we are.[3] It is insofar as an understanding of moral reflection as impartial is inseparable from this form of dissociation that, according to the criticisms just outlined, it is in tension with conditions of our moral identity.[4]

Although it is widely recognized that there is a family of (what might be called) *impartiality criticisms* that agree in thus attacking the idea of an impartial morality, it is generally overlooked that there is a subtle division within this family. Many impartiality criticisms are concerned to show not only that we need to abandon moral impartiality in order to preserve our integrity but, moreover, that the abandonment of such impartiality is equivalent to the abandonment of an understanding of moral reflection as a rational pursuit. The impartiality criticisms that proceed along these lines are helpfully understood as taking for granted what I am calling the narrower conception of rationality (i.e., the conception on which it must be possible to grasp the connections that make up a rational line of thought independently of the possession of any particular routes of feeling) (4.1; see also 3.2.ii). Within the context of this conception it appears that modes of thought that depart from impar-

---

3. This is the point that, Bernard Williams is making when, in a famous gesture, he declares that the problem with Kantian ethical theories is not that they prevent us from sanctioning specific considerations but rather that they force us to think "one thought too many" ("Persons, Character and Morality," p. 18).

4. Moral philosophers who aim to rebut the criticisms sometimes fail to register that it is this specific form of dissociation which is in question. Consider here a relatively early paper in which Barbara Herman responds to the criticisms on behalf of Kant's ethical theory. In "Integrity and Impartiality"—reprinted in *The Practice of Moral Judgment* (Cambridge, MA: Harvard University Press, 1993), pp. 23–44—Herman argues, allegedly against the criticisms, that Kant's theory does not keep us from acting on reasons supplied by our personal attachments as long as those reasons are regulated by the motive of duty serving as a sort of limiting condition. This argument fails as a response to the relevant criticisms, since it does nothing more than assert the need for the kind of dissociation that they contest. In more recent work, Herman acknowledges that this earlier rejoinder to the criticisms fails and she presents what she takes to be a more adequate rejoinder. For a comment on her more recent efforts, see note 6.

tiality in being directly informed by feelings have an inherent tendency to fall short of rationality. By the same token, it appears that, if we reject the idea of an impartial morality and make room for modes of moral reflection that are directly informed by feelings, we at the same time distance ourselves from an understanding of moral reflection as fully rational. We can thus justly say that it is because some impartiality criticisms at least tacitly rely on the narrower conception of rationality that they conclude that rejecting the idea of an impartial morality is tantamount to rejecting the idea of a rational one.[5]

There are also other impartiality criticisms that, far from relying on the specific conception of rationality that seems to underwrite this conclusion, are expressly concerned to challenge it. Some of these undertake to show—in a manner that implies a rebuke to the narrower conception of rationality—that emotional endowments we possess as people with emotional attachments of different kinds may be essential to who we are in the sense of being internal to our rational moral capacities. These impartiality criticisms maintain both that there are moral values that are intelligible only in terms of certain attitudes and that the (at least imaginative) possession of certain attitudes is a necessary precondition of following fully rational lines of thought about such values. This position is clearly laid out, for instance, in the writings of Bernard Williams, the advocate of the most influential impartiality criticism that proceeds along these lines. Williams claims not only that concepts for moral values function within particular attitudes or interests but also that it may not be possible to grasp (what he sees as) rational connections among individual applications of such concepts apart from an appreciation of the relevant attitudes or interests. Williams himself once put it this way:

> How we "go on" from one application of a concept to another is a function of the kind of interest that the concept represents, and we should not assume that we could see how people "go on" if we did

5. For a representative example of an impartiality criticism that takes this form, see e.g., Lawrence Thomas, "Trust, Affirmation, and Moral Character: A Critique of a Kantian Morality," in *Identity, Character and Morality: Essays in Moral Judgment*, ed. Owen Flanagan and Amélie Rorty (Cambridge, MA: MIT Press, 1990), pp. 235–257.

not share the evaluative perspective in which this kind of concept has its point.[6]

Part of what is striking about the view of moral concepts that Williams describes is that it represents a direct challenge to the authority of the narrower conception of rationality. This is striking because, in mounting such a challenge, the view implies that insistence on an abstract or impartial survey of a situation may, instead of helping us to arrive at a more accurate assessment of it, serve to limit or distort rational, moral understanding. We might accordingly say that it is by turning on the narrower conception of rationality that some impartiality criticisms— such as Williams's—attempt to justify the repudiation of traditional impartialist approaches in ethics.[7]

Impartiality criticisms encounter a great deal of resistance, and it should come as no surprise that rejoinders to them are generally formulated in terms of the narrower conception of rationality. What originally drives insistence on the enormously influential understanding of moral reflection that the criticisms target—an understanding of it as

6. Bernard Williams, *Ethics and the Limits of Philosophy* (Cambridge, MA: Harvard University Press, 1985), p. 141. Even the most nuanced rejoinders to impartiality criticisms typically overlook the fact that some of the criticisms aim to bring certain emotional endowments inside our rational capacities. Thus, e.g., one of Barbara Herman's more recent rejoinders to impartiality criticisms is grounded in the thought, which she takes to be foreign to the criticisms, that "the affective life is not in general independent of various norms of rationality" ("Agency, Attachment and Difference," in *The Practice of Moral Judgment*, pp. 184–207, p. 189). Herman presents herself as adding a fresh insight to conversations about impartiality criticisms when she argues that our interests and emotional attachments are often products of reflection that can be "'normalized' to varying degrees to the principles of practical agency, both moral and nonmoral" (ibid., p. 198). Although in developing this argument Herman makes room for considerations supplied by our attachments that do not require abstract scrutiny and that accordingly do not call for the kind of dissociation that fans of impartiality criticisms oppose (compare note 4), she nevertheless overlooks the fact that some advocates of impartiality criticisms, such as Williams, agree with her in thinking that our interests and attachments can be "normalized" and disagree only in thinking that the exercises of reflection internal to "normalization" essentially presuppose certain emotional endowments. Or, to put it in other words, she overlooks the fact that some advocates of impartiality criticisms are prepared go significantly further than she is in denying that "affective life is in general independent of various norms of rationality."

7. For relevant references to Williams's work, see note 1. See also Williams's *Shame and Necessity* (Berkeley, CA: University of California Press, 1993), a work that contains a rich discussion, in connection with ancient Greek thought, of the understanding of ethical identity that Williams prefers and that he thinks is excluded by traditional impartialist ethical theories. For references to other impartiality criticisms that, like Williams's, start from the critique of the narrower conception of rationality just described, see note 9.

impartial in a sense that includes an abstraction from all feelings—is a commitment to an understanding of such reflection as fully rational, together with a commitment to the narrower conception on which an abstraction from all feelings is a mark of the rational. However, although it is unsurprising that rejoinders to impartiality criticisms are generally formulated in narrowly rational terms, it is nevertheless interesting that such rejoinders by and large fail even to register that some of the criticisms specifically aim to question this conception. Impartiality criticisms are typically received as if they constituted a uniform family whose members all simply took for granted a problem-space determined by the narrower conception. Their call to reject an impartialist approach in ethics is for the most part greeted as a call for an understanding of moral reflection as failing to attain to our ideals of rationality and fairness. And their claim that it is only by abandoning an impartialist approach in ethics that we can place the right sort of importance on personal attachments is for the most part greeted as a claim to the effect that we are forced to choose between, on the one hand, placing the right sort of importance on such attachments and, on the other, preserving an understanding of moral reflection as intrinsically rational and fair.

Although there is a sense in which, as I just argued, this uniform rejoinder to impartiality criticisms fails to do justice to the concerns of those who challenge the authority of the narrower conception of rationality, there is also a competing sense in which the rejoinder is in fact justified. Even those impartiality criticisms that proceed by defending permissive conceptions of moral rationality generally do so on the basis of what might be described as merely local challenges to the narrower conception's authority. These criticisms do not typically engage in a gesture of wholesale rejection of the idea, distinctive of this conception, that our rational capacities essentially exclude our capacities of feeling. Instead, they typically suggest that the narrower conception of rationality governs non-moral discourse and that moral discourse is anomalous in failing to be governed by it. They thus present us with a view of moral thinking on which it is beholden to considerations that, while rational, are not only different from but also less stringent than considerations that get adduced in non-moral thinking.

One of the more striking implications of impartiality criticisms that have this basic form is that our moral conclusions, even when in some sense 'rationally' justified, are essentially at risk of being undermined by non-moral reflections. Bernard Williams is, to return for a moment to his work on these matters, refreshingly frank about this. The point, in Williams's well turned phrase, is that "reflection destroys [ethical] knowledge."[8] Bearing this point in mind, we can say that even thinkers who frame their critiques of moral impartiality as calls for a more permissive conception of moral rationality effectively represent the abandonment of such impartiality as tantamount to the abandonment of an understanding of moral reflection as rational in the fullest sense.[9] This means that there is a respect in which these thinkers' opponents are right to group them together with advocates of less nuanced impartiality criticisms and to depict the members of both groups as in agreement in rejecting the idea of moral rationality.

I just argued that both critics and defenders of the idea of an impartial morality tend to take for granted, at least to a significant extent, restrictions internal to the narrower conception of rationality. My argument reveals the possibility of making an original contribution to debates about impartiality in ethics as follows. The idea would be to change the debates' structure by defending a position in ethics that resembles impartiality criticisms of different stripes in attacking an understanding of morality as abstracting from all feelings but that differs from them in grounding such an attack in a thoroughgoing repudiation of the logic of the narrower conception of rationality. It is not difficult to see that the view of ethics presented in this book has the structure of just such a position. This view is grounded in the rejection of the idea of an abstraction requirement and in the consequent endorsement of an image of our discursive capacities as necessarily informed by acquired sensitivities (1.2, 2.1–2.2 and 3.2). Insofar as the view takes this image for granted, it both implies a deep criticism of the assumption, distinctive of the narrower conception of rationality, that it must in theory be possible to grasp the connections constitutive of rational line of thought

8. Williams, *Ethics and the Limits of Philosophy*, p. 148. See also Bernard Williams, "Who Needs Ethical Knowledge?" in *Making Sense of Humanity and Other Philosophical Papers* (Cambridge: Cambridge University Press, 1995), pp. 203–212.

9. See also in this connection the writings of Michael Stocker (e.g., "How Emotions Reveal Value and Help Cure the Schizophrenia of Modern Ethical Theories," in *How Should One Live? Essays on the Virtues*, ed. Roger Crisp [Oxford: Clarendon Press, 1996], pp. 173–190) and Lawrence Blum (e.g., "Moral Perception and Particularity," *Ethics* 101 (1991): 701–725).

independently of the possession of any particular sensitivities and provides support for the assumption, distinctive of what I am calling the wider conception of rationality, that our ability to grasp the connections constitutive of a rational line of thought invariably presupposes the possession of certain sensitivities (3.2.ii and 4.1). One significant consequence of this reliance on the wider conception is that the view of ethics developed here equips us to defend the claim—championed with at best qualified success within Williamsian impartiality criticisms— that insistence on surveying a situation from a maximally abstract vantage point may as such limit or distort rational moral understanding.

While this view of ethics resembles impartiality criticisms in targeting the idea of an abstract morality, it would be misleading to characterize it as opposed to moral *impartiality*. "Impartiality" refers to an epistemic ideal with close ties to our ideals of rationality and fairness, an ideal that we attain to the extent that we recognize and treat the same as the same. But the view I advocate is not in the business of challenging this ideal or of representing it as beyond our reach in the moral sphere. It would be more accurate to say that what is in question in my preferred view of ethics is a challenge to a philosophically influential conception of the ideal that stipulates, in a manner respectful of the logic of the narrower conception of rationality, that an abstraction from all feelings is necessary to the ideal's attainment.[10]

It might seem as though this philosophically influential conception of impartiality is simply dictated by our ordinary modes of thought and speech and is accordingly compulsory. We ordinarily say things to the effect that, for example, "in order to be impartial you need to look at things dispassionately." But this ordinary way of talking is in fact philosophically quite innocent. When we use "impartial" in such ordinary contexts, we are using it to mean an abstraction from those routes of feeling that threaten to distort moral judgment, but we are not taking a

10. It would be no less misleading to describe my preferred view as calling for moral *partiality*. "Partiality" refers to bias or distance from the ideal of impartiality, and the view I favor is not in the business of insisting on such bias or suggesting that it is inevitable in the moral sphere. This view might more aptly be described as challenging a philosophically influential interpretation of the notion of partiality that stipulates, in a manner respectful of the logic of the narrower conception of rationality, that any emotional influence has an essential tendency to make us partial in the sense of removing us from a fair or impartial stance.

stand on the philosophical question of whether every affective propensity we have as such represents a potential threat to such judgment. This is the question that the view I favor answers in the negative. It follows that it would be more accurate to describe the position as aiming not to impugn moral impartiality per se but rather to replace a philosophically influential conception of such impartiality with an alternative conception that stipulates, in accordance with the logic of the wider conception of rationality, that there is something confused about the assumption that an abstraction from everything affective is necessary to attaining it. We might say that, far from rejecting impartiality, my view takes for granted a widely rational conception of it and stands opposed only to approaches in ethics that insist on conceiving impartiality in narrowly rational terms.

Moreover, to the extent that this view thus resolutely repudiates the narrower conception of rationality, it is properly regarded as containing a criticism of traditional approaches in ethics that is more fundamental than any impartiality criticism. Where the view in question goes all the way to the conception of rationality that originally makes traditional approaches seem compulsory, impartiality criticisms, insofar as they preserve this conception at least to some extent, continue to bear a significant kinship to traditional approaches. Indeed, although within conversations about impartiality in ethics we are typically invited to focus on the gulf separating traditional approaches in ethics from impartiality criticisms, it is fair to say that there is a more basic philosophical difference running between, on the one hand, an approach in ethics that plainly rejects the narrower conception of rationality and, on the other, more traditional approaches in ethics together with the set of impartiality criticisms that agree with them in relying on it.

My reflections in this section derive their piquancy from the fact that debates about impartiality in ethics adjudicate specifically moral concerns about traditional, narrowly impartialist approaches in ethics. Thus far I have limited myself to describing these concerns in terms of a worry about whether traditional approaches allow us to do justice to conditions of our moral identity. I have argued that, although advocates of impartiality criticisms develop such a worry in different ways, they uniformly fail to proceed in a manner that leaves our entitlement to the notion of moral rationality intact and that in this respect the approach in ethics taken in this book is superior. What interests me now is a respect in which the worry is often further developed. This brings me to my main topic, the topic of moralism.

## 6.2 "Moralism" as a Term of Criticism

> Suppose we think of [a] background of responsiveness [to life] as what gives rise to explicit moral thought and particular decisions. Then it looks as if moral philosophers, and (more generally) people reflecting on ethics, should attend to the texture of life, to modes of responsiveness, and to the relation between texture of life and particular acts, thoughts, responses . . . But the conclusion may be resisted; the kind of approach to morality that gets called *moralistic* can lead to a rejection of the argument that we should attend to modes of responsiveness to life.
>
> ~ Cora Diamond, *"Moral Differences and Distances:*
> *Some Questions" in* Commonality and Particularity in
> Ethics, *ed. Lilli Alanen et al. (1997), pp. 221–222.*

Consider what, at the most fundamental level, seems to speak for the form of dissociation from feelings that is under investigation within debates about impartiality in ethics. Within more traditional approaches in ethics, the relevant form of dissociation appears to be nothing more and nothing less than a basic requirement of moral responsibility. It takes on the aspect of such a requirement against the background of the assumption, distinctive of the narrower conception of rationality, that it must be possible to grasp the connections constitutive of a rational line of thought independently of the possession of any particular endowments of feeling. Against this background, it appears that our affective propensities are necessarily external to any rational, moral capacities we possess and that these propensities accordingly lack any inherent tendency to correspond to the deliverances of such capacities. Further, it also appears that if we want to insure that our feelings don't lead us morally astray we therefore need to regulate them in accordance with prior moral judgments, where such judgments are understood as presupposing a vantage point that abstracts from all feelings. The result is that it seems as though, in order to be morally responsible, we need to adopt an approach to managing our feelings that is characterized by a form of reflective abstraction or dissociation from them. For, given these considerations, it seems reasonable to think that any willingness we manifest to allow our feelings to be engaged apart from the guidance of prior (dissociation-involving) moral judgments will leave us vulnerable to a charge of moral laxity or worse.

One way of capturing the interest of impartiality criticisms is to say that they suggest that this worry about moral laxity is misplaced. This suggestion is made especially clearly within those members of the group of impartiality criticisms that contain local challenges to the narrower conception of rationality. These impartiality criticisms presuppose that it is impossible to make moral discriminations apart from the possession of particular endowments of feeling and that in this respect some endowments of feeling are internal to moral understanding. By the lights of these impartiality criticisms, it appears that, in order to remain receptive to certain kinds of moral growth, we need to leave ourselves open to new emotional influences (say, influences that run counter to our moral beliefs as they stand). Further, it appears that moral responsibility speaks for an approach to managing feelings that is free from any tendency, of the sort characteristic of traditional approaches in ethics, to insist on regulating them in accordance with prior moral judgments. The problem with this tone of insistence, as it now seems, is that in adopting it we wrongly exclude the possibility that certain forms of moral instruction (viz., those that directly address our feelings) may be rationally up to snuff, and we thereby cut ourselves off from modes of thought that may enable us to recognize defects in our own moral outlook or virtues in someone else's. The result is that insistence on allowing our feelings to be engaged only in accordance with prior moral judgments, far from seeming like a morally responsible austerity measure (as it does within traditional approaches in ethics), seems like an unnecessarily harsh and morally dangerous one.

This tone of insistence is sometimes described, within impartiality criticisms, as the mark of a species of *moralism*. Williams, for instance, condemns as "richly moralistic" efforts to subject feelings to the governance of prior moral judgments—or, as he at one point puts it, efforts to bring feelings within morality "from the beginning."[11]

The charge of moralism that Williams and others thus level has by no means been ignored by advocates of more traditional approaches in ethics. But the style of its reception has tended to repeat what I described above as a basic limitation of rejoinders to impartiality criti-

11. Williams, "Persons, Character and Morality," p. 16.

cisms. Although the charge is developed most fully within impartiality criticisms that contain partial attacks on the authority of the narrower conception of rationality, it is for the most part received as if it were addressed to moral defects—such as judgmentalism and rigorism—that are recognizable as the kinds of moral problems they are within the framework of this conception. Thus, although it is, for instance, possible to find many genuinely convincing arguments to the effect that Kant's ethical theory remains untainted by "moralism" understood as a matter of judgmentalism or rigorism,[12] it is difficult to find even one such argument that addresses a kind of moralism that resists analysis in narrowly rational terms—and, by the same token, difficult to find even one that succeeds in addressing the specific worry about moralism to which some impartiality criticisms give voice.

There is a sense in which impartiality criticisms are themselves responsible for this failure. Because, as I have been arguing, they continue to draw at least to some extent on the logic of the narrower conception of rationality (see 6.1), they in effect preserve for their interlocutors the idea of a vantage point from which to discern that insistence on regulating our emotional lives in accordance with prior moral judgments (i.e., the very tone of insistence that they themselves hope to get us to see as moralistic) is nothing more than a basic requirement of moral responsibility. And, in this way, they make it difficult to recognize the species of moralism that they originally set out to elucidate as even a conceptual possibility.

The view of ethics laid out in this book is fundamentally different. This view takes for granted the logic of the wider conception of rationality, and in consequence it differs from impartiality criticisms in suggesting that there is something confused about the very idea of a vantage point outside individuals' affective lives from which to determine that moral responsibility calls for bringing these lives within morality "from the beginning." At the same time, the view also differs from impartiality criticisms, not only in making the widely rational sug-

12. See, e.g., Thomas Hill Jr., "Kant's Anti-Moralistic Strain," *Dignity and Practical Reason in Kant's Moral Theory* (Ithaca, NY: Cornell University Press, 1992), pp. 176–195; Christine Korsgaard, "The Reasons We Can Share," *Creating the Kingdom of Ends* (Cambridge: Cambridge University Press, 1996), pp. 275–310; and Onora O'Neill, "Kant After Virtue," *Constructions of Reason: Explorations of Kant's Practical Philosophy* (Cambridge: Cambridge University Press, 1989), pp. 145–164.

gestion that (without regard to its form) rational moral thought is essentially informed by and expressive of individuals' sensibilities, but also in thereby suggesting that demands for regulating the play of sensibility in accordance with prior moral judgments represent an unqualified and entirely general threat to the development of moral understanding.

This particular concern about moralism, which is rarely registered in contemporary moral philosophy,[13] bears directly on the different moral judgment-centered approaches in ethics that I am criticizing in this book. A tendency toward modes of thought and conduct that are moralistic in this sense is, as I just pointed out, a direct expression of respect for the narrower conception of rationality. This conception in turn is held in place by the abstract epistemological requirement that I am calling an abstraction requirement (3.2.ii and 4.1), and the idea of such a requirement, in addition to seeming to speak for the narrower conception of rationality, seems to speak for the narrower conception of objectivity that leads moral philosophers to fixate on moral judgments (1.1). So, to the extent that it is driven by allegiance to the narrower conception of objectivity and the abstraction requirement that fixes this conception in place, moral philosophers' preoccupation with moral judgments is rightly represented as a sign of a trend toward a moralistic attitude that directly threatens the growth of moral understanding—and that we can only overcome by directing attention in ethics beyond moral judgments to the whole rich fabrics of individuals' lives. *This* is the moral criticism of moral-judgment centered approaches in ethics implied by this book's central argument.

## 6.3 Additional Examples of Moralism

> There is no escaping the fact that want of sympathy condemns us to a corresponding stupidity.
>
> ~ *George Eliot*, Daniel Deronda *(1995), p. 596.*

If we help ourselves to this book's description of forms of moral thought that do not involve the application of moral concepts, we can capture

---

13. For some notable exceptions, see Cora Diamond, "Moral Differences and Distances: Some Questions"; Stanley Cavell, *Conditions Handsome and Unhandsome* (Chicago: University of Chicago Press, 1990); and Annette Baier, "Moralism and Cruelty: Reflections on Hume and Kant," in *Moral Prejudices: Essays on Ethics* (Cambridge, MA: Harvard University Press, 1994), pp. 268–293, esp. 275 and 283–285.

what is striking about the complaint about moralism that I just leveled against traditional moral judgment-centered views of ethics as follows. We can say that this complaint about moralism has to do with moral differences that are functions of divergences in our stances toward the sensibilities that compose the (individual) images of the world we pre-suppose in applying moral concepts. Further, we can say that the complaint is thus concerned with moral differences—of a type described earlier in this book—that are not as such a matter of disagreements about how or whether to apply particular moral concepts (1.4). The point here is not that the problem of moralism monopolizes the field of such moral differences. We are justified in speaking of moral differences that cannot be wholly captured in terms of disagreements about how or whether to apply moral concepts whenever we encounter substantial divergences between individuals' sensibilities or entire personalities. The complaint about moralism I just isolated is simply concerned with one subset of these moral differences, and it is with an eye to showing that the kind of moral differences in question is anything but unfamiliar that in this section I offer a set of further illustrations of this complaint.

### 6.3.i  *Theodor Fontane's* Effi Briest

> He had a great deal of good in his nature and was as fine a man as any one can be who doesn't really love.
> ∼ *Effi on Innstetten in Theodor Fontane*, Effi Briest *(1967), p. 266.*

One good place to turn for examples of the relevant species of moralism (hereafter simply "moralism") is the novels of Theodor Fontane. Fontane's novels, which are largely written in the 1880s and 1890s and are for the most part set in and around contemporaneous Berlin, depict a society pervaded by moralism. The novels describe a social world in which there is widespread agreement on an alleged need to subject feelings to the prior guidance of established moral principles. Further, they represent this tendency, in a manner that expresses a recognition of it as a moral problem of the relevant kind, as a threat to the growth of moral intelligence and the flourishing of personal relationships. Fontane's different literary evocations of this moralistic trend, considered together, are part of a larger picture of Bismarck's Prussia in which the aristocracy is in decline and the newly ascendant middle class is shallow and culturally barren. Again and again, Fontane invites his readers to understand the pertinent trend as an expression of the morally dangerous efforts of a fading aristocratic elite to exert itself and to preserve its authority. He thus effectively presents readers with a number of socially and historically quite specific portraits of the dangers of moralism. One of the most compelling of these portraits is drawn in his best known novel, *Effi Briest*, and in this section I want to make a case for thinking of moralism as a recognizable moral problem by describing this particular novel's treatment of it.

I proceed by first commenting on a reading of *Effi Briest* by Julia Annas. In a 1984 paper, Annas invites us to understand Fontane's novel as containing (what I am calling) an impartiality criticism.[14] Annas's main thesis is that the novel illustrates, in her words, "dangers implicit in regarding morality as essentially a matter of impartiality" and, more specifically, that, given the novel's Protestant Prussian setting, it is appropriate to take this illustration as implying a rebuke to Kant.[15] Annas's reading is attractive in that she successfully brings out how the novel represents certain features of our lives as available only to the person of refined feelings and how it thus effectively repudiates the idea that the vantage point of moral reflection is an abstract one. But there is also a respect in which her reading is plainly unsatisfactory. Like other advocates of impartiality criticisms, Annas assumes that rejecting the idea of an abstract morality is equivalent to rejecting an understanding of moral reflection as rational in the fullest sense. Annas tends to impose this—by my lights, wrongheaded—assumption on the novel, and this tendency leads her to overlook some of the subtlety and intricacy of its moral vision. One of my ambitions in what follows is to underline aspects of Fontane's novel that Annas in this manner obscures. My larger ambition is thereby to show that the novel contains a philosophically more provocative criticism of Kantian approaches in ethics (and, indeed, also of other traditional, narrowly impartialist approaches) than Annas ultimately describes—a criticism that might aptly be summarized by speaking, in my terms, of "the problem of moralism."

14. Julia Annas, "Personal Love and Kantian Ethics in *Effi Briest*," *Philosophy and Literature* 8, no. 1 (April 1984): 15–31.
    15. Ibid., pp. 15–16.

Annas's discussion of *Effi Briest* focuses largely on the character of Innstetten and, more particularly, on the dramatically central scene, toward the end of the novel, in which Innstetten deliberates about how to respond to his discovery of an adulterous affair that his wife—Effi— had six years earlier. In just a moment, I turn to Annas's claims about how Fontane's portrait of Innstetten implies a criticism of Kant's conception of morality. But before considering Annas's work, I want to briefly sketch relevant elements of the narrative.

Effi and Innstetten become engaged and marry, in an arrangement that is both blessed by Effi's parents and also sanctioned by aristocratic mores, when Effi is sixteen and Innstetten is already an accomplished middle-aged bureaucrat embarked on a promising career. The difference between Effi's and Innstetten's ages, in itself striking, is easily matched by differences between their characters. Where Innstetten is a man of "- fundamental principles" who also has an inclination toward sententious- ness, Effi is an impetuous and imaginative teenager who sees herself, more or less accurately, as someone who "hasn't got any" principles.[16] These differences seem to promise trouble, and once Effi and Innstet- ten are married and installed in Kessin, the sleepy northern port town in which Innstetten is provincial governor, trouble is indeed quick to arrive. While a dutiful husband, Innstetten is an insensitive and tepid lover who doesn't cater to his wife's craving for affection and amuse- ment. Effi grows predictably restless and is easily seduced by a member of the local militia—a Major von Crampas—whose only real recom- mendation is that he desires her sexually. The affair is broken off when Innstetten is promoted to a ministry in Berlin, and the family moves. Neither Effi nor Crampas is sorry to see it end. Indeed, for her part, Effi is positively relieved. She has learned from the experience and is no longer attracted to the excitement of danger. Her marriage with Innstet- ten is now healthier, and it flourishes for six years—until one day Innstetten accidentally discovers Effi's letters from Crampas. Innstet- ten's response to his discovery is violently punitive. He challenges Crampas to a duel and then, having killed him, divorces Effi and cuts her off from her child.

What leads Innstetten to take this drastic step? Annas's answer to this question forms the centerpiece of her reading of the novel. She stresses,

---

16. Theodor Fontane, *Effi Briest*, trans. Douglas Parmée (London: Penguin, 1967), p. 39.

to begin with, that Innstetten is not driven by anger or lust for revenge. This is brought out, she observes, by the fact that he at one point says to his friend and confidante Wüllersdorf:

> I love my wife, yes, strange to say, I still love her, and however frightful all these things appear to me, yet I'm so much under her spell, she's so lovable and so gay, she has such a special charm all her own, that, in spite of myself, I feel tempted, in my heart of hearts, to forgive her.[17]

When he starts to explain to Wüllersdorf his reason for acting as he does, Innstetten declares that "individuals cannot escape society." Later, he adds that in any case he cannot live with the awareness that someone else knows of the "stain" on his honor.[18] At first it accordingly appears that Innstetten, far from taking himself to be morally obliged to act in a certain way, simply feels beholden to certain social conventions. But—and this is something that Annas takes pains to point out—the novel emphasizes that Innstetten has significant resources of character and that, despite his talk about what society demands, he in fact honestly believes that it is his duty to categorically condemn Effi's conduct. This is made clear in a late scene in which Innstetten, besieged by doubts about whether he was right to fight Crampas, reassesses his own conduct. What is striking is that even at this point forgiving Effi does not occur to him as an option. He now says to himself:

> I should have burnt the letters and the world should never have heard of them. And when she came to me, all unsuspecting, I should have said to her: "There's where you belong" and cut myself off from her. Inwardly, not in the eyes of the world.[19]

The main point here is not that we (contemporary readers) find even this envisioned gesture of inward alienation extreme but that the novel itself invites us to regard it as disproportionate. After all, we are shown that Effi's marriage was never one of romantic love and that certain ob-

---

17. Ibid., p. 214. For Annas's discussion of this passage, see "Personal Love," p. 19.
18. Fontane, *Effi Briest*, pp. 215–216.
19. Ibid., p. 222. For Annas's discussion of this passage, see "Personal Love," p. 20.

vious pitfalls for her were built into it from the start. Moreover, we are also repeatedly shown that Prussian society has an accepting and even light hearted attitude toward men's liaisons and at least a tolerant one toward their adulterous affairs. The novel's suggestion at this juncture is accordingly that Innstetten's fixation on condemning Effi bespeaks not merely a failure to pursue an appropriate course of conduct but, moreover, a failure even to perceive it.

This suggestion is central to Annas's account of the novel's criticism of Kant. Annas is not interested in arguing that Innstetten's deliberations conclude with a principle of action that qualifies as morally permissible by Kant's lights. What interests her is observing that his deliberations can be seen as having "the *form* of Kantian moral thinking."[20] When Annas describes Innstetten's characteristic modes of thought as thus formally Kantian, she means that it is characteristic of Innstetten to try to satisfy Kant's conditions on appropriate moral modes of thought by distancing himself as far as he can from every emotional influence. She points out that Innstetten is a man for whom duty is something "grasped by abstracting from all personal considerations," and she argues that the novel is best read as illustrating that there is something morally troubling about Innstetten's reflections insofar as they take this Kantian form.[21] On her reading, the novel depicts Innstetten as someone who has a glimmering of "the depth and significance of a shared life of mutual affection" as long as he has his feelings for Effi before his mind and who loses touch with his understanding of these matters when he insists on abstracting from "feelings that go against his principles."[22] This is the basic criticism of Kant that, according to Annas, Fontane's treatment of Innstetten implies. It implies that if, like Innstetten, we insist on trying to survey our lives in an impersonal and hence formally Kantian manner, we run the risk of degrading feelings that are essential to who we are and, at the same time, also of thereby handicapping our own moral understanding.

Annas argues very persuasively that this criticism gets developed not only in connection with Innstetten but also in connection with a range of other characters. Effi's parents resemble her husband in that they both suppress their own feelings for her in reflecting on what duty re-

20. Ibid., p. 23; stress in the original.
21. Ibid., p. 19.
22. Ibid., p. 20.

quires and conclude that they are obliged to categorically condemn her actions. (For them, this involves banishing her from their home.) To be sure, the Briests differ from Innstetten in that they eventually let Effi back into their lives. But, as Annas points out, they do so partly because Effi's father is, with the passage of time, inclined to allow his love for his daughter to shape his view of her transgression and also because he is accordingly happy to let Effi's doctor persuade him to take care of her. The case of the Briests thus provides further support for a reading of *Effi Briest* as attacking the idea that the proper standpoint of moral reflection is one that abstracts from all feelings.[23] And something similar can also be said about the case of the character Roswitha, another of Annas's examples. Although Roswitha, a Catholic peasant employed as one of Effi's maids, is clearly not very bright, she nevertheless differs from Innstetten and the Briests both in her possession of strong and responsive feelings and in her consistently good understanding of the human significance of Effi's ordeal.[24] The novel's treatment of this humble character thus reinforces the message that some features of our lives are available only to the person with a developed heart.

Annas's account of how Fontane's sketches of his characters thus spell out an anti-Kantian moral message is, in these respects, genuinely helpful. There are, however, further respects in which her account is simply inaccurate. Annas takes Fontane to be suggesting that in order to grasp certain features of their lives characters like Innstetten and the Briests need not only to abandon their insistence on abstract modes of moral scrutiny but, by the same token, to give up any adherence to moral *principles*. This is very clear, for instance, in Annas's discussion of Innstetten. After posing the question of why Innstetten is unable to forgive Effi, Annas delivers the following answer: "It is because he is a man of principle."[25] Annas thinks that Fontane must be targeting moral principles as such because she assumes, in a manner respectful of what I am calling the narrower conception of rationality, that if we allow feelings to directly inform moral reflection there can no longer be any question of our authoritatively picking out modes of conduct that are principled in the sense of being composed of rationally respectable regularities. We

23. See Annas's discussion of the Briests, ibid., p. 28.
24. See Annas's discussion of Roswitha, ibid., p. 27.
25. Ibid., p. 20.

might accordingly say that Annas tacitly excludes the possibility of a—wider—conception of rationality that is capable of underwriting principled modes of conduct in the absence of a demand for abstraction from all feelings. This gesture of exclusion, far from being peculiar to Annas, is, as we saw, characteristic of advocates of impartiality criticisms. What gives it interest here is that it leads Annas to obscure some of the moral complexity of Fontane's novel.

The characters in *Effi Briest* who are presented as morally most admirable are those who, in addition to possessing deep feelings, *also* adhere to principle. This includes Gieshübler, the hunchbacked chemist of Kessin. Gieshübler is Effi's most devoted friend during her years in Kessin, and as readers we are invited to admire the modest grace with which he manages his relationship with Effi and also his relationships with other friends and acquaintances. It is accordingly noteworthy that Gieshübler, in addition to having the kind of warm and responsive nature that allows him to sympathize quickly with Effi's desires and fears,[26] is also clearly, as Innstetten at one point puts it, "a man with principles."[27] Any adequate list of the novel's morally most admirable characters would also need to include the elderly Frau von Padden. Frau von Padden, a representative of the aristocracy around Kessin, is distinguished in the novel by the fact that, when she first meets Effi at a ball, she is capable not only of immediately detecting Effi's weakness for Crampas but also of recognizing that, despite this weakness, Effi is nevertheless supremely innocent. Given the positive moral assessment that the novel thus invites, it is apposite that Frau von Padden is described as equally admirable for the rigor of her principles as for her humane and richly cultivated sense of humor.[28]

Nor do we need to rely on observations about auxiliary characters like Gieshübler and Frau von Padden to establish that *Effi Briest* treats a commitment to moral principles as consistent with the kind of emotional responsiveness that it extols. There can be no understanding of the basic moral predicament of the novel's central characters, Effi and Innstetten, apart from the recognition that the novel is not concerned

---

26. Upon learning the news of Effi's adultery and Innstetten's duel, years after the two have left Kessin, Gieshübler breaks down in tears (ibid., p. 223).

27. Ibid., p. 122.

28. Ibid., pp. 154–155 and 188.

to impugn moral principles as such. Effi is originally presented as a free-spirited and largely unprincipled girl who slides easily into error.[29] But by the end of her life, several years after her divorce, she has matured significantly. Although shortly after the divorce she cursed Innstetten for turning her child against her, she now tells her own mother that she wants Innstetten to know that she died believing that he was right. Effi concludes her speech about Innstetten with these words: "He had a great deal of good in his nature and was as fine a man as any one can be who doesn't really love."[30] It is important to appreciate that this is both genuine praise and also deeply insightful criticism. Innstetten attempts to act on sound principles, and we miss what is right about Effi's approval of him if we assume that there is something intrinsically wrong with doing that. But Innstetten also refuses to let his heart run free of an ossified set of inherited moral principles. This is what Effi has in mind when she says that "he doesn't really love," and what she now sees clearly is that it is a tragic flaw. Innstetten's failure to love in this sense is what prevents him—until after he has destroyed all of the emotional attachments that once gave his life meaning—from suspecting that a more enlightened and still principled mode of conduct was open to him.

In the final analysis, it is wrong to follow Annas in reading *Effi Briest* as structured by narrowly rational assumptions that force us to choose between allowing feelings to directly inform moral reflections and remaining committed to the pursuit of impartially available, principled modes of conduct. It would be more appropriate to read the novel as containing not a narrowly rational lesson about how there is something amiss with moral principles as such but rather a widely rational one about how understanding the world in a way that allows us to formulate and apply sound moral principles requires the resources of an educated heart. Moreover, read in this manner, the novel can be seen as suggesting a more interesting criticism of Kant than Annas describes—a criticism that depends for its force on a thoroughgoing repudiation of the narrower conception of rationality that, within the framework of Kant's thought, seems to speak for construing the moral standpoint as ideally abstract.

---

29. Thus, at the time at which Effi is conducting her affair with Crampas, we see her hypocritically reprimanding Roswitha for telling salacious tales and for flirting with the coachman (ibid., pp. 163–164 and 173).

30. Ibid., p. 266.

This correction to Annas's reading of *Effi Briest* permits us to characterize the novel as concerned with moralism. The point here is not that the correction permits us to read the novel as inviting us to regard a tendency to insist on mistrusting any feelings that don't accord with prior moral judgments as unduly harsh and morally dangerous. It is true that the novel issues an invitation on these lines—above all, via its descriptions of Innstetten and the Briests—and it is also true that the fact that it does so is, in significant part, what licenses us to describe it as preoccupied with moralism. But if nothing more were at stake we would be able to fully capture what *Effi Briest* has to teach us about moralism without going beyond Annas's reading. The point here is that we need the above correction to Annas's reading to see that the novel is preoccupied with moralism in my sense. We need to register that the novel helps itself to the logic of the wider conception of rationality. For it is only insofar as we at least tacitly register this fact that we can recognize that many of Fontane's characters (e.g., Innstetten and the Briests) suffer from a moral defect, of the sort that I am describing as "moralistic," that involves refusing to trust feelings that oppose one's current moral beliefs and, at the same time, refusing to entertain certain rationally respectable considerations that speak for a different understanding of situations in which one finds oneself. It is thus in the light of this proposed correction to Annas that it first seems reasonable to credit *Effi Briest* with furnishing a vivid illustration of the kind of concern about moralism that interests me.

Notice that we are clearly justified in characterizing this concern about moralism as having to do with the distinctive kind of moral differences, touched on earlier in this book, that don't take the form of disagreements about how or whether to apply particular moral concepts. To say that Innstetten and the Briests are moralistic in my sense is to make a claim about the stances they adopt toward the development of feelings or sensibility. These characters inhibit the growth of their own feelings in ways that check their development of visions of the world to ground their projections of moral concepts. Insofar as the gulf Innstetten's and the Briests' moralistic manners create between Effi and themselves is thus in the first instance a gulf between visions of the world to which moral concepts apply, it follows that it resists being fully captured in the form of a disagreement (or set of disagreements) about the employment of moral concepts. Indeed the novel foregrounds the fact that it is concerned with this particular kind of moral difference by showing us that at the end of her life Effi agrees with Innstetten and her parents in judging that her affair with Crampas was wrong and that nevertheless, morally speaking, she continues to stand worlds apart from them.

It is not difficult to see that the concern about moralism I am here discussing is immune to the kind of rejoinder that routinely gets made, on behalf of traditional approaches in ethics, within ongoing conversations about moralism. Consider in this connection the efforts of a critic of Julia Annas—Marcia Baron—to show that *Effi Briest* fails to underwrite talk of "Kant's moralism."[31] Baron argues, against what she takes to be Annas's position, that it is wrong to think that Innstetten exhibits any forms of harshness or judgmentalism that Kant condones and hence wrong to take Fontane's description of Innstetten as showing that Kant is moralistic. The particular forms of harshness and judgmentalism that Baron takes Innstetten to exhibit include placing value on actions that defy inclination, insisting on rigid compliance with established principles and tending to pass judgment on others. Baron argues, compellingly, and along lines well drawn in recent conversations about Kant's moral philosophy, that Kant in no way sanctions any of *these* modes of conduct.[32] But Baron never even considers the possibility that Innstetten suffers from a moral defect, of the sort that I am placing under the heading of "moralism," that depends for its cogency on a conception of what rationality is like that is very different from Kant's. Moreover, although this means that there is an important sense in which she is thus a fitting interlocutor for Annas, who likewise leaves unquestioned the conception of rationality that informs Kant's ethical theory, it also means that Baron ultimately fails even to engage the worry about moralism that the novel in fact expresses. Indeed, it would not be inaccurate to say that Baron betrays a deafness to this worry of the sort that is, as we saw, characteristic of recent conversations about the problem of moralism.

*Effi Briest* is not the only work of Fontane's that addresses moralism

31. See Marcia Baron, "Was Effi Briest a Victim of Kantian Morality," *Philosophy and Literature* 12, no. 1 (April 1998): 95–113.

32. Ibid., esp. pp. 97–98. For other attempts to defend Kant against the kinds of charges of moralism Baron considers, see note 12, above.

as I have defined it. Fontane frequently represents a moralistic insistence on regulating feelings in accordance with prior moral judgments as a mannerism of members of a fading Prussian aristocracy. In *The Poggenpuhl Family*, a short novel concerned with the efforts of an impoverished officer's widow and her children to preserve the appearance of gentility, Therese von Poggenpuhl, a character who is stubbornly attached to aristocratic forms, adopts this tone of insistence—and does so in a manner that leads her to slight or wound several members of her family. Again, in *Delusions, Confusions*, a short novel concerned with the breaking off of a serious affair between a young, aristocratic officer and a Berlin seamstress, the young officer's aristocratic peers and family members adopt a similar tone of insistence to similarly hurtful effect. In these further works, as in *Effi Briest*, Fontane depicts a trend toward moralism as infecting and threatening the relationships of members of a relatively cohesive Prussian society. Of course, such a trend might also be shown to represent a threat to relationships that span significant cultural gulfs. This brings me to a second example.

### 6.3.ii  Henry James's The Europeans

> What is life, indeed, without curtains?
>
> ∼ *Gertrude Wentworth in Henry*
> *James,* The Europeans *(1985), p. 79.*

Another good source of examples is the novels of Henry James. Throughout his career, James is concerned with characters who are— this is one of his own terms of art—"moralistic" in that they insist on regulating their feelings in accordance with prior moral judgments. In various works, James undertakes studies of moralism in this sense in connection with what gets called his "international theme." Thus, for instance, in several novels he presents American characters who veer toward refusing to allow their feelings to be engaged except in conformity with their established moral convictions, and he also brings these characters into contact with European characters who incline toward contrasting kinds of emotional permissiveness.[33] One thing that

33. See in this connection esp. *The American, The Ambassadors* and *The Europeans*, the last of which is discussed in this section. James varies this international theme in different ways. In *The Tragic Muse*, it is not American but rather British characters who lean toward moralism

James's explorations of this particular sort of international episode are designed to suggest is that the kind of emotional restraint exercised by some of his American characters encourages them to overlook flaws in their own moral outlooks and to favor prejudicial estimates of the moral outlooks of others. This suggestion is the mark of preoccupation with the species of moralism that I have been discussing, and a helpful place to turn for a version of it is James's early novel *The Europeans*.[34]

The main claim that I want to advance is that, considered thematically, *The Europeans* opposes the idea of an abstract morality and asks us to believe that an undistorted understanding of our lives is available only via the sorts of developments of sensibility afforded by a willingness to explore different responses to life. Moreover, as I read it, James's novel not only suggests that refinements of sensibility are sometimes a necessary prerequisite of understanding features of our shared lives but, moreover, makes this suggestion without inviting us to disparage the kind of understanding in question as less than fully rational or impartial. So it is appropriate to describe the novel as unfolding thematically in a way that, instead of being hostile to the concept of moral impartiality in the manner of impartiality criticisms, takes for granted a wider conception of it. These are the kinds of textual observations that position us to see that *The Europeans* is concerned with moralism in my

---

and encounter European characters inclined toward contrasting kinds of emotional permissiveness. In *The Author of Beltraffio*, James describes a confrontation between an intensely moralistic British character and an anti-moralistic American. And in *The Bostonians*, he explores a national variation on his international theme, bringing a moralistic New Englander into contact with a non-moralistic southerner.

34. Many commentators have regarded this novel as too insubstantial to reward serious consideration. This critical tendency originates with Henry James's older brother, the philosopher William James. In the year in which *The Europeans* was first published, William wrote to Henry, attacking the novel's action as "thin" and "slight," and there is good reason to think that Henry ultimately came to regard William's attack as justified. So it is worth emphasizing that—as the following discussion is designed to demonstrate—even if we follow the Jameses (as many readers do, but I do not) in regarding the simplicity of the novel's main story line as a significant defect, a case for its interest can still be made on the ground of the delicacy and sophistication with which it develops its central moral themes. For a couple of helpful accounts of the relevant correspondence between William and Henry, and of its effect on Henry's estimate of the novel, see Leon Edel, *The Life of Henry James*, vol. 2: *The Conquest of London: 1870–1881* (New York: Avon Books, 1962), pp. 383–385, and Richard Poirier, *The Comic Sense of Henry James: A Study of the Early Novels* (New York: Oxford University Press, 1960), pp. 96–98.

sense, and I here approach a discussion of relevant issues by focusing on the novel's treatment of the Baroness Eugenia—the character who, in addition to being arguably central to the action of the novel, might seem to pose the biggest problem for things I say about it.

The story is set in the mid-nineteenth century just outside Boston, and it features a visit that Eugenia and her brother Felix, the book's eponymous Europeans, make to a family of wealthy Americans. The Americans are Eugenia's and Felix's deceased mother's half brother and his family, relatives whom the European siblings have never before met. At the time of the visit, Felix, a handsome and lighthearted bohemian artist, is twenty-eight, and Eugenia, a person both less gay and more sophisticated, is thirty-three. Eugenia has acquired the title "baroness" through marriage to a financially strapped German prince who now wants to divorce her, and, in proposing the visit, she is motivated in significant part by the thought of a rich marriage. Moreover, at first her prospects for success seem good. Although there is no obviously suitable match in her uncle's household—Mr. Wentworth's family consists of two daughters in their early twenties, Gertrude and Charlotte, and a twenty-year-old son, Clifford, whose drinking habit has forced him to take a break from his studies at Harvard—the Wentworth family has close ties with a middle-aged bachelor named Robert Acton, who, because he is relatively sophisticated and more than relatively affluent, seems an immediately acceptable candidate. There is an initially promising rapprochement between Acton and Eugenia, but this romantic possibility is never actualized. The Europeans' visit does produce one marriage that crosses the family's continental divide, namely, one between Felix and Gertrude. Nevertheless, Eugenia ultimately feels that her own efforts have been a failure. She leaves America, even before her brother's wedding, having concluded that "the conditions of action on this provincial continent [are] not favorable to really superior women."[35]

The interest in Eugenia that the novel inspires is not, however, exhausted by this kind of simple list of events leading up to her return to Europe. As readers, we are encouraged to ask what accounts for her failure within the society of her American cousins, and we are encouraged to look for an answer in her characteristic modes of conduct and habits of thought. The novel consistently emphasizes that Eugenia is

35. Henry James, *The Europeans* (Oxford: Oxford University Press, 1985), p. 156.

artful in the sense of having a refined and mannered demeanor. Her artfulness is represented—and there is a contrast here with Felix, who is described as possessing but a certain measure of his sister's art—as extending markedly to her style of dress as well as to her characteristic modes of speech and gesture. As early as the novel's opening scene, we are shown Eugenia standing in front of a mirror, adjusting her hair, clothes and facial expression, and we are also given a glimpse of her wit and gift for repartee.[36] Further, this early image of Eugenia is quickly brought into relief by a dramatically different portrait of her American relatives. Far from cultivating artfulness, the Wentworths are for the most part distinguished by the simplicity of their manner or, alternately, by their repudiation of anything that they recognize as manner. Their house, though well furnished, is without "splendors, guildings or troops of servants"; Charlotte and Gertrude dress in a relatively unadorned style; and the whole Wentworth family tends to speak in such a plain manner that Eugenia immediately acquires a reputation for brilliancy.[37] Indeed, Clifford is stupidly amused at one point by the simple fact that he is capable of understanding something she tells him even though she says it using figurative language.[38]

Within the novel, the Wentworths' preference for simple and straight-forward comportment—the preference that distinguishes them most conspicuously from Eugenia and, to a lesser degree, also from Felix—is portrayed as the expression of deep-seated moral convictions. The Wentworths take simplicity to be the mark of both naturalness and honesty. They believe that any refinements of speech or manner that are designed to elicit emotional or imaginative responses should at bottom be regarded as deceptive extravagances, and they believe this because they also believe that emotional or imaginative responses have an essential tendency to cloud moral perception.[39] These closely connected beliefs lead most of the Wentworths, not only to insist on simplicity in their own conduct, but, by the same token, also to be suspicious of Eugenia's less than simple manner and to regard her presence among them as a source of moral danger. The one exception to this is Gertrude, and her

36. Ibid., pp. 1–2 and 4.
37. See ibid., pp. 26, 15, 30 and 34.
38. Ibid., p. 99.
39. For the Wentworths' emphasis on duty, see ibid., pp. 29, 37, 144 and 151. For their general hostility to imagination, see pp. 41, 52, 145, 148–9 and 150.

family's reactions to her prove the rule. Perceiving that Gertrude is greatly excited about the arrival of her foreign cousins, Mr. Wentworth warns her that she is going to be "exposed to peculiar influences."[40] And, in a protective gesture that reflects a touching naivete, Mr. Wentworth and Charlotte attempt to shield Gertrude from what they see as moral risk by putting Eugenia up, not in the main house with the rest of the family, but rather in a small, freestanding cottage nearby.

Granted that the Wentworths are suspicious of Eugenia, what are we as readers supposed to make of her? At first blush, it might seem as though the novel endorses the Wentworths' attitude. After all, Eugenia possesses, in addition to a sophisticated, artful manner, also a propensity to tell lies. In the course of the action, she is shown coming out not merely with a variety of relatively trivial social fibs,[41] but also with several quite substantive untruths. Here we might consider, for instance, two significant lies that she tells to Robert Acton. The backdrop for the first of these is the fact that, although Eugenia pins her marital ambitions chiefly on Acton and eventually takes herself to be in love with him, she also briefly toys with the idea of seducing young Clifford Wentworth. When Acton surprises her at her house one night and finds Clifford already there, Eugenia claims—falsely—that Clifford is enamored of her and has taken to making impromptu romantic visits.[42] The backdrop for Eugenia's second significant lie to Acton is the fact that, as Eugenia herself informs Acton early on, her princely husband wants her to sign a paper formalizing their divorce. When toward the end of her stay Acton asks her whether she has sent off the paper, she answers him—again, falsely—in the affirmative.

Given that Eugenia tells these and other lies, we might think it reasonable to read the novel as suggesting that her artful manner is necessarily tied to a lack of respect for the truth. The idea might be—and this is what the Wentworths in fact believe—that her manner invites an emotional engagement that as such has a tendency to distort our view of what she is saying and doing and, furthermore, that it is therefore properly regarded as essentially dishonest. Notice, moreover, that if we

40. Ibid., p. 41.

41. Thus, e.g., upon first meeting Mr. Wentworth, she politely but dishonestly compliments him on his daughters' beauty; and upon first meeting Robert Acton's invalid mother, she politely but dishonestly declares that Acton has spoken a great deal of her.

42. Ibid., pp. 109–110.

endorse this idea, as some commentators think we should,[43] we are in effect opposing the larger claim about *The Europeans* that interests me here. The Wentworths are led to regard Eugenia's artful manner as essentially dishonest by the assumption that sound moral thought demands an abstraction from feelings, and what primarily interests me is a claim about how this assumption is foreign to James's novel.

Setting aside for a moment the question of the foreignness of the assumption to the novel's treatment of Eugenia, I want to say a word about its foreignness to the novel's treatment of Gertrude Wentworth. Gertrude has an active imagination, and within the novel it is quite clearly indicated that she allows her view of her cousins to be informed by her imaginative responses to them. Consider, for instance, Gertrude's first encounter with Felix. Gertrude is sitting alone in the house, on a sunny Sunday morning, reading *Arabian Nights*. When her handsome cousin appears before her, it seems to her for a moment that she is gazing upon Prince Camaralzaman himself. Presently she and Felix begin to talk, and Felix tells her about Eugenia's marriage to Prince Silberstadt-Schreckenstein. By the time the return of the rest of the Wentworths interrupts the newly acquainted cousins, Gertrude is so captivated by both real and fictional royal tales that she confusedly introduces Felix to her assembled family as "the Prince—the Prince of Silberstadt-Schreckenstein!"[44] While it is thus made comically clear that Gertrude engages with her European cousins in an imaginative and emotionally charged manner, there is no suggestion that this style of engagement distorts her fundamental understanding of them. On the contrary, Gertrude is the only Wentworth who has a grasp of Eugenia's needs and motives.[45] In this respect the portrait we are given of her, far from encoding the idea that sound moral thinking requires an abstrac-

43. See in this connection, Leo Bersani's influential article "The Jamesian Lie" (in *A Future for Astyanax: Character and Desire in Literature* [New York: Columbia University Press, 1984], pp. 128–155, esp. pp. 136–137). Bersani argues, along roughly Wentworthian lines, that the novel treats responses Eugenia's sophisticated manner elicits as distancing us from the real and that it thus asks us to regard her manner as essentially dishonest. Moreover, although Bersani's overall account of *The Europeans* is nuanced (specifically, in that it involves a story about how James writes this novel at an intermediate stage in the development of his thought), Bersani never qualifies his Wentworthian suggestion about how to understand Eugenia.

44. Ibid., p. 24.

45. Thus, Gertrude rightly tells her assembled family not only that Eugenia will not like staying with them in the main house but also that Eugenia will be interested in Robert Acton (ibid., pp. 38–39).

tion from feelings, is suggestive of the opposing idea that some aspects of our lives may be accessible only in terms of further refinements of feeling.

Something similar can be said about the novel's portraits of the rest of the Wentworths—Charlotte, Clifford and Mr. Wentworth—as well as of its portrait of Mr. Brand, the young unitarian minister who has been enlisted by Charlotte and Mr. Wentworth to help Gertrude with her troubles and who is now expected to marry Gertrude. All of these characters are described as people whose emotional reticence limits their capacities of imagination. Charlotte has an imagination that she keeps "in her pocket" where it takes "no journeys whatever."[46] While Clifford is crudely dense and Mr. Brand is earnestly dull, they resemble each other in their general lack of imagination. And, for his part, Mr. Wentworth seems to have "no imagination at all."[47] These observations are interesting in part because we are repeatedly asked to connect the imaginative deficits of these characters with their failures to bring various basic features of their lives properly into focus. Block-headed Clifford is as such incapable of recognizing that a woman as 'ancient' as thirty-three-year-old Eugenia might yet have romantic designs on him; prim and literal Charlotte is as such incapable of recognizing that Gertrude could never be happy with Mr. Brand; flatfooted Mr. Brand's flatfootedness prevents his detecting "poor Charlotte's hidden flame" for him;[48] and unfanciful Mr. Wentworth's failure is quite general.

Mr. Wentworth has never allowed his "imagination to hover" around the thought of his half sister's children and, as a result, cannot conceive that there was anything less than admirable either about his family's neglect of them in the past or about his own insouciance about them more recently.[49] Further, his unimaginativeness also obstructs his grasp of present circumstances. For instance, when Felix asks for permission to marry Gertrude, and Mr. Brand, now persuaded of Charlotte's love for him, eagerly proposes to perform the ceremony, Mr. Wentworth is completely at a loss and finds himself left by all in a state of "unillumined perplexity."[50] Hence it is correct to conclude that in its portrait of Mr. Wentworth, no less than in its portraits of Gertrude, Charlotte, Mr. Brand and Clifford,

46. Ibid., p. 41.
47. Ibid., p. 150.
48. Ibid., p. 125.
49. Ibid., p. 52.
50. Ibid., p. 150.

the novel implies that certain features of our lives may be unavailable apart from new developments of sensibility and imagination.

This brings me back to the novel's portrait of Eugenia and to how, despite a superficial appearance to the contrary, it has the same implication. To see this, it is helpful to have before us a more detailed account of the circumstances in which Eugenia lies to Acton. What emerges is that a great deal of her lying, far from being a simple outgrowth of her personality, is a defense against Acton's refusal to involve himself with her in an unguarded and sympathetic manner. To be sure, Acton is from the beginning keenly and openly interested in Eugenia. Further, he is more cultivated and responsive than the Wentworths, and is accordingly capable, unlike them, of appreciating that her marital situation and family history make her position in local Boston society delicate. Nevertheless, Acton resembles the Wentworths in approaching Eugenia with "vague mistrust."[51] In the beginning, he exhibits this by demanding confidences from her without any compensating emotional commitment.[52] Later on, he increasingly confronts her with intrusive questions and comments that are actively designed to get her to lie. He is, for instance, far too sophisticated and worldly to believe that Eugenia would formalize her divorce in the absence of a compensating marital offer, and, when he asks her whether she has in fact formalized it, he is primarily motivated not—we are led to believe—by the desire to learn something but rather by the aim of eliciting a demonstration of what he sees as her dishonesty.[53]

Thus, although Acton ultimately tells himself that he has to give up the thought of marrying Eugenia because "she is a woman who will lie,"[54] it would be more accurate to say that he makes her into a woman who will lie because he is afraid of the kind of openness to her that would permit him to take seriously the idea of marriage and that he uses the narrow morality of the Wentworths as a cover for his own emotional reluctance. This observation speaks against taking the novel's treat-

51. Ibid., p. 66.

52. Acton peppers his conversations with Eugenia with questions about her personal life—about why she came to Boston (ibid., p. 67), about the circumstances of her marriage (ibid., p. 70), about whether she would, if asked, return to her husband (ibid., pp. 71–72), and about whether she missed him (i.e., Robert Acton) when he was away from her for a few days (p. 106).

53. Ibid., p. 134.

54. Ibid., p. 133.

ment of Eugenia as illustrating an alleged "necessary deduction of dishonesty from the art of appearances."[55] To be sure, Eugenia might prove
to be deeply dishonest. While the novel does not insist on this possibility, it also does not exclude it. (Eugenia remains something of a cipher.)
It is noteworthy, in this connection, that in later novels James is often
preoccupied with characters whose artfulness and manner are expressions of their unwillingness to be accountable for facts of their lives.
But my point here is simply that Acton is not in a position to draw any
firm conclusions about Eugenia's relationship to truth. And since it is
his refusal to explore feelings that challenge his moral misgivings about
her that prevents him, in the final analysis, from arriving at a good understanding of her character, we can justly conclude that in its portrait
of Eugenia's interaction with Acton the novel reinforces one of the
morals internal to its portraits of the members of the Wentworth clan—
namely, that there are aspects of our shared lives that we grasp only insofar as we allow ourselves to grow emotionally in various ways.

Having just argued that, considered thematically, *The Europeans* contains an attack on the idea of an abstract morality, I want to add that it
would be wrong to extend my argument so that the novel is now represented as resembling impartiality criticisms in engaging in a gesture of
rejection of the very concept of moral impartiality. The novel invites its
readers to regard a kind of emotional depth that most of the Wentworths
lack as a necessary condition of a grasp of its social world that, far from
being partial and optional, is sound and consistent. By its lights, reliance
on the sort of refined sensibility that we acquire by opening ourselves, in
the manner of Gertrude Wentworth, to different responses to life is a
requirement, for instance, not only of understanding that it would be
wrong for Mr. Wentworth to oppose a marriage between Gertrude and
Felix but also of understanding that, for closely connected reasons, Mr.
Wentworth's family was wrong to condemn his half sister's marriage to
an undistinguished European and to cut themselves off from her children, and that the members of the present Wentworths' circle are wrong
to approach Eugenia with suspicion and mistrust. The novel's narrative
is thus aptly characterized as unfolding in a manner that presupposes
the logic of the wider conception of rationality.

There is therefore a straightforward sense in which *The Europeans*

55. Bersani, "The Jamesian Lie," p. 136.

can be seen as concerned with the kind of moralistic attitude I am investigating. The novel presents us with characters—specifically, most of the members of the American Wentworth clan and their close affiliates—who, while in other respects thoughtful, typically refuse to explore modes of response that run counter to their moral convictions, and it also depicts this gesture of refusal as hampering their development of sound images of the world and leading them to neglect moral insights they could glean from a more open engagement with others. This basic complaint about moralism is, as I have already noted, concerned with a kind of moral difference that cannot be explained exhaustively in terms of disagreements about how or whether to use particular moral concepts. For it has to do with discrepancies between the images of the world that ground individuals' use of moral concepts—images that individuals (e.g., Gertrude Wentworth and her father) have in virtue of their distinct sensibilities.

Moreover, as I have also noted, this complaint about moralism is immune to the kinds of rejoinders that routinely get made, on behalf of traditional approaches in ethics, within ongoing conversations about moralism. The suggestion I am making is not that members of the Wentworth clan are inclined to exhibit the forms of rigorism and judgmentalism that are for the most part in question within such conversations. That is, I am not specifically suggesting that they are inclined to insist on rigid compliance with established moral principles or to pass judgment on others. It is possible to recognize these tendencies of conduct as moral defects without raising a question about the credentials of the conception of rationality that informs most treatments of moralism, and what interests me here is a suggestion to the effect that, whatever else we want to say about them, James's characters also suffer from a moral defect that depends for its cogency on a very different conception of what rationality is like. It is for this reason that the novel is aptly described as containing a clear and compelling study of the logic of moralism.[56]

56. The best discussion of James's work I'm familiar with that represents James as developing, in a range of different novels, the kind of anti-moralistic concern I've been considering in reference to the *Europeans* is Cora Diamond, "Henry James, Moral Philosophers, Moralism," *Henry James Review* 18, no. 3 (1997): 243–257.

## 6.3.iii A Further Comment on These Examples

The subject doesn't matter, it's the treatment, the treatment!
~ *Biddy Dormer in Henry James,*
The Tragic Muse *(1995), p. 22.*

The examples of moralism adduced in the last two sections are drawn from novels, and, before concluding my discussion of them, I want to comment on a sense in which it is unsurprising to find treatments of moralism in literary texts. The point, in brief, is that works of literature are capable of contributing to our grasp of this problem in ways that go beyond supplying the kinds of narrative treatments of it that I have been discussing. Given that it is distinctive of literary works to engage our feelings in various ways, and given that—as I argued in sections 4.3 and 4.4—literary works may present us with rational modes of moral instruction insofar as they do so, it follows that they are as such capable of addressing the problem of moralism, not only by describing it, but also by eliciting emotional responses that give us direct access to features of the world that a moralistic bearing prevents us from understanding. Literary works are, as we might put it, capable of addressing the problem of moralism in virtue of their distinctive forms. So it should not surprise us to find that they sometimes also work treatments of moralism into their narrative contents.

It is not a stretch to claim that the novels considered in the last two sections combine a narrative preoccupation with moralism with this sort of formal opposition to it. We could defend this claim in reference to Fontane's *Effi Briest* by observing that this novel presents us with delicately (if also pointedly) humorous descriptions of its social world and that, by inviting us to explore a range of responses to that world, it aims to enable us to make more sense of the lives of its moralistic characters than they can themselves. Consider, in this connection, the novel's treatment of Innstetten. The novel shows us circumstances in Innstetten's life from perspectives that diverge markedly from his own. We are often shown his wife in a light very different from that in which he sees her. Where Innstetten for the most part regards Effi's desire to be amused and spoiled as weakness of character, as readers of the novel we are invited to adopt a more charitable attitude. We are asked to place importance on Effi's craving for attention and physical tenderness from her husband and to view with both indulgence and sympathy the child-ishness of her efforts to solicit these things.

We are also occasionally given glimpses of Innstetten that reveal un-witting comedy. Innstetten arranges to devote his honeymoon with seventeen-year-old Effi to traveling through Italy and, as Effi's father sardonically puts it, "recatalogu[ing] all the art galleries," and Innstet-ten fails to register anything comic about thus immediately escorting his captivating young wife on an educational excursion.[57] A few years later, during a winter in Kessin in which he has more time than usual at home, Innstetten proposes to spend a series of evenings reviewing with Effi the works of art that they saw. And just as he once failed to see any-thing humorous about his wedding journey, he is now incapable of rec-ognizing the self-parody, revealed to us as readers, in his expectation that Effi will delight in the prospect of hours dedicated to "fixing [what they saw] permanently in [their] minds."[58]

How do the responses that the novel thus elicits position us to un-derstand features of Innstetten's life that he himself never fully grasps? When Innstetten discovers Effi's adultery, he fixates on the wrongheaded idea that what she did is "an unforgivable sin . . . in man's eyes."[59] The re-sponses elicited by the novel are supposed to help us arrive at a better grasp of his situation by positioning us to recognize the importance of features of it that he himself, to the extent that he registers them at all, is inclined to treat as insignificant (e.g., his unjust interpretation of cer-tain of Effi's innocent impulses and his more general tendency toward pedantry). They are supposed to direct our sense of what is and is not important with a view to facilitating the realization that, even by his own lights, Innstetten's reaction to what Effi did is disproportionate and that her misstep is analogous to similar missteps that Prussian soci-ety in general (and, indeed, also Innstetten in particular) treat as for-givable in men. These are the kinds of observations that speak for describing Fontane's novel as formally opposed to moralism. And inso-far as things the novel's emotional strategy positions us to recognize are things that Innstetten's moralistic demeanor prevents him from seeing,

57. For the inset quotation, see *Effi Briest*, p. 45.
58. Ibid., p. 134.
59. Ibid., p. 124.

the novel is correctly described as offering a formal demonstration of how a moralistic demeanor can block moral understanding.

James's *The Europeans* might also aptly be characterized as offering such a demonstration. A good case could be made for representing this novel both as showing us many of its narrative circumstances from perspectives more ironic than those occupied by its most moralistic characters (viz., Mr. Wentworth, Charlotte and Mr. Brand) and as aiming—by means of reactions that it thus produces, and hence by means of a formally anti-moralistic method—to get us to grasp things that these characters' moralistic proclivities prevent them from seeing.

Once we recognize that novels such as Fontane's *Effi Briest* and James's *The Europeans* are opposed to moralism in virtue of their forms as well as their contents, we are well situated to see that an anti-moralistic posture is part of a proper receptivity to literature. By the same token, we are well situated to recognize that it is reasonable to look for examples of moralism not only in literature but in certain kinds of resistance to it. Interestingly, we need to look no further than the reception of certain of Fontane's and James' own works to find resistance of the relevant type. Fontane's *Delusions, Confusions* (i.e., the short novel of his, touched on briefly at the end of section 6.3.i, that concerns an affair between a Berlin seamstress and a young aristocrat) provoked a wave of moralistic criticism when it was first serialized. Although some of the indignation it aroused stemmed simply from anger at the novel's suggestion that affairs of the kind it depicts were common within the aristocracy, a significant part of it also stemmed from opposition, of a moralistic sort, to its sympathetic treatment of what was thought of as the debased topic of free love. The newspaper in which the story first appeared, the *Vosische Zeitung*, received letters calling on this ground for its termination, including one, allegedly by a member of the family of the paper's owner, that demanded, "Isn't that awful whore's story going to be over soon?"[60] Similarly, James reports confronting moralistic criticism of his treatment, in *What Maisie Knew*, of a young girl's efforts to understand the sexual liaisons of her parents and stepparents. According to James, some

---

60. For accounts of the controversy surrounding *Confusions, Delusions*, see Gordon Craig, *Theodor Fontane: Literature and History in the Bismarck Reich* (Oxford: Oxford University Press, 1999), pp. 193–194, and William Zweibel, *Theodor Fontane* (New York: Twayne Publishers, 1992), p. 59.

of his readers took offense at his amused, novelistic portrait of Maisie's efforts because they held that, in his words, "nothing could well be more disgusting than to attribute to Maisie so intimate an 'acquaintance' with the gross immoralities surrounding her."[61] In connection with these anecdotes, we might credit some of Fontane's and James's least sympathetic readers with unwittingly contributing to what these literary authors have to teach us about the dangers of moralism.

## 6.4 Conclusion: Beyond Moral Judgment

> Try to take hold of your sensibility, and use it as if it were a faculty, like vision.
>
> ⁓ *Daniel Deronda to Mrs. Grandcourt in*
> *George Eliot, Daniel Deronda (1995), p. 452.*

These remarks conclude this book's case for a view on which the concerns of ethics extend beyond moral judgments to individuals' entire sensibilities or modes of responsiveness to life. In making this case, I argued that moral philosophers' tendency to restrict the concerns of ethics to moral judgments is philosophically problematic, and I also claimed that this tendency is morally problematic. While my emphasis in earlier parts of the book was on the former of these projects, my emphasis in this closing chapter has been on the latter.

To summarize my philosophical moves in the latter direction: After first discussing how the conception of rationality that I am calling "narrower" structures a prominent set of conversations in ethics (6.1), I pointed out that insistence on the constraints of this conception is inseparable from a kind of moral arrogance that is rightly characterized as moralistic, and I then observed that some of the main philosophical considerations that lead advocates of traditional moral judgment-centered ethical theories to fixate on moral judgments also commit them to accepting the conception (6.2). Finally, having argued that moral judgment-centered theories are vulnerable to a charge of moralism, I observed that the pertinent charge has to do with moral differences that cannot be accounted for exclusively in terms of disagreements about how or whether to use particular moral concepts, and I complemented my ob-

---

61. Preface to Henry James, *What Maisie Knew* (New York: Modern Library, 2002), p. xxxi.

servation with a series of further examples of moralism intended to bring out the familiarity of moral differences of this kind (6.3).

This is how I defended the conclusion that a traditional focus on moral judgments, in addition to being philosophically questionable, is also morally problematic and that, if we want to avoid its moral pitfalls, we need to direct attention in ethics past moral judgments to all of individuals' ways of thinking and speaking and to the rich and variegated sensibilities these ways of thinking encode. This conclusion highlights the fact that the dispute between traditional moral judgment-centered views of ethics and the non-traditional view championed here has a significant moral dimension and that, in consequence, the dispute deserves a kind of serious philosophical consideration that it has yet to receive.

# Credits

Chapter 1 contains a brief extract from "Why Can't Moral Thought Be Everything It Seems?" *Philosophical Forum* 33, no. 4 (Winter 2002): 373–392.

Chapter 2 reprints, with additions, "The Happy Truth: J. L. Austin's *How to Do Things with Words*," *Inquiry* 45, no. 1 (Spring 2002): 1–22. It also contains a brief extract from "Austin and the Ethics of Discourse," in *Reading Cavell*, ed. Alice Crary and Sanford Shieh (London: Routledge, 2006), pp. 42–67.

Chapter 3 contains a shortened and revised version of "Wittgenstein and Ethics: A Discussion in Reference to *On Certainty*," in *Readings of Wittgenstein's* On Certainty, ed. William Brenner and Daniele Moyale-Sharrock (London: Palgrave Macmillan, 2005), pp. 275–301. It is reproduced here with permission of Palgrave Macmillan.

Chapter 4 reprints, with revisions and additions, "Does the Study of Literature Belong in Moral Philosophy? Some Reflections in the Light of Ryle's Thought," *Philosophical Investigations* 23, no. 4 (October 2000): 315–350.

Chapter 5 contains a revised excerpt from "What Do Feminists Want in an Epistemology?" in *Re-Reading the Canon: Feminist Interpretations of Wittgenstein*, ed. Peg O'Connor and Naomi Scheman (University Park, PA: Penn State Press, 2002), pp. 97–118.

# Index